WHAT I WOULD HAVE SAID...

What I Would Have Said...

If You Had Only Asked

Thomas R. Wallin
September 1999 to January 2012

Copyright © 2013 by Thomas R. Wallin.

Library of Congress Control Number:		2013905945
ISBN:	Hardcover	978-1-4836-1850-0
	Softcover	978-1-4836-1849-4
	Ebook	978-1-4836-1851-7

All rights reserved. No part of this book may be reproduced or transmitted in any form or by any means, electronic or mechanical, including photocopying, recording, or by any information storage and retrieval system, without permission in writing from the copyright owner.

This book was printed in the United States of America.

Rev. date: 04/30/2013

To order additional copies of this book, contact:
Xlibris Corporation
1-888-795-4274
www.Xlibris.com
Orders@Xlibris.com

Contents

Dedication 27
Introduction 29
Why The Book In The First Place? 29

1   Introduction: Part II . . . A Father's Instructions For Life 33

1A.	Compliment Three People Each Day............................	36
1B.	Watch A Sunrise At Least Once A Year	37
1C.	Overtip Breakfast Waitresses...	39
1D.	Look People In The Eye	40
1E.	Say "Thank You" A Lot..	41
1F.	Say "Please A Lot"..	42
1G.	Live Beneath Your Means	43
1H.	Buy Whatever Kids Are Selling On Card Tables In Their Front Yards	45
1I.	Treat Everyone You Meet As You Want To Be Treated	46
1J.	Donate Two Pints Of Blood Every Year	48
1K.	Make New Friends But Cherish The Old Ones	49
1L.	Keep Secrets	51
1M.	Don't Waste Time Learning The "Tricks Of The Trade"; Instead, Learn The Trade.	52
1N.	Admit Your Mistakes...	54
1O.	Be Brave. Even If You're Not, Pretend To Be. No One Can Tell The Difference.	55
1P.	Choose A Charity In Your Community And Support It Generously With Your Time And Money................	56
1Q.	Read The Bill Of Rights	58
1R.	Use Credit Cards Only For Convenience, Never For Credit........	71
1S.	Never Cheat	72
1T.	Give Yourself A Year And Read The Bible Cover To Cover	74
1U.	Learn To Listen. Opportunity Sometimes Knocks Very Softly	76
1V.	Never Deprive Someone Of Hope; It Might Be All He Or She Has...	78

1W.	Pray Not For Things, But For Wisdom And Courage	79
1X.	Never Take Action When You're Angry	81
1Y.	Have Good Posture. Enter A Room With Purpose And Confidence	82
1Z.	Don't Discuss Business In Elevators	83
1AA.	Never Pay For Work Before It's Completed	84
1BB.	Be Willing To Lose A Battle In Order To Win The War.	85
1CC.	Don't Gossip	86
1DD.	Beware Of The Person Who Has Nothing To Lose	87
1EE.	When Facing A Difficult Task, Act As Though It Is Impossible To Fail. If You Are Going After Moby Dick, Take Along The Tartar Sauce.	88
1FF.	Don't Spread Yourself Too Thin. Learn To Say No Politely And Quickly.	89
1GG.	Expect Life To Be Fair. Never Underestimate The Power Of Forgiveness. Instead Of Using The Word "Problem," Try Substituting The Word "Opportunity."	90
1HH.	Never Walk Out On A Quarrel With Your Wife (Unless One Or Both Of You Are Angry; If One Or Both Of You Are Angry, Walk Out And Finish The Discussion When You Have Cooled Off).	91
1II.	Regarding Furniture And Clothes, If You Think You'll Be Using Them Five Years Or Longer, Buy The Best You Can Afford.	92
1JJ.	Be Bold And Courageous. When You Look Back On Your Life, You'll Regret The Things You Didn't Do More Than The Ones You Did.	94
1KK.	Forget Committees! New, Noble, World-Changing Ideas Always Come From One Person Working Alone.	96
1LL.	Street Musicians Are A Treasure. Stop For A Moment And Listen, Then Leave A Small Donation.	97
1MM.	When Faced With A Serious Health Problem, Get At Least Three Medical Opinions.	98
1NN.	Wage War Against Littering.	99
1OO.	After Encountering Inferior Service, Food, Or Products, Bring It To The Attention Of The Person In Charge. Good Managers Will Appreciate Knowing.	100
1PP.	Don't Procrastinate. Do What Needs Doing When It Needs To Be Done	101
1QQ.	Get Your Priorities Straight. No One Ever Said On His Deathbed, "Gee, If I'd Only Spent More Time At The Office."	103

1RR.	Don't Be Afraid To Say "I Don't Know."	105
1SS.	Don't Be Afraid To Say "I'm Sorry."	106
1TT.	Make A List Of Twenty-Five Things You Want To Experience Before You Die. Carry It In Your Wallet And Refer To It Often	108
1UU.	Call Your Mother	112
2	"How To Pursue Happiness" By Adair Lara, Reader's Digest, P. 155, June 1993.	113
3	"Do Unto Others As You Would Have Them Do Unto You. The Golden Rule Is Where It All Begins And Ends . . ." By James R. Fisher Jr., Reader's Digest, P. 130, June 1993.	116
3A.	The Golden Rule Is Where It All Begins And Ends	117
3B.	To Have A Friend, You Must Be A Friend, Starting With Yourself. "Do Unto Others . . ." By James R. Fisher Jr., Reader's Digest, P. 130, June 1993.	120
3C.	The Greatest Virtue Is Kindness. You Can't Love Everyone, But You Can Be Kind To Everyone. "Do Unto Others . . ." By James R. Fisher Jr., Reader's Digest, P. 130, June 1993.	122
3D.	Be Enthusiastic. Nothing Of Consequence Was Ever Been Achieved Without Enthusiasm. "Do Unto Others . . ." By James R. Fisher Jr., Reader's Digest, P. 130, June 1993.	123
3E.	Be Positive. Positive People Attract Others, While Negative People Repel. "Do Unto Others . . ." By James R. Fisher Jr., Reader's Digest, P. 130, June 1993.	124
3F.	Gossip Cheapens The One Who Gossips More Than The One Gossiped About. "Do Unto Others . . ." By James R. Fisher Jr., Reader's Digest, P. 130, June 1993.	126
3G.	Communicate Cheerfulness. "Do Unto Others . . ." By James R. Fisher Jr., Reader's Digest, P. 130, June 1993.	127
3H.	If You Are Given To Make Fun Of Someone, Be Sure It Is Of Yourself. "Do Unto Others . . ." By James R. Fisher Jr., Reader's Digest, P. 130, June 1993.	129
3I.	A Smile Doesn't Cost Anything And Pays Big Dividends. Not Only Does It Make You Feel Good, But It Makes Everyone Else Be Better Too. "Do Unto Others . . ." By James R. Fisher Jr., Reader's Digest, P. 130, June 1993.	130

4   "Trust In God But Lock Your Car," From Life's Little Instruction Book, Vol. II. H. Jackson Brown Jr..131

4A. Never Laugh At Anyone's Dreams, From Life's Little Instruction Book, Vol. II, H. Jackson Brown Jr..........................132

4B. Believe In Love At First Sight, From Life's Little Instruction Book, Vol. II, H. Jackson Brown Jr..........................134

4C. Remember That No Time Spent With Your Children Is Ever Wasted. Time Is A Commodity—We All Have Some Of, Some More; Some Less Than Others, From Life's Little Instruction Book, Vol. II, H. Jackson Brown Jr................136

4D. When Traveling, Take Two Big Safety Pins So You Can Pin The Motel Drapes Shut, From Life's Little Instruction Book, Vol. II, H. Jackson Brown Jr. 138

4E. Accept A Breath Mint If Someone Offers You One, From Life's Little Instruction Book, Vol. II, H. Jackson Brown Jr. 139

4F. Keep The Porch Light On Until All The Family Is In For The Night, From Life's Little Instruction Book, Vol. II, H. Jackson Brown Jr..140

4G. Rehearse A Joke Before Telling It, From Life's Little Instruction Book, Vol. II, H. Jackson Brown Jr..........................141

4H. Always Try The House Dressing, From Life's Little Instruction Book, Vol. II, H. Jackson Brown Jr..........................142

4I. Don't Let A Little Dispute Injure A Great Friendship, From Life's Little Instruction Book, Vol. II, H. Jackson Brown Jr. 143

4J. Once In A While, Invite The Person In Line Behind You To Go Ahead Of You, From Life's Little Instruction Book, Vol. II, H. Jackson Brown Jr..145

4K. Send Your Mother-In-Law Flowers On Your Spouse's Birthday, From Life's Little Instruction Book, Vol. II, H. Jackson Brown Jr..146

4L. Buy Ladders, Extension Cords, And Garden Hoses Longer Than You Think You'll Need, From Life's Little Instruction Book, Vol. II, H. Jackson Brown Jr. 147

4M. Never Be The First To Break A Family Tradition, From Life's Little Instruction Book, Vol. II, H. Jackson Brown Jr.................149

4N. Steer Clear Of Any Place With A "Ladies Welcome" Sign In The Window, From Life's Little Instruction Book, Vol. II, H. Jackson Brown Jr. 151

4O. Don't Stop The Parade To Pick Up A Dime, From Life's Little Instruction Book, Vol. II, H. Jackson Brown Jr.................152

4P.	Ask Anyone Giving Directions To Repeat Them At Least Twice, From Life's Little Instruction Book, Vol. II, H. Jackson Brown Jr.	153
4Q.	Don't Wash A Car, Mow A Yard, Or Select A Christmas Tree After Dark, From Life's Little Instruction Book, Vol. II, H. Jackson Brown Jr.	155
4R.	Hold Your Child's Hand Every Chance You Get. The Time Will Come When He Or She Won't Let You, From Life's Little Instruction Book, Vol. II, H. Jackson Brown Jr.	157
4S.	Own A Hammock, From Life's Little Instruction Book, Vol. II, H. Jackson Brown Jr.	159
4T.	Never Be Photographed Holding A Cocktail Glass, From Life's Little Instruction Book, Vol. II, H. Jackson Brown Jr.	160
4U.	Give People More Than They Expect, And Do It Cheerfully, From Life's Little Instruction Book, Vol. II, H. Jackson Brown Jr.	161
4V.	Someone Will Always Be Looking At You As An Example Of How To Behave. Don't Let Them Down, From Life's Little Instruction Book, Vol. II, H. Jackson Brown Jr.	162
4W.	Do Your Homework And Know Your Facts, But Remember It's Passion That Persuades, From Life's Little Instruction Book, Vol. II, H. Jackson Brown Jr.	163
4X.	Be As Friendly To The Janitor As You Are To The Chairman Of The Board, From Life's Little Instruction Book, Vol. II, H. Jackson Brown Jr.	164
4Y.	When Someone Asks You A Question You Don't Want To Answer, Smile And Say, "Why Do You Want To Know?" From Life's Little Instruction Book, Vol. II, H. Jackson Brown Jr.	165
4Z.	Overestimate Travel Time By 15 Percent, From Life's Little Instruction Book, Vol. II, H. Jackson Brown Jr.	166
4AA.	Never Wear A White Bathing Suit, From Life's Little Instruction Book, Vol. II, H. Jackson Brown Jr.	168
4BB.	Don't Dismiss Any Good Idea Regardless Of The Source, From Life's Little Instruction Book, Vol. II, H. Jackson Brown Jr.	169
4CC.	When You Say "I'm Sorry," Look The Person In The Eye. When You Say You Are Sorry, Make Sure You Mean It, From Life's Little Instruction Book, Vol. II, H. Jackson Brown Jr.	171
4DD.	Put The Strap Around Your Neck Before Looking Through The Binoculars, From Life's Little Instruction Book, Vol. II, H. Jackson Brown Jr.	172

4EE.	Trust In God But Lock Your Car, From Life's Little Instruction Book, Vol. II, H. Jackson Brown Jr.	173
4FF.	Never Say Anything Uncomplimentary About Your Wife Or Your Children In The Presence Of Others, From Life's Little Instruction Book, Vol. II, H. Jackson Brown Jr.	174
4GG.	No Matter How Old You Get, Hug And Kiss Your Mother Whenever You Greet Her, From Life's Little Instruction Book, Vol. II, H. Jackson Brown Jr.	175
4HH.	Pray. There's Immeasurable Power In It, From Life's Little Instruction Book, Vol. II, H. Jackson Brown Jr.	176
4II.	Brush Your Teeth Before Putting On Your Tie, From Life's Little Instruction Book, Vol. II, H. Jackson Brown Jr.	179
4JJ.	Never Ask A Barber If You Need A Haircut, From Life's Little Instruction Book, Vol. II, H. Jackson Brown Jr.	180
4KK.	Phone Home If You're Going To Be More Than Twenty Minutes Late, From Life's Little Instruction Book, Vol. II, H. Jackson Brown Jr.	182
4LL.	Remember That Everyone Is Influenced By Kindness, From Life's Little Instruction Book, Vol. II, H. Jackson Brown Jr.	184
4MM.	Overpay Good Baby-Sitters, From Life's Little Instruction Book, Vol. II, H. Jackson Brown Jr.	185
4NN.	If You're Away From Home And Hear Church Bells, Think Of Three People Who Love You! From Life's Little Instruction Book, Vol. II, H. Jackson Brown Jr.	187
4OO.	Leave A Quarter Where A Child Can Find It, From Life's Little Instruction Book, Vol. II, H. Jackson Brown Jr.	189
4PP.	When It Comes To Worrying Or Painting A Picture, Know When To Stop, From Life's Little Instruction Book, Vol. II, H. Jackson Brown Jr.	190
4QQ.	Avoid Using The Word "Impacted" Unless You're Describing Wisdom Teeth, From Life's Little Instruction Book, Vol. II, H. Jackson Brown Jr.	192
4RR.	Be Bold. Providence Loves Boldness And Will Assist You In Ways You Wouldn't Imagine. Providence Is A Nonentity, From Life's Little Instruction Book, Vol. II, H. Jackson Brown Jr.	193
4SS.	Never Order Chicken Fried Steak In A Place That Doesn't Have A Jukebox, From Life's Little Instruction Book, Vol. II, H. Jackson Brown Jr.	195
4TT.	Go On A Blind Date; That's How I Met Your Mother, From Life's Little Instruction Book, Vol. II, H. Jackson Brown Jr.	196

4UU.	Call Your Dad, From Life's Little Instruction Book, Vol. II, H. Jackson Brown Jr.	197
5	"Win With Your Strengths" By Donald O. Clifton And Paula Nelson, Reader's Digest, P. 74, May 1993	198
5A.	Pick At Least One Strength To Use And To Pursue For Success.	199
5B.	"Exercise Your Strength Daily" By Donald O. Clifton And Paula Nelson, Reader's Digest, P. 74, May 1993.	200
5C.	"Ignore Weaknesses That Don't Hinder You," By Donald O. Clifton And Paula Nelson, Reader's Digest, P. 74, May 1993.	201
5D.	"Look For Complementary Partners" By Donald O. Clifton And Paula Nelson, Reader's Digest, P. 74, May 1993.	203
5E.	"Develop A Support System" By Donald O. Clifton And Paula Nelson, Reader's Digest, P. 74, May 1993.	205
6	"What Winners Know," Reader's Digest, March 1994, And Condensed From The Winner Within: A Life Plan For Team Players By Pat Riley.	207
6A.	"Be A Team Player," Reader's Digest, March 1994, And Condensed From The Winner Within: A Life Plan For Team Players By Pat Riley.	209
6B.	"Welcome Change," Reader's Digest, March 1994, And Condensed From The Winner Within: A Life Plan For Team Players By Pat Riley.	211
6C.	"Beware Of Complacency," Reader's Digest, March 1994, And Condensed From The Winner Within: A Life Plan For Team Players By Pat Riley.	212
6D.	"Remember, Attitude Is Mother Of Luck," Reader's Digest, March 1994, And Condensed From The Winner Within: A Life Plan For Team Players By Pat Riley.	214
7	The 7 Habits Of Highly Effective People: Powerful Lessons In Personal Change By Stephen R. Covey.	216
7A.	Be Proactive	217
7B.	Begin With The End In Mind: A Powerful Lessons In Personal Change, By Stephen R. Covey.	218

7C.	Put First Things First: Powerful Lessons In Personal Change, By Stephen R. Covey.	219
7D.	Think Win/Win: Powerful Lessons In Personal Change, By Stephen R. Covey.	220
7E.	Seek First To Understand, Then To Be Understood: Powerful Lessons In Personal Change, By Stephen R. Covey.	222
7F.	Synergize: Powerful Lessons In Personal Change, By Stephen R. Covey.	224
7G.	Sharpen The Saw: Powerful Lessons In Personal Change, By Stephen R. Covey.	226
8	"People Need Trouble—A Little Frustration To Sharpen The Spirit On, Toughen It . . ." By William Faulkner, Reader's Digest, March 1994.	228
9	"It Says Something About The Capacity Of Government To Manage The Health Care System When A Private Publisher Had A 192-Page Summary Of The Clinton Health Plan In Bookstores For More Than A Month While Only A Thirty-Two-Page Summary Was Available From The Government printing Office . . ." By Malcolm S. Forbes Jr., Reader's Digest, March 1994.	230
10	"Hope Is Not The Same As Joy . . ." By Vaclav Havel, Reader's Digest, March 1994.	233
11	"The Sight Of A Gravestone, Weighty Not Only In Its Granite, Allows Us Perspective On Problems As Pressing As Burnt Toast, Taxes, And Hay Fever . . ." By Donald Hall, Reader's Digest, March 1994.	235
12	"Genius Is A Bend In The Creek Where Bright Water Has Gathered, And Which Mirrors The Trees, The Sky And The Banks," By Edgar Lee Masters, Reader's Digest, March 1994.	237
13	"Snobs Talk As If They Had Begotten Their Own Ancestors," By Herbert Agar, Reader's Digest, March 1994.	239
14	"Self-Esteem Cannot Be Sought As An End In Itself But Must Come As A By-Product Of Meeting Standards Of Excellence, Taking Pride In Work, Supporting A Family, Bringing Up Decent Children, Learning About Life And Imparting That Wisdom" By Aaron Wildavsky, Reader's Digest, March 1994.	241
15	"This Grand Show Is Eternal. It Is Always Sunrise Somewhere, The Dew Is Never All Dried At Once; A Shower Is Forever Falling . . ." By John Muir, Reader's Digest, March 1994.	243

16	"It Doesn't Matter If You Win Or Lose, Until You Lose" By Angie Papdikis, Reader's Digest, March 1994.	245
17	Are We Demanding Enough Of Our Kids? By Edwin Kiester Jr. And Sally Valente Kiester.	247
17A.	Remember Who's Who, Are We Demanding Enough Of Our Kids? By Edwin Kiester Jr. And Sally Valente Kiester	248
17B.	Don't Let Them Quit, From Are We Demanding Enough Of Our Kids? By Edwin Kiester Jr. And Sally Valente Kiester	249
17C.	Give Them Chores, From Are We Demanding Enough Of Our Kids? By Edwin Kiester Jr. And Sally Valente Kiester	251
17D.	Build Scaffolding, From Are We Demanding Enough Of Our Kids? By Edwin Kiester Jr. And Sally Valente Kiester	253
17E.	Hands Off The Answer Sheet, From Are We Demanding Enough Of Our Kids? By Edwin Kiester Jr. And Sally Valente Kiester	254
17F.	Encourage Worthwhile Fun, From Are We Demanding Enough Of Our Kids? By Edwin Kiester Jr. And Sally Valente Kiester	256
17G.	Don't Solve Their Problems, From Are We Demanding Enough Of Our Kids? By Edwin Kiester Jr. And Sally Valente Kiester	258
17H.	Point The Way To The Stars, From Are We Demanding Enough Of Our Kids? By Edwin Kiester Jr. And Sally Valente Kiester	259
18	The Book Of Virtues, By William J. Bennett, 1993, By Simon And Schuster.	261
18A.	Self-Discipline, From The Book Of Virtues, By William J. Bennett, 1993, By Simon And Schuster	263
18B.	Compassion, From The Book Of Virtues By William J. Bennett	265
18C.	Responsibility, From The Book Of Virtues By William J. Bennett	267
18D.	Friendship, From The Book Of Virtues By William J. Bennett	269
18F.	Work From The Book Of Virtues By William J. Bennett	271
18F.	Courage, From The Book Of Virtues By William J. Bennett	273

18G.	Perseverance, From The Book Of Virtues By William J. Bennett	274
18H.	Honesty, From The Book Of Virtues By William J. Bennett	275
18I.	Loyalty, From The Book Of Virtues By William J. Bennett	276
18J.	Faith, From The Book Of Virtues By William J. Bennett	277
19	Are You Trying Real Hard? John H. Johnson And Lerone Bennett Jr.	278
20	"I Will Permit No Man To Narrow And Degrade My Soul By Making Me Hate Him." Booker T. Washington.	280
21	"Of Course, It's The Same Old Story. Truth Usually Is The Same Old Story," Margaret Thatcher.	282
22	"We Are All Worms, But I Do Believe I Am A Glowworm." Winston Churchill.	284
23	"What Really Is Worthwhile?" Nardi Reader Campion, Reader's Digest, July 1994	286
23A.	Drop Pretense, From "What Really Is Worthwhile?" By Nardi Reeder Campion, Reader's Digest, July 1994	287
23B.	Drop Worry, From "What Really Is Worthwhile?" Nardi Reeder Campion, Reader's Digest, July 1994.	288
23C.	Let Go Of Discontent, From "What Really Is Worthwhile?" By Nardi Reeder Campion, Reader's Digest, July 1994.	289
23D.	Let Go Of Self-Seeking, From "What Really Is Worthwhile?" By Nardi Reeder Campion, Reader's Digest, July 1994.	290
23E.	What Are The Things In Life That We Should Keep, Guard, Use? Ar Brown. From "What Really Is Worthwhile?" By Nardi Reeder Campion, Reader's Digest, July 1994.	291
23F.	Be Wise In The Use Of Time, From "What Is Worthwhile?" By Anna Robertson Brown, Reader's Digest, July 1994.	292
23G.	Value Work, From "What Is Worthwhile?" By Anna Robertson Brown, Reader's Digest, July 1994.	293
23H.	Seek Happiness Each Day, From "What Is Worthwhile?" By Anna Robertson Brown, Reader's Digest, July 1994.	294
23I.	Cherish Love, From "What Is Worthwhile?" By Anna Robertson Brown, Reader's Digest, July 1994.	295
23J.	Keep Ambition In Check, From "What Is Worthwhile?" By Anna Robertson Brown, Reader's Digest, July 1994.	297
23K.	Embrace Friendship, From "What Is Worthwhile?" By Anna Robertson Brown, Reader's Digest, July 1994.	299

23L.	Do Not Fear Sorrow, From "What Is Worthwhile?" By Anna Robertson Brown, Reader's Digest, July 1994.	300
23M.	Cherish Faith, From "What Really Is Worthwhile?" By Anna Robertson Brown, Reader's Digest, July 1994.	301
24	"Raising A Can-Do Kid: Seven Traits That Encourage Self-Esteem In Your Children," John Rosemond, Better Homes And Gardens, March 1990	302
24A.	Resourcefulness, From "Raising A Can-Do Kid: Seven Traits That Encourage Self-Esteem In Your Children," John Rosemond, Better Homes And Gardens, March 1990	303
24B.	Imagination And Creativity, From "Raising A Can-Do Kid: Seven Traits That Encourage Self-Esteem In Your Children," John Rosemond, Better Homes And Gardens, March 1990	305
24C.	Determination, From "Raising A Can-Do Kid: Seven Traits That Encourage Self-Esteem In Your Children," John Rosemond, Better Homes And Gardens, March 1990	306
24D.	Self-Sufficiency, From "Raising A Can-Do Kid: Seven Traits That Encourage Self-Esteem In Your Children," John Rosemond, Better Homes And Gardens, March 1990	307
24E.	Responsibility, From "Raising A Can-Do Kid: Seven Traits That Encourage Self-Esteem In Your Children," John Rosemond, Better Homes And Gardens, March 1990	308
24F.	Respectfulness, From "Raising A Can-Do Kid: Seven Traits That Encourage Self-Esteem In Your Children," John Rosemond, Better Homes And Gardens, March 1990	310
24G.	Autonomy, From "Raising A Can-Do Kid: Seven Traits That Encourage Self-Esteem In Your Children," John Rosemond, Better Homes And Gardens, March 1990	311
25	A Millionaire's Notebook: How Ordinary People Can Achieve Extraordinary Success, Copyright 1996, By Steven K. Scott.	312
25A.	Insight 1: Past Achievement Is Not A True Predictor Of Future Success.	313
25B.	Insight 2: If You Can Do One Thing Well, Even If It Doesn't Seem Significant, You Have The Potential For Phenomenal Success, From A Millionaire's Notebook: How Ordinary People Can Achieve Extraordinary Success, Copyright 1996, By Steven K. Scott.	314

25C.   Insight 3: Take A Close Look And Discover What "Insignificant" Successes You Have Had And Focus On Them. They Could Well Become The Foundation Of Your Future Achievement, A Millionaire's Notebook: How Ordinary People Can Achieve Extraordinary Success, Copyright 1996, By Steven K. Scott.....315

25D.   Insight 4: Past Failures Don't Have To Limit Your Future, From A Millionaire's Notebook: How Ordinary People Can Achieve Extraordinary Success, Copyright 1996, By Steven K. Scott.....317

25E.   Insight 5: "Three Strikes, You're Out" Applies Only In Baseball, From A Millionaire's Notebook: How Ordinary People Can Achieve Extraordinary Success, Copyright 1996, By Steven K. Scott.....318

25F.   Insight 6: Work To Meet Your Needs But Dream To Get Ahead. Your Dream Or Vision Of Your Future Is The Focus Of Your Work, From A Millionaire's Notebook: How Ordinary People Can Achieve Extraordinary Success, Copyright 1996, By Steven K. Scott.....319

25G.   Insight 7: Don't Let Small Minds Limit Your Thinking, From A Millionaire's Notebook: How Ordinary People Can Achieve Extraordinary Success, Copyright 1996, By Steven K. Scott.....321

25H.   Insight 8: "Young And Inexperienced" Is Not A Valid Reason To Ignore Or Stifle Creative Ideas And Activities, From A Millionaire's Notebook: How Ordinary People Can Achieve Extraordinary Success, Copyright 1996, By Steven K. Scott.....322

25I.   Insight 9: You May Be A Lot Smarter Than Your Bosses, From A Millionaire's Notebook: How Ordinary People Can Achieve Extraordinary Success, Copyright 1996, By Steven K. Scott.....324

25J.   Insight 10: A Person Who Believes In You Is A Tremendous Source Of Power, From A Millionaire's Notebook: How Ordinary People Can Achieve Extraordinary Success, Copyright 1996, By Steven K. Scott.....325

25K.   Insight 11: Don't Be Greedy, Share The Wealth, Don't Hoard It, From A Millionaire's Notebook: How Ordinary People Can Achieve Extraordinary Success, Copyright 1996, By Steven K. Scott.....327

25L.   Insight 12: Whom You Work For Is As Important As What You Do, From A Millionaire's Notebook: How Ordinary People Can Achieve Extraordinary Success, Copyright 1996, By Steven K. Scott.....329

25M.   Insight 13: There Is No Greater Motivation Than Love, From A Millionaire's Notebook: How Ordinary People Can Achieve

	Extraordinary Success, Copyright 1996, By Steven K. Scott.	330
25N.	Insight 14: Commitment And Motivation Are More Important Than Credentials Or Resumes, From A Millionaire's Notebook: How Ordinary People Can Achieve Extraordinary Success, Copyright 1996, By Steven K. Scott.	331
25O.	Insight 15: It Is Important To Never Overestimate The Incredible Worth Of The Right Partners (Friends, Teammates, Mate), From A Millionaire's Notebook: How Ordinary People Can Achieve Extraordinary Success, Copyright 1996, By Steven K. Scott.	333
25P.	Insight 16: Do Everything You Can To Make Those You Work With Successful, From A Millionaire's Notebook: How Ordinary People Can Achieve Extraordinary Success, Copyright 1996, By Steven K. Scott.	335
25Q.	Insight 17: Share The Wealth, From A Millionaire's Notebook: How Ordinary People Can Achieve Extraordinary Success, Copyright 1996, By Steven K. Scott.	337
25R.	Insight 18: Consumers (People Who You Are Trying To Convince To Need You And What You Have To Offer) Are A Lot Smarter Than You Think, From A Millionaire's Notebook: How Ordinary People Can Achieve Extraordinary Success, Copyright 1996, By Steven K. Scott.	338
25S.	Insight 19: Artistic Swells. Logic Sells, From A Millionaire's Notebook: How Ordinary People Can Achieve Extraordinary Success, Copyright 1996, By Steven K. Scott.	340
25T.	Insight 20: You Have To Take A Lot Of Swings To Hit A Lot Of Home Runs, From A Millionaire's Notebook: How Ordinary People Can Achieve Extraordinary Success, Copyright 1996, By Steven K. Scott.	341
25U.	Insight 21: No Recriminations For Failures, From A Millionaire's Notebook: How Ordinary People Can Achieve Extraordinary Success, Copyright 1996, By Steven K. Scott.	343
25V.	Insight 22: Shoot For The Moon. If You Miss, You're Still High! From A Millionaire's Notebook: How Ordinary People Can Achieve Extraordinary Success, Copyright 1996, By Steven K. Scott.	344
25W.	Insight 23: Prepare. Do Your Homework, From A Millionaire's Notebook: How Ordinary People Can Achieve Extraordinary Success, Copyright 1996, By Steven K. Scott.	346
25X.	Insight 24: Go For It.	348
25Y.	Insight 25: Minimize The Losses. Share The Winnings, From	

	A Millionaire's Notebook: How Ordinary People Can Achieve Extraordinary Success, Copyright 1996, By Steven K. Scott.	349
25Z.	Insight 26: If It's Not Fun, You Probably Won't Succeed, From A Millionaire's Notebook: How Ordinary People Can Achieve Extraordinary Success, Copyright 1996, By Steven K. Scott.	351
25AA.	Insight 27: Any Other Way Of Getting Rich Is A Waste Of Life, From A Millionaire's Notebook: How Ordinary People Can Achieve Extraordinary Success, Copyright 1996, By Steven K. Scott.	353
26	"How To Be The Best," My Conversation With Jimmy Johnson, Rush Limbaugh Newsletter, June 1996	355
26A.	"Two Things Make A Champion. Pride And Work. I Don't Know That I've Ever Been Around A Champion, A True Champion Year In And Year Out, Unless He Was Working, Always Trying To Get Better."	356
26B.	"The Only Way I Know How To Play The Game Is To Give It My All," My Conversation With Jimmy Johnson, Rush Limbaugh Newsletter, June 1996.	357
26C.	"As Head Coach, I (Jimmy Johnson) Do Three Things:	358
27	My American Journey, By Colin Powell, Copyright 1995. Colin Powell's Rules:	360
27A.	It Ain't As Bad As You Think. It Will Look Better In The Morning.	361
27B.	Get Mad, Then Get Over It, From My American Journey, By Colin Powell.	362
27C.	Avoid Having Your Ego So Close To Your Position That When Your Position Falls, Your Ego Goes With It, From My American Journey, By Colin Powell.	364
27D.	It Can Be Done! From My American Journey, By Colin Powell.	366
27E.	Be Careful What You Choose; You May Get It, From My American Journey, By Colin Powell	367
27F.	Don't Let Adverse Facts Stand In The Way Of A Good Decision, From My American Journey, By Colin Powell	368
27G.	You Can't Make Someone Else's Choice. You Shouldn't Let Someone Else Make Yours, From My American Journey, By Colin Powell.	369

27H.	Check Small Things, From My American Journey, By Colin Powell.	370
27I.	Share Credit, From My American Journey, By Colin Powell.	372
27J.	Remain Calm. Be Kind, From My American Journey, By Colin Powell.	373
27K.	Have A Vision. Be Demanding, From My American Journey, By Colin Powell.	375
27L.	Don't Take Counsel Of Your Fears Or Naysayers, From My American Journey, By Colin Powell.	377
27M.	Perpetual Optimism Is A Force Multiplier, From My American Journey, By Colin Powell.	378
28	Pres. James A. Garfield's Cherished Personal Principles:	379
28A.	"Never Be Idle", One Of Pres. James A. Garfield's Cherished Personal Principles.	381
28B.	"Make Few Promises", One Of Pres. James A. Garfield's Cherished Personal Principles.	382
28C.	"Always Speak The Truth", One Of Pres. James A. Garfield's Cherished Personal Principles.	383
28D.	"Live Within Your Income", One Of Pres. James A. Garfield's Cherished Personal Principles.	384
28F.	"Never Speak Evil Of Anyone", One Of Pres. James A. Garfield's Cherished Personal Principles.	386
28F.	"Keep Good Company Or None", One Of Pres. James A. Garfield's Cherished Personal Principles.	387
28G.	"Live Up To Your Engagements", One Of Pres. James A. Garfield's Cherished Personal Principles.	388
28H.	"Never Play Games Of Chance", One Of Pres. James A. Garfield's Cherished Personal Principles.	389
28I.	"Drink No Intoxicating Drinks", One Of Pres. James A. Garfield's Cherished Personal Principles.	391
28J.	"Good Character Is Above Everything Else", One Of Pres. James A. Garfield's Cherished Personal Principles	392
28K.	"Keep Your Own Secrets," One Of Pres. James A. Garfield's Cherished Personal Principles.	393
28L.	"Never Borrow If You Can Possibly Help It," One Of Pres. James A. Garfield's Cherished Personal Principles	394
28M.	"Do Not Marry Until You Are Able To Support A Wife," One Of Pres. James A. Garfield's Cherished Personal Principles.	395

28n.	"When You Speak To A Person, Look Into His Eyes, One Of Pres. James A. Garfield's Cherished Personal Principles.	396
28O.	"Save When You Are Young To Spend When You Are Old," One Of Pres. James A. Garfield's Cherished Personal Principles	397
28P.	"Never Run Into Debt Unless There Is A Way Out Again," One Of Pres. James A. Garfield's Cherished Personal Principles.	398
28Q.	"Good Company And Good Conversation Are The Sinews Of Virtue," One Of Pres. James A. Garfield's Cherished Personal Principles.	399
28R.	"Your Character Cannot Be Essentially Injured Except Through Your Own Acts," One Of Pres. James A. Garfield's Cherished Personal Principles.	400
28S.	"If Anybody Speaks Evil Of You, Let Your Life Be So That No One Believes Him," One Of Pres. James A. Garfield's Cherished Personal Principles.	401
28T.	"When You Retire At Night, Think Over What You Have Done During The Day," One Of Pres. James A. Garfield's Cherished Personal Principles.	402
28U.	"If Your Hands Cannot Be Employed Usefully, Attend To The Culture Of Your Mind," One Of Pres. James A Garfield's Cherished Personal Principles.	403
28V.	"Read The Above Carefully And Thoughtfully At Least Once A Week," One Of Pres. James A. Garfield's Cherished Personal Principles.	404
29	The Only Cure To An Identity Crisis Is Involvement In Life Outside Of Self; Sermon, December 15, 1996, Naperville, Illinois, St. Margaret Mary Parish, Pastor Rev. William O'shea.	405
30	Idleness, Selfishness, Recklessness, Envy, And Irresponsibility Are The Vices Upon Which Socialism In Any Form Flourishes And Which It, In Turn, Encourages," Margaret Thatcher, Washington Times Weekly, December 1996.	407
30A.	Envy	409
30B.	Idleness	410
30C.	Irresponsibility	411
30D.	Recklessness	412
30E.	Selfishness	413

31 "Maturity Is A High Price To Pay For Growing Up," Tom Stoppard, The Plays For Radio 1964-91 (Faber And Faber), Reader's Digest, August 1996. 414
32 "When We Seek To Discover The Best In Others, We Somehow Bring Out The Best In Ourselves," William Arthur Ward, Reader's Digest, August 1996. 416
33 "Hot Heads And Cold Hearts Never Solved Anything," Billy Graham, Reader's Digest, August 1996. 418
34 "A Great Many People Mistake Opinions For Thoughts," Herbert V. Prochnow, Reader's Digest, August 1996. 420
35 "Freedom, After All, Is Simply Being Able To Live With The Consequences Of Your Decisions," James X. Mullen, The Simple Art Of Greatness (Viking Penguin), Reader's Digest, August 1996 422
36 "Slow Down, Simplify, And Be Kind," Naomi Judd, Reader's Digest, August 1996. 424
37 "We May Pass Violets Looking For Roses. We May Pass Contentment Looking For Victory," Bern Williams; Reader's Digest, August 1996. 426
38 "Words Are Plentiful, But Deeds Are Precious," Lech Walesa, Reader's Digest, August 1996. 428
39 "The Harder I Work, The Luckier I Get," Unknown Speaker, Talk Radio, December 26, 1996. 430
40 "If You Are Going To Get Anywhere In Life, You Are Going To Have To Go Into Business For Yourself!" Unknown Speaker, Talk Radio, December 26, 1996. 432
41 "Be Fair; Only Agreed-To Need Comes Before Fairness," The Author . . . Unless Someone Else Claims It 434
42 "The Most Important Trip You May Take In Life Is Meeting People Halfway," Henry Boye In National Enquirer; Reader's Digest, January 1997. 436
43 "In Politics, There's A Fine Line Between Too Much Conviction And Too Little," Robert J. Samuelson In Newsweek, Reader's Digest, January 1997 438
44 "High Station In Life Is Earned By The Gallantry With Which Appalling Experiences Are Survived With Grace," Tennessee Williams, Memoirs (Doubleday), Reader's Digest, January 1997. 440
45 "The Attempt To Silence A Man Is The Greatest Honor You Can Bestow On Him. It Means That You Recognize The Other Person As Superior To Yourself," Joseph Sobran,

	Universal Press Syndicate, Reader's Digest, January 1997..................442
46	"Never Let A Problem To Be Solved Become More Important Than A Person To Be Loved," Barbara Johnson, The Joy Journal (Word); Reader's Digest, January 1997..............................444
47	"Love Is What's Left In A Relationship After All The Selfishness Has Been Removed," Cullen Hightower, Reader's Digest, January 1997...447
48	"Treat A Person As He Is, And He Will Remain As He Is. Treat Him As He Could Be, And He Will Become What He Should Be," Jimmy Johnson, Quoted By Jarret Bell In Usa Today; Reader's Digest, January 1997...452
49	"Suggestions For Making Life More Vivid, More Enjoyable, More Rewarding: Try To Be Surprised By Something Every Day; Wake Up In The Morning With Specific Goals To Look Forward To; Make Time For Reflection And Relaxation," Mihaly Csikszentmihalyl, Creativity: Flow And The Psychology Of Discovery And Invention..454
50	"Honesty, Hope, Faith, Courage, Integrity, Willingness, Humility, Brotherly Love, Justice, Perseverance, Spiritual, And Service," Alcoholics Anonymous, Bill Wilson And Robert Smith, 1935...........457

50A.	Honesty 459
50B.	Hope..460
50C.	Faith 461
50D.	Courage 462
50E.	Integrity..463
50F.	Willingness...464
50G.	Humility...465
50H.	Brotherly Love..466
50I.	Justice 467
50J.	Perseverance 468
50K.	Spiritual 469
50L.	Service 470

51	Salada Tea Taglines: 471
51A.	Salada Tea Taglines: A Pat On The Back Is More Powerful Than A Kick In The Pants. 472
51B.	Salada Tea Taglines: You Can't Improve Your Physical Fitness By Running Down Your Friends. 473

51C.	Salada Tea Taglines: No Man Can Do More Than His Best Nor Should He Do Less	474
51D.	Salada Tea Taglines: Be Sure Of Your Facts Or Be Prepared For Disappointment.	475
51E.	Salada Tea Taglines: Drive Defensively. An Accident That Doesn't Happen Helps Both You And The Other Driver.	476
51F.	Salada Tea Taglines: A Job Well Done Requires An Enthusiastic Beginning Followed By Intelligent Determination.	477
51G.	Salada Tea Taglines: Think How Happy You Would Be If You Lost Everything—Then Found It Again	478
51H.	Salada Tea Taglines: People Who Get Discovered And Those Who Get Found Out Are Very Different.	479
51I.	Salada Tea Taglines: Almost Always The Last Key You Try Opens The Door.	480
51J.	Salada Tea Taglines: The Greater The Problem, The More Glory In Solving It.	481
51K.	Salada Tea Taglines: The True Worth Of Water Is Seldom Realized Until The Well Runs Dry	482
51L.	Salada Tea Taglines: Be Friendly And You Will Never Want For Friends	483
51M.	Salada Tea Taglines: Figures Can Be Misleading—But Those On The Cost Of Living Are On The Up And Up.	484
51N.	Salada Tea Taglines: Your Mind Is Somewhat Like A Parachute—Neither Work Unless Open.	485
51O.	Salada Tea Taglines: Time Spent Getting Even Would Be Better Spent In Getting Ahead.	487
51P.	Salada Tea Taglines: You're A Diplomat If You Can Cut A Cake So Everybody Thinks He Has The Biggest Slice.	488
51Q.	Salada Tea Taglines: You Have Poise If You Can Be Ill At Ease Inconspicuously.	489
51R.	Salada Tea Taglines: Politicians Are Very Adept At Answering Questions Nobody Asks.	490
51S.	Salada Tea Taglines: All Too Often, When Nothing Remains To Be Said, Somebody Says It.	491
51T.	Salada Tea Taglines: To Avoid Making Mistakes, You Must Gain Experience—But To Do That, You Often Make Mistakes.	492
51U.	Salada Tea Taglines: Friendships Earned Before You Need Them Are Almost Certain To Be More Lasting.	493

51V.	Salada Tea Taglines: Fly Into A Rage Only At The Risk Of Making A Bad Landing.	494
51W.	Salada Tea Taglines: A Spoiled Child Is A Perfect Example Of Minority Rule In The House.	495
51X.	Salada Tea Taglines: Even Though You May Fail To Attain—You Must Never Fail To Aspire.	496
51Y.	Salada Tea Taglines: Even Nature Is Not Perfect. She Lets Spring Fever And House Cleaning Come At The Same Time.	498
51Z.	Salada Tea Taglines: Always Put Off Until The Day After Tomorrow The Things You Shouldn't Do At All.	499
51AA.	Salada Tea Taglines: Alimony Is Sometimes Known As Bounty On The Mutiny.	500
51BB.	Salada Tea Taglines: To End A War Is Fine, But To Keep One From Starting Is Better.	501
51CC.	Salada Tea Taglines: Like Tea, Getting Into Hot Water Tends To Bring Out The Best In You.	502
51DD.	Salada Tea Taglines: An Oversimplification Can Get Mighty Complicated Before Becoming Practical.	503
51EE.	Salada Tea Taglines: A Person Is Happy Only When He Believes He Is!	504
51FF.	Salada Tea Taglines: If You Must Kill Time, Try Working It To Death.	506
51GG.	Salada Tea Taglines: If You Could Remember All Salada Taglines, You'd Be A Better Conversationalist.	507
51HH.	Salada Tea Taglines: It's Better To Face Up To Trouble Squarely Than To Live In Fear Of It Forever.	508
51II.	Salada Tea Taglines: It's A Recession When Others Meet Financial Adversity; A Depression When You Do.	509
51JJ.	Salada Tea Taglines: Everybody Being Pleasant To Everybody Else Would Make For A Better World.	510
51KK.	Salada Tea Taglines: There May Be Times When You Can't Find Help—But You Can Always Give It.	511
51LL.	Salada Tea Taglines: Some People Are So Eager To Find Fault That You'd Think There Was A Reward.	512
52	"Regardless Of Your Excitement Over A Snowfall, Be Mindful That The Snow Will Soon Melt, And You Will Be Left With Just Your Overall Zest For Life To Provide Your Excitement For Living," Thomas R. Wallin.	513
53	"A Temptation Resisted Is A True Sense Of Character," Quote From The Movie Papillon, 1973.	515

54 "Doing What's Right When You Know No One Is Looking Is A True Measure Of Character," Congressman J. C. Watts In His Rebuttal To Pres. William Jefferson Clinton's State Of The Union Address, January 1997..517
55 "It Is Ok To Disagree Without Hating Someone," T. R. Wallin..519
56 "Assess Their Passion Before You Commit," T. R. Wallin..521
57 "Decisions, Not Conditions, Determine Who A Man Is," Vicktor Frankl, Unknown Media Quote, 9/2/, 1997. 523

Bibliography 525

DEDICATION

I wish to dedicate this book to the near "holiness" of the US Constitution and the equally near perfect set of operational rules for our Country

George Washington, a founding father and first President believed:

- that preserving the Union should be most important bottom line for all of our citizens.
- Regional trade, ie North with the South, the South with the West, and for example the Eastern portion of the country with the Southern are all preferential to trade with Foreign interests.

Avoid foreign military entanglements

- The United States of America is a Constitutional Republic; therefore, we vote for and elect leaders who we believe will represent our interests as well as the interests of the people of the United States of America. Labor unions, lobbying groups, as well as regional interest groups represent interests of isolated groups . . . often contrary to the long term good of our country.

Our country, our Union and our Liberty should be bound together by Love
We would then avoid seeing jealousies coming in with a shove.
Regional issues may come in like a dove . . . .
By the time all side issues play out, the USA will need help from above.
(a limerick from Washington's Wisdom and My Limericks)

We are there now . . . needing help from above! Labor unions, lobbying groups, as well as regional interest groups represent interests of people who are more interested in what their country can do for them than what they can do for our country. Our country and our people are tough but our system of Liberty and Freedom is breakable by decades of our people choosing their interests over those of this great Constitutional Republic.

On a lighter note, I wish to dedicate this "writing exercise" to my dear wife Judy and my family who endured while I formulated these philosophies. Also thanks to Judy, as a former reading and writing teacher, for trying to minimize my writing errors and point out dumb statements I may wish to rethink.

Introduction

Why The Book In The First Place?

Ayn Rand in her classic novel, *Atlas Shrugged,* used a character (Francisco d'Anconia, a genius, flamboyant industrialist) to put one's stating gratuitous opinions in perspective when she wrote, "It is not advisable, James, to venture unsolicited opinions. You should spare yourself the embarrassing discovery of their exact value to your listener."

So many times . . . I should have followed the advice of Ayn Rand's Francisco . . . and kept my mouth shut. Often, people really aren't interested in gratuitous opinions. Why cause them, your friends and family, to expend energy to deal with your opinion when they don't have to and mostly aren't interested? You may think or hope they are, but they usually aren't interested. If they didn't ask you for an opinion and if one is offered, they have to put effort into the conversation as needed to politely respond. Maybe, even with the emotion involved or fear of "hurting your feelings," they may feel a need to explain why they are not going to take the advice being offered. Repeated "opinionaters" are the worst kind!

Talk about the weather, their kids, their grandkids, or what kind of activities with which they are involved . . . but not a constant stream of opinions and suggestions.

Did you ever notice how fast someone's eyes glaze over when you start to offer an unsolicited opinion concerning what someone should do or how they should think about an issue? About a nanosecond is all it takes for their eyes to glaze over.

Never offer an opinion to someone unless either the person sincerely asks for your opinion or the outcome significantly and materially affects you. And if the outcome does significantly and materially affects you . . . be prepared to implement your opinion over the objections of the other person(s) involved because they are not likely to take advantage of your "wisdom."

Everyone speaks from where they are . . .
Some speak as if they're pondering afar.
Just a few lines to share with you . . .
Small tips from my venue.

It is not that I pretend to know it all.
For sure it is not just from what I recall.
I recognize wisdom from my quests, my heroes.
So, these thoughts are worth saying . . . I propose.

KEEP YOUR OPINIONS RARE LIKE DIAMONDS OR GOLD
Keep your opinions rare like diamonds, gold, or silver rather than everywhere like raindrops.

I have often said that I wish to keep my opinions rare and valued like diamonds or gold rather than spew them out of my mouth, lowering their value to the copper or zircon level.

This book is a collection of jewels preserved over the years which inspired my thoughts and opinions.

ADVICE FROM OTHERS
Don't take advice from someone who doesn't!
Another one of my thoughts on the subject is that I try not to take any advice from someone who doesn't . . . take advice themselves . . . just as a matter of principle . . . unless they have a "good" idea.

We . . . everyone does I am sure . . . have family and friends who truly could use a little advice. You ask . . . how do I know that? and I would say that I really don't know for sure . . . it's kinda like when you see someone trying to change a flat tire on a car by taking off the lug bolts before they block the wheels and jack up the wheel that is flat. Some things a person just understands, and you just know that they could use some advice. If they don't ask for advice or suggestive opinions . . . don't waste your and their time and energy.

One thing you can always say is that you can't . . . it is insane to . . . expect different results when one does something the same . . . reacts to the same situation . . . over and over. They should not expect different results when performing the same activity over and over . . . but surprisingly, some do!

PHILOSOPHY AND PHILOSOPHERS

People in Socrates', Plato's, and Aristotle's times used to follow the philosophers around and considered them the great minds and intellects of their day. In simplest terms, the greatest philosophers of all time said what they thought . . . gave their opinions about the great issues of their day. Even then their philosophies . . . demanding society to be responsible, were not received well by the masses. Socrates was executed because the government leaders did not agree with what he taught and were not otherwise able to silence him.

According to the Thorndike-Barnhart Dictionary/Worldbook-Childcraft International Inc., the word philosophy means

- < the study of the truth or principles of all real knowledge;
- < the study of most general causes and principles of the universe;
- < a system for guiding life;
- < the broad general principles of a particular subject;
- < a calm and reasonable attitude;
- < accepting things as they are and making the best of them; and
- < the love or pursuit of wisdom in its broadest sense.

Yes, this definition describes what is being presented in this book . . . my opinions . . . philosophies if you will . . . on important issues and ideas of the day.

CREDIBILITY FOR MY OPINIONS ... PHILOSOPHIES

To establish credibility for my opinions ... philosophies ... I have included within this book one-line sayings, quotes, wise sayings, or key points of people who have many big-time achievements, positive life experiences, and successes. I have written an essay and a limerick within this "book" for each for future reference as to why I believe each individual's opinion, comment, or saying is truly a wise statement.

My opinions are just that ... opinions and represent my life experiences and observations. Beyond borrowing the credited author's one-liners as topics, I have personal credibility by living a successful life to this point at age sixty-nine ... sixty-nine! ... can that be possible? While I may lack some authority or notoriety, by inserting my own words, and including my own philosophies of life, into the framework of quotes or sayings of many very wise and successful people, I try to achieve some level of credibility in the "outside world" for my thoughts.

Writing opinions and limericks citing my philosophies are much more satisfying and less confrontational than trying to seriously engage others with opinions or thoughts on this or that topic of the day.

Socrates, Plato, and Aristotle were scholars representing the early Greek.
There have been many since, knowledge is what they seek.
Why can't we all who think ... speak ...
Thoughts that will take us beyond a critique.

The whole of our earth ...
Needs rules to set society's worth.
Pardon me if there is a dearth!
This 'ol philosopher's rules give opinionators a wide berth.

1

Introduction: Part II . . . A Father's Instructions For Life

The concept for this book of philosophy or advice began with the September 1992 issue of *Reader's Digest* and an article titled "Father's Instructions For Life" by H. Jackson Brown Jr. Brown's list of individual instructions included in *A Father's Instructions for Life*, such wise suggestions as COMPLIMENT THREE PEOPLE EACH DAY; WATCH A SUNRISE AT LEAST ONCE A YEAR; OVERTIP BREAKFAST WAITRESSES; LOOK PEOPLE IN THE EYE; and SAY "THANK YOU" A LOT. His booklet served as a starting point. The list of broad suggestions offered by Jackson Brown seemed very appropriate. However, with just the headings, many details and "father's insights" would not be transferred to the children. The cute little sayings and one-liners mean something to a person who has had sufficient life experiences to appreciate their value and wisdom. But without the life experiences to understand the significance of the one-liners, the wisdom would not and could not be appreciated. Actually, the original author of *A Father's Instructions for Life*, H. Jackson Brown Jr., may have included more details when he originally wrote the text, but it was just the list in the *Reader's Digest* that prompted this effort.

I liked and valued the topics as an outline and felt that they were totally appropriate for subject areas to be passed down from one generation to another. The outline for *A Father's Instructions for Life* represented an excellent start to record a basic philosophy of life and a personalized collection to share with my family.

1. Beginning with *A Father's Instructions for Life*, I have collected examples of the great issues of our day or the topics of today in the form of sayings and quotes of numerous famous and accomplished people. Key words, quotes, or sayings of many very wise and successful people have been included. Some of these individuals are basketball coach, Pat Riley; famous author, William Faulkner; businessman and presidential candidate, Malcolm Forbes; former U.S. secretary of education and author, William Bennett; inventor, Booker T. Washington; statesman and former prime

ministers of Great Britain, Margaret Thatcher and Winston Churchill; football coach, Jimmy Johnson; four-star general and former chairman of the Joint Chiefs of Staff, Colin Powell; and former president, James A. Garfield, to name a few.

The collection depicted herein is a truly great collection of sayings, quotes, or key points written by the credited authors. Often the credited line or quote could stand alone to convey its meaning. However, I believe that most needed to be expanded or enhanced to make them meaningful to those without sufficient life experiences to fully appreciate the wisdom. And although the credited lines were so impressive, I wanted to add my thoughts for family and others should they ever wish to know what I thought on these very impressive concepts. Near the end, I sprinkled in a few of my own "one-liners" and expounded upon them.

1A. COMPLIMENT THREE PEOPLE EACH DAY

And why stop at three?

Remembering to be complimentary is the biggest obstacle to overcome and is something at which I am the weakest. Not only should you compliment three people each day . . . you should start early.

The first must come within five minutes of waking up in the morning, and the last must come within fifteen minutes of going to bed.

Yes, that means family must receive the first and last compliments each day.

It does not hurt us at all to give someone a compliment. It feels good to look for something good to say about family and friends.

Personally, I find myself being willing to give compliments to people who are the underdogs—the less fortunate. I am less likely to give a compliment to those who are riding a crest of luck or good fortune or just doing well and would be more inclined to seek someone out who seems to be having a tougher time.

Regardless—if someone does a task the very best or just well, I am, and I believe we all should be complimentary to them.

However, if someone is obviously down on their luck, a compliment might help perk them up. Make sure your compliments are credible. Only compliment actions of someone who actually tried. If they made an attempt, there will be some aspect of what they accomplished on which to base a compliment. Don't hesitate—give them a compliment.

Everyone—I don't care who they are and what they do—everyone has something about them that warrants a compliment. Looks, dress, accomplishment—something that warrants a compliment. Compliments based on an accomplishment will be appreciated and may be just the support they need to encourage them along on the road to excellence.

You are the best;
You cannot be beat;
In life's test,
You are a treat!

1B. WATCH A SUNRISE AT LEAST ONCE A YEAR

Watch a sun rise at least once a year. Stop and smell the roses. This is not a plea to merely watch the sun come over the horizon or stoop and sniff a flower. This is a plea to our children to take the time to enjoy life. We all can get too totally caught up in the busy day-to-day activities of our jobs and volunteer activities and churches.

Enjoy life: that is a nebulous charge. Are you laughing or smiling a lot and having pleasant thoughts about your situation, friends, and family? These are keys to look for that sunrise everywhere and all day long.

Another key is the question whether you have a balance between doing activities that focus on helping others, leisure and activities that are focused on accomplishing work.

We must have direction or focus on all three; we must have focus on helping others. We must have direction and focus in our work life so that we end up where we want to end rather than just ending up someplace. And we must have direction and focus in our leisure life. The idea here is to have objectives and direction so that we know what we are trying to accomplish.

Life can be complex, and setting time aside for leisure may be difficult.

Leisure is more than a grandiose vacation; it is daily, weekly, monthly opportunities for enjoying each other and the sheer joy of being alive. It is an opportunity to lean back and think, to appreciate our health, our friends, the nice people we know, and our family.

Immediately following our son Jeff's death—this was easier to do—easier to keep things in perspective. Now some twenty-eight years later . . . keeping things in perspective seems more difficult, and it shouldn't be.

There are so many things we can and should be thankful for and enjoy.

Our family, each other, our health, our jobs . . . all represent key objects for which we should be extremely thankful. To watch a sunrise is not the key to enjoying our blessings—the key is to appreciate the little things in life; appreciate what we have and do not dwell on problems.

Each day . . .
Offers for sure . . .
Many bouquets . . .
To enrich our tour.

1C.   OVERTIP BREAKFAST WAITRESSES

Overtip a breakfast waitress.

The focus here is to be kind and generous to those in need—especially those who are trying to help themselves. A breakfast waitress would be a great example. They are probably the lowest paid of even the waitresses. They must get up early, probably leave their family before breakfast and before helping their family get ready for school and other activities. They are generally a hard working group, and they are trying to help support their family.

Be kind and generous to them.

Similarly—be kind and generous to others.

Be focused on the importance of being kind and generous to those in need who are trying to be productive members of society. Don't pass the Salvation Army kettle without making a contribution. Always buy at least one box of Girl Scout cookies. Help the elderly to their car . . . at night and especially if there is ice. The kind word or smile to the stranger on the street corner will always be appreciated. Appreciate the waitress who is up early and out while her family needs her too. They are the jewels to appreciate.

The lady must roll out early you know!
Then, when there, she's on the go.
Pancakes and sausage pay the rent.
Without big tips, she may live in a tent!

1D. LOOK PEOPLE IN THE EYE

Look people in the eye; they will trust you more, and it forces you to be confident or at least appear confident to face people and issues head on.

It is often difficult for people to face others straight in the eye when you speak to them.

The head-down approach to meeting people makes them suspicious and offers them a chance to feel pity for you for fear that you have no confidence or you have done something wrong and feel guilty.

We must either, naturally or by developing a habit, meet people and issues head on! Look them in the eye when speaking. They will be more apt to trust you; they will appreciate you as a person.

Young children need to be reminded to keep their head up and never look away or down when they are meeting someone. This is just one of those rules. There are some in the family who, it seems, almost stare at my eyes when we are talking. Their eyes seem to "bulge" out while I am talking to them, and that seems a bit unnatural.

Do your best and mostly look into people's eyes when you are speaking with them. Also remember to keep your chest out and shoulders back!

Look at people in the eye . . .
When you speak to them . . . not the sky!
The same for shaking their hand—you ask why.
Eye contact shows your character so no alibi!

1E.   SAY "THANK YOU" A LOT

Say "thank you" a lot. Also, say "please" and "excuse me," and other expressions of courtesy . . . a lot.

In this world, there are many, many mean, inconsiderate, or unscrupulous people without a conscience.

Everyone appreciates courtesy and respectfulness.

Treat people with kindness—it costs nothing and leaves people with a warm feeling about themselves and you.

The waiter or waitress appreciates a "thank you" every time they make a delivery to your table. Anytime someone opens a door for you or does any favor, large or small, say "thank you"!

Avoid the "I am sorry." Don't be in a position to truly need to say "I am sorry," and you will not need to use the phrase often, or not at all.

"Thank you" cannot be used enough, but avoid needing to say that you are sorry.

Say thank you when you receive;
Say thank you a lot.
There is no cost to thanking, you must believe;
Say thank you when you receive; don't say I forgot.

1F. SAY "PLEASE A LOT"

Say please a lot; people do not owe us anything.

Consequently, when we must ask someone to do something for us, we should show our appreciation by saying "please".

To ask someone to do something for us is to ask them to do us a favor. It is a courtesy from others who do something for us.

Please is a positive courtesy word, which we should use often.

Please is a word that cannot be overused. As was said before though, "I am sorry" can be overused. So can the words "relationship" or "diversity" or "frankly." All are words I quickly tire from hearing. Never can one say please too much, I believe.

Try me; I'll let you know if you manage to say please too much. The word just is humbling and expresses your appreciation of small favors enough to say—please.

Please for this, please for that;
Being courteous should be old hat.
Say please, please, let's not get in a spat!
So dear friend . . . use please to show your grat!

1G. LIVE BENEATH YOUR MEANS

What are you trying to accomplish?

The American dream, the American ego is geared toward achieving.

Work hard toward a dream and achieving! When you do achieve—accomplishing something and it results in a monetary reward—people naturally want to enjoy the fruits of their labors.

The American ego—perhaps the ego of achievers around the world, will push some of us to achieve partly because we are goal oriented and partly because we ultimately want to be able to use, enjoy, and display the fruits of our labor.

The problem, and the basis for the premise for this section, is that situation where living high creates a motivation for continuing these high-living standards. The stress of maintaining the high and expensive living standard adds to life's stresses.

It is fine to set goals, ambitious goals, and try to achieve them. But living and spending at or above one's earning power will create unnecessary stress.

Your conscious effort to consume a significant amount less than your full income is best—say 25 percent less. Save and prepare for emergencies or a rainy day. This coupled with a confident entrepreneurial spirit—a striving, achieving spirit will be best. Work hard, achieve, grow rich—but do not spend or use your resources anywhere close to the limit of what you earn.

Watch—observe people—but it is difficult to know exactly what goes on inside the personal lives of people with whom we come in contact. What you see is not necessarily the way it is. Often, they are living beyond their means and are struggling just to maintain the status quo. Envy no one. Respect achievers for what they have done—not for what they spend but for what they have accomplished.

The importance of this advice is that the continuous stress of being forced to work to maintain something you already have and are using is unnecessary. Strive, achieve, and enjoy the fruits of your labor is to be commended; but do not plan to spend all you bring in . . . save a rainy-day fund of around 25 percent of your income.

Much of life's joy comes with being successful at what you do . . . but a habit of high spending will be a burden.

Live beneath your means . . .
Means spend less than you make!
That will leave you a surplus it seems . . .
To grow in time for your trip to the lake.

1H. BUY WHATEVER KIDS ARE SELLING ON CARD TABLES IN THEIR FRONT YARDS

Many of these simple instructions involve appreciating the little things of life. The sunset or sunrise, the little kindnesses we can show each other—these are the important things in life.

A lemonade stand with little kids out in their front yard is a perfect example. They have the right idea—the entrepreneurial spirit. A dime or a quarter means nothing to you, but that really may excite the child and ignite their ambitions to achieve.

Your kindness of stopping and paying for a cup of lemonade gives them joy. It is nothing more than making them feel good and successful and is enough reason to buy whatever they are selling. Now . . . whether you actually drink the lemonade from an open pitcher with bugs and fingers is up to you. I don't unless I can buy a sealed can of lemonade or water.

The same goes for kids selling cookies, candy, Christmas wrapping around their neighborhood. Stop and make a purchase.

Buy something no matter what they are selling. Granted—not everyone can do this—$1 here, $3 there—just is not always possible. But if at all possible, that is money well spent. Why reject a little child with a fragile ego. Buy one item at least. They truly will receive joy from your effort, and you will feel good about your good deed.

Buy, yes, buy what they sell!
But dear me, I do not tell . . .
To drink or eat; I want you to stay well!
Those kids try hard and use their fingers swell.

1I. TREAT EVERYONE YOU MEET AS YOU WANT TO BE TREATED

The Golden Rule—do unto others as you would have them to do unto you.

Everyone—treat everyone you meet as you would want to be treated.

This is a universal truth; in fact, treat those with special problems, or handicaps, better than you would want or expect to be treated.

Always protect the smaller, the younger, the delicate.

Never abuse or unfairly take advantage of a situation because of your superior size or intelligence. Never take an unfair advantage at the expense of others.

Sports is an exception in most cases, but not always. As long as they keep score, play to win . . . but play by the rules and be fair and play clean too.

Take only your share.

Do your share.

If the thought were constantly on the minds of everyone on earth, what a great, great place this would be. You know that you would want to be treated fairly, with appreciation and respect. If everyone treated everyone else this way, there would be no war, and total peace would exist in our time.

The ol' do unto others clause;
As you wish to be treated—did you pause?
What a common and simple verse that's true!
And if all followed our phrase; we'd be merrier and happier too.

1J. DONATE TWO PINTS OF BLOOD EVERY YEAR

For most people—it is possible to donate six pints of blood each year. It is relatively painless, and I think it is a tremendous favor to the recipient. Donating blood gives the donor a major sense of accomplishment and sense of well-being. I have given about fourteen gallons. That represents about 114 times of contributions of blood. That really does not seem like much. One hundred and fourteen times in sixty-nine years.

Men and older women can benefit from donating blood for the same reason. Adult men do not need all the iron they get in vitamins and food. Women, after menopause, need no more iron than men. In both cases, the buildup of iron may cause blood clotting.

Recent medical evidence confirms the actual medical benefits to being a blood donor.

The long-term buildup iron in the blood has been connected to heart attacks and heart disease. The long-term build up of iron is reduced because iron is taken along with the blood contribution. Monitoring your blood chemistry and blood pressure are additional benefits of being a blood donor.

How else can you do so much good to help someone with a critical health emergency so easily and still do something to benefit you as well? I contend . . . really no where!

Donate blood . . . a life may be saved!
That life may be one who you don't know . . .
Or it may be your life that is saved,
Getting rid of old blood of is more than just show.

1K. MAKE NEW FRIENDS BUT CHERISH THE OLD ONES

This is part of the balancing of priorities, which is so much a part of life.

Life can get so full with family, job, and fitness activities that there is little time left for friends.

Friends, new and old, who are part of the family often result.

Friends who enjoy the same sport—physical fitness, golf, tennis, walking, etc.

Friends per se without common interests or separated by space often drop out of the picture.

That doesn't mean that these friendships can't be easily rekindled when you have an opportunity to be together again.

Friendships can be a spin-off from work, from church, from neighbors, from school/college, children's activities.

Seemingly, with life being so full, it is necessary for friendships to be spin-offs from other activities, which bring people together.

Make new friends but cherish the old ones, is one of life's little instructions, which I wish I would have done better.

Not only have I personally not made new friends—I haven't cherished the old ones enough to stay in close contact.

At times I feel lonely, without someone to discuss problems or issues.

There has not been time—it seems to do justice to family, job, and friendships.

This is good advice; try to strike a better balance than I did.

Seemingly so much time goes into children's entertainment, education, sports, and just care needs; there is little time left for friends. Time will tell if that was worth the tremendous investment of time and energy which must be put into the lives of children.

Friends are a must not to sweep.
I can advise but not show.
Family has been on my list to keep.
Mike, TA, and John were lost long ago.

1L.   KEEP SECRETS

Earn the trust of others. If they tell you something—don't spread that secret to everyone or anyone you know. Telling a secret to even one additional person opens the secret to everyone and out of your control. Once you tell one other person, you have no control whether the whole world or just one more person knows about the secret.

If someone tells you something and asks you not to spread that around, don't tell anyone.

Nothing destroys a friendship, hurts feelings or brings anger, faster than being told something in confidence and breaking that confidence by telling others.

This is a matter of trust.

We/you have to earn the trust of others. To do this, people must gain confidence in us by experience. As long as we maintain the trust, their confidence in us will grow. Telling the secrets of others, lying, breaking confidences will cause them to lose confidence in us.

A secret is too important to trust to just one?
A secret is no longer if shared even as a pun.
Resist if you must tell just one under the sun.
Telling secrets must be fun.
But if you get an urge, please run!

1M. DON'T WASTE TIME LEARNING THE "TRICKS OF THE TRADE"; INSTEAD, LEARN THE TRADE.

It is best to have the broadest, all-around education before you start to specialize. Young people are not necessarily wise enough early to know what they want to do later. A broad-based education will be helpful to identify topics, which the young person might enjoy or have special aptitude. Then when a preferred "lifetime" activity becomes apparent . . . specialized and deeper study can be targeted on the necessary information. If you had any math or/and chemistry, physics aptitude, take those classes as for and as soon as you can.

A clean slate mind does not know enough to make lifetime decisions without a broad, general education.

If you do something, such as painting, wood working, engineering, and so on—it is best to understand the basics of the trade before short-cut measures and specialization are implemented.

In all cases though, thinking about improvement should always be practiced. Understand in detail the "why something is done," and that process can be improved. Blindly doing something because that is the way it's always been done is not the preferred approach.

There was an example at home when our son was showing me how to solve word problems by the method he was taught at school. They were taught to guess and check rather than thinking about the problem and writing an equation to solve the problem and obtain the correct answer.

"Guess and check" is a trick of the trade, while solving the problem is the trade.

Learn the skill first, and then if you want—apply the short cuts. Adding, subtraction, multiplication, and division all should be learned before going to the calculators as a shortcut.

Work smart, though! Working smart is not a trick as implied with this little instruction.

In the study and perfection of math skills, learn the trade by practicing sample problems over and over. There are no short cuts to working the sample problems and absolutely understanding every single aspect of what you are doing. The calculator, as a trick of the trade, should be avoided while doing school-type practice problems.

A play on words is to learn a trick . . .
When skills are needed for most, it is true!
A trick of the trade makes life's path pretty slick.
Of course, I am only thinking of you!

1N. ADMIT YOUR MISTAKES

Personal confidence is the key to being able to admit your mistakes. And having the confidence to admit that you made a mistake, if you are wrong, will build stronger confidence.

Keep in mind that it is far easier to explain why you are going to do something to be successful at an activity that you were supposed to or expected to have a appreciable degree of competence than to explain why you didn't do something you supposedly should have been able to perform and were committed to do.

This requires thought and a plan. Action that needs to be taken must be taken. Omissions may occur as a result of a plan—not because there was no plan.

Accidents are accidents and should easily be admitted—once. Multiple "accidents" of the same event are not acceptable. Fear of admitting your mistake comes from the thought that you have done wrong and will be punished, ridiculed, or lectured.

In one sense, that is positive because it implies a conscience. In this day and age, the presence of a conscience in a person is a positive attribute.

However, one's actions must be planned enough to avoid the multiple accidents—or all "accidents" if possible.

In all cases—the first mistake should more easily be forgiven. From then on—once you understand the rules, accidents are not a satisfactory reason for an inappropriate event.

Come on my friend, admit a mistake.
It wipes your conscience clean.
Don't fear, it's clear . . . make your break.
You will want to be seen!

10. BE BRAVE. EVEN IF YOU'RE NOT, PRETEND TO BE. NO ONE CAN TELL THE DIFFERENCE.

My advice is a little different. Be honest; be courageous; be and act with intelligence and honesty.

You can be brave, even just acting brave, and end up dead!

Accepting a dangerous dare is an act of bravery—or pretended bravery and very stupid! You would be courageous—but you would not be honest and definitely would not be acting with intelligence.

Be honest; your true feelings will be shared by quality people in all of life's situations. Of course, there are many people in this world with limited scruples, and with no ethics, kindness, or compassion. Your feelings and values may not match theirs, however, and that's good.

Be courageous; consistent with honesty and intelligence. It is courageous to act with honesty and intelligence, and don't accept dangerous and thoughtless dares.

Be brave but act with intelligence; think before you act and stay focused on your life's vision rather than trying to impress someone with mindless bravery.

Never cheat, be brave . . . but I repeat, never cheat.
Truth to self . . . on our team . . . is at the seat . . .
For all our lives I must repeat . . .
Be brave but never cheat.

1P.   CHOOSE A CHARITY IN YOUR COMMUNITY AND SUPPORT IT GENEROUSLY WITH YOUR TIME AND MONEY

This certainly is a judgment call: which charity you choose, what you define as a charity, and how do you define supporting your charity generously?

Your family, your wife, your parents, and your children should be your number-one charity in line for earliest and most support.

I consider your job, provided you approach your job with dedication and extra commitment, such as teaching and support of children, completely satisfying the commitment to choose a charity and supporting it generously. Similarly, a job with state or any government or private sector and focused on accomplishing some public good qualifies in my mind as a charity if you have a commitment in time and money for that public or private job.

Most private or government jobs would qualify for a charity in my mind if the tasks are pushed with a passion and have some intrinsic positive worth to others. Even though you are performing the public or private job for a paycheck, your service provided makes for the hardworking and dedicated worker, a job sufficient to qualify for a charity. Besides if you were not earning a paycheck, you would need charity support yourself.

The difference between government pay and private sector pay is no longer certain enough to make any big deal of the differences. The good accomplished by both public and private jobs should qualify as public service and the public good—similar to a charity.

Even private sector jobs have a strong element of service. If you devote your passion to your job no matter whether it is public or private, it should count in my mind as a charity.

Contributions to church, the Leukemia Foundation, school-based foundations, and political parties are all opportunities for contributions to a charity.

Choose a cause and give it your support.
Why look to the IRS for your call?
They tax it away, you must report.
In the spring you give it, it's no ball.
There is no choice; no way to contort;
Your generous gift is taken or you fall.

1Q. READ THE BILL OF RIGHTS

People in the United States have rights. From these ten rights listed in the Bill of Rights plus the remainder of the United States Constitution and other amendments thereof, Americans have many, many expressed and implied rights.

These rights should come with certain responsibilities from our Christian heritage.

Written rights, which are protected, without adherence to responsibilities, will bring down the country. Protects the rights without addressing responsibilities will contribute to chaos.

RESPONSIBILITIES

We have a responsibility to follow the laws of the city, county, state, and the United States to the best of our ability.

We have the responsibility to treat others as we would hope to be and expect to be treated.

We have the responsibility to work and earn our own keep as an adult.

Children have the responsibility to keep their rooms clean, to do their share of family chores, study and do their best in school, and to determine one thing to be as good or better at as anyone else.

We have the responsibility to eat healthy, live a healthy lifestyle, and exercise.

We have the responsibility to love and nurture our families.

We have the responsibility to make a positive contribution to society.

BILL OF RIGHTS

AMENDMENT 1
Congress shall make no law respecting an establishment of religion or prohibiting the free exercise thereof; or abridging the freedom of speech,

or of the press; or the right of the people peaceably to assemble, and to petition the government for a redress of grievances.

COMMENT: Congress shall make no laws establishing a state religion. Also, the Congress shall not prohibit the free exercise of religion. Since Amendment 10 says that powers not given to congress, or prohibited by the constitution to the states, are reserved for the states or people. And since the first amendment itself is fairly restricted, today's absolute separation of church and state is erroneous—but real. State and local governments should be able to take whatever approach to religion that they deem appropriate as long as they do not prohibit the free exercise of religion by other individuals.

AMENDMENT 2
A well-regulated militia being necessary to the security of a free State, the right of the people to keep and bear arms shall not be infringed.

COMMENT: Based on *World Book Encyclopedia—Thorndike-Barnhart Dictionary*, "militia" means military force, army of citizens who are not regular soldiers but who undergo training for emergency duty or national defense, etc. The state national guard units are in the definition of militia. As a second point of the amendment the right of people to own and bear arms is so very clear. It has to be one of the clearest of the amendments. The right of our citizenry to be armed is assured by the Second Amendment.

AMENDMENT 3
No soldier shall, in time of peace, be quartered in any house, without the consent of the owner; nor in time of war but in a manner to be prescribed by law.

COMMENT: Soldiers shall not be quartered in our homes during peace. OK. And soldiers cannot be quartered in our homes during war except by act of congress. OK. These are OK, and I do not know of current violations or misinterpretations of this amendment.

AMENDMENT 4
The right of the people to be secure in their persons, houses, papers, and effects, against unreasonable searches and seizures, shall not be violated, and no warrants shall issue, but upon probable cause, supported by oath or

affirmation, and particularly describing the place to be searched, and the persons or things to be seized.

COMMENT: Our persons, our property shall not be searched or seized without reasonable cause. But what is a "reasonable cause" for searching and seizing? A body of law exists and ideally defines what is reasonable and unreasonable. I think and expect that if you have not taken something that doesn't belong to you, you will not have a problem with the unreasonable searches and seizures.

Keep your "act" clean and work for what you have—I have to believe that this advice will serve you well and keep you free of unreasonable searches and seizures.

No warrants, or approvals, shall be given for arrests or for searches unless it can be shown that with a high degree of confidence that there is some illegal activity going on. Then a judge, for example, could give the police written approval to search for certain specific information connected to the suspicion of illegal activity.

AMENDMENT 5
No person shall be held to answer for a capital, or otherwise infamous crime, unless on a presentment or indictment of a grand jury, except in cases arising in the land or naval forces, or in the militia, when in actual service in time of war or public danger; nor shall any person be subject, for the same offense, to be twice put in jeopardy of life or limb; nor shall be compelled, in any criminal case, to be a witness against himself, nor be deprived of life liberty, or property, without due process of law; nor shall private property be taken for public use, without just compensation.

COMMENT: No person shall be tried for a crime unless indicted by a grand jury or specifically charged clearly based on the evidence. An exception is when you are with the military in time of war. No person shall be tried for the same crime twice. This is circumvented these days by first charging the person with the criminal charge. Then if found innocent of the criminal charge, they could be tried for violating the person's civil rights or some other similar charge. This is double jeopardy in my mind, but the Supreme Court allows it by the way they interpret the constitution. I believe this is wrong.

No person shall be required to give information to convict himself or herself.

No person shall be deprived of freedom, liberty, or his or her life without the complete process of the laws of our country.

Also your property cannot be taken from you for public use without just compensation.

As with many topics that come up relative to our constitution over time, interpretation and application of laws and rules have gotten so complicated.

The Ten Commandments might be comparable to our constitution. The laws and subsequent regulations of the Old Testament have made the application of the Ten Commandments almost impossible. Similarly, the U.S. Constitution and Bill of Rights have become almost ridiculous with some of the expanding interpretation of the courts aided by legislation hungry legislators.

AMENDMENT 6
In all criminal prosecutions, the accused shall enjoy the right to a speedy and public trial, by an impartial jury of the State and district wherein the crime shall have been committed, which district shall have been previously ascertained by law; and to be informed of the nature and cause of the accusation; to be confronted with the witness against him; to have compulsory process for obtaining witness in his favor; and to have the assistance of counsel for his defense.

COMMENT: People accused of a crime shall have a right to a speedy and public trial by a fair and impartial jury from the area where the crime was committed. A person tried shall be told the nature and reason why he or she was charged and why he will be tried.

The person being accused and tried shall have the right to confront his or her accusers.

Further the person accused shall have the assistance of a lawyer and may have witnesses in his behalf if they exist.

AMENDMENT 7
In suits at common law, where the value in controversy shall exceed twenty dollars, the right of trial by jury shall be preserved; and no fact tried by a jury, shall be otherwise reexamined in any court of the United States other than according to the rules of the common law.

COMMENT: A jury trial may be requested where the value in question exceeds $20. And once a jury reaches a decision, the case may not be examined further or again unless the law allows. And with the Sixth Amendment, it is difficult to see how the case could be retried. If the person were determined to be guilty under the criminal side, it may be possible to get civil action. But, double jeopardy prohibition shouldn't prevent it being possible to get civil case though if the person is determined to be innocent of the crime.

AMENDMENT 8
Excessive bail shall not be required, nor excessive fines imposed, nor cruel and unusual punishments inflicted.

COMMENT: If a person has been arrested, the bail charged to get the person out of jail until trial must not be excessive. As with many things, the courts determine what is excessive. And the amount of bail needs to be commensurate with the likelihood of the person appearing for trial and the severity of the crime. Big, serious crimes will have the higher bails, especially if there are minimal ties to the community and lots of money is involved.

Cruel and unusual punishment shall not be allowed. Modeling our prisons and punishments after the way they were at the time of the constitution would be fine. They were definitely not cruel and unusual because the founding fathers were satisfied with them at time the founding fathers started the country. A prison system identical to the system at the time of our founding fathers should be OK for us and our criminals today.

AMENDMENT 9
The enumeration in the Constitution, of certain rights, shall not be construed to deny or disparage others retained by the people.

COMMENT: Listing certain rights in the Bill of Rights should not be interpreted as limiting in any way the other rights of the people that they wish to retain or provide . . . not specifically listed in this Bill of Rights.

AMENDMENT 10

The powers not delegated to the United States by the Constitution, nor prohibited by it to the States, are reserved to the States respectively, or to the people.

COMMENT: This is a key amendment too. Powers not given to the United States government by the constitution and are not a prohibited function of the States, by the constitution, are set aside and reserved to the States. If the Constitution did not give the power to the United States government, then the power must be left for the States to carry out. This is a major issue with federal government taking more and more power into itself . . . contrary to the United States Constitution.

The bill of rights you see . . .
Lack an important piece, if you ask me!
Rights without responsibility . . .
Is like a ship without a sea . . .
Or like a car without a key!

READ THE U.S. CONSTITUTION

Read the Constitution of the United States. The following is my summary of the U.S. Constitution although much of the document has been quoted verbatim.

Preamble

We the People of the United States, in order to form a more perfect union, establish justice, ensure domestic tranquility, provide for the common defense, promote the general welfare, and secure the blessing of liberty to ourselves and our posterity, do ordain and establish the Constitution of the United States of America.

Article 1: Congress
Article 1 Describes and lists the powers ascribed to the congress; who shall be in congress; numbers of congressmen and that taxes shall be apportioned by numbers of people in the states; two senators from each state; qualification for members of the House and Senate; composition of the Senate; frequency of House and Senate meetings; compensation for serving in Congress; revenue bills must start in the House; the president must sign all bills before they can become law; limits on states to sign treaties or tax commerce without Congress's approval; Congress has the power to lay and collect taxes; collect duties; borrow money on the credit of the U.S.; regulate commerce; regulate immigration; print currency; establish a post office and a system of roads; raise and support an army, navy, and militia; make rules for government; regulate the land; decide the punishment for piracy; and to establish them within government. The president, vice president, and all civil officers of the United States shall be removed from office on impeachment for, and conviction of treason, bribery, or other high crimes and misdemeanors.

Article 2: The President
Article 2 describes the power of the president; the process for electing and replacing the president including the Electoral College; the compensation of the president; the oath of office of the president; the presidential commander in chief of the Armed Services powers; the president fills vacancies in the Supreme Court and other high offices within government; the president must be a natural born citizen or a citizen of the U.S. at time of signing of constitution, the same for the vice president; the president shall from time to time make a report to Congress as to the state of the

nation; and the president shall be removed from office on impeachment for, and conviction of treason, bribery, or other high crimes and misdemeanors;.

Article 3: Judicial Powers
Article 3: describes the judicial powers of the United States including the Supreme Court and such inferior courts as the congress may establish; the judges shall hold their office during good behavior and shall be compensated; judicial power shall extend to all cases and laws; the trials in all cases except impeachment shall be by jury. Treason against the United States shall consist only in levying war against them or in adhering to their enemies, giving them aid and comfort; it will take two witnesses to convict one of treason, and the Congress shall have the power to declare the punishment of treason, but one cannot be convicted of treason through the treasonous act of a family member.

Article 4: State's and Citizen's Rights
Article 4: Full faith and credit shall be given in each state to the public Act, records and judicial proceeding of every other state; citizens of one state shall be entitled to the privileges and immunities of citizens in the other states; commitments owed in one state are still owed even when going to another state; states may not be created out of other states without the consent of the forming state; and each state is assured of the right to have a Republican form of government.

Article 5: Amending the Constitution
Article 5: The constitution may be amended if two-thirds of both Houses shall deem it necessary. The Congress shall propose the amendments to the Constitution or on the application of the legislatures of two-thirds of the states, shall call a convention for proposing amendments, which, in either case, shall be valid to all intents as a part of the Constitution when ratified by the legislatures of three-fourths of the states or by convention in three-fourths of the states.

Article 6: Pre Constitution Debts Good Post
Article 6: All agreements, including debts, agreed to by the Confederation of States shall be binding after the Constitution; the Constitution and laws shall be the supreme law of the land; the judges in every state shall be bound thereby; Congress and offices of the states shall be bound by oath or affirmation to support the Constitution, but no religious test shall ever be required as a qualification to any office or public trust under the United States.

Article 7: Ratification of the Constitution Process
Article 7: Nine of the states must ratify.

AMENDMENTS:
AMENDMENT 1
Congress shall make no law respecting an establishment of religion or prohibiting the free exercise thereof; or abridging the freedom of speech, or of the press; or the right of the people peaceably to assemble, and to petition the government for a redress of grievances.

AMENDMENT 2
A well-regulated militia being necessary to the security of a free state, the right of the people to keep and bear arms shall not be infringed.

AMENDMENT 3
No soldier shall, in time of peace, be quartered in any house, without the consent of the owner; nor in time of war but in a manner to be prescribed by law.

AMENDMENT 4
The right of the people to be secure in their persons, houses, papers, and effects, against unreasonable searches and seizures, shall not be violated, and no Warrants shall issue, but upon probable cause, supported by oath or affirmation, and particularly describing the place to be searched, and the persons or things to be seized.

AMENDMENT 5
No person shall be held to answer for a capital, or otherwise infamous crime, unless on a presentment or indictment of a grand jury, except in cases arising in the land or naval forces, or in the militia, when in actual service in time of war or public danger; nor shall any person be subject, for the same offense, to be twice put in jeopardy of life or limb; nor shall be compelled, in any criminal case, to be a witness against himself, nor be deprived of life liberty, or property, without due process of law; nor shall private property be taken for public use, without just compensation.

AMENDMENT 6
In all criminal prosecutions, the accused shall enjoy the right to a speedy and public trial, by an impartial jury of the State and district wherein the crime shall have been committed, which district shall have been previously ascertained by law; and to be informed of the nature and cause

of the accusation; to be confronted with the witness against him; to have compulsory process for obtaining witness in his favor; and to have the assistance of counsel for his defense.

AMENDMENT 7
In suits at common law, where the value in controversy shall exceed twenty dollars, the right of trial by jury shall be preserved; and no fact tried by a jury, shall be otherwise reexamined in any court of the United States other than according to the rules of the common law.

AMENDMENT 8
Excessive bail shall not be required, nor excessive fines imposed, nor cruel and unusual punishments inflicted.

AMENDMENT 9
The enumeration in the Constitution, of certain rights, shall not be construed to deny or disparage others retained by the people.

AMENDMENT 10
The powers not delegated to the United States by the Constitution, nor prohibited by it to the States, are reserved to the States respectively, or to the people.

AMENDMENT 11
The judicial power of the United States shall not be construed to extend to any suit in law or equity, commenced or prosecuted against one of the United States by citizens of another state, or by citizens or subjects of any foreign state.

AMENDMENT 12
Electors shall meet in their respective states and vote by ballot for president and vice president, one of whom, at least, shall not be an inhabitant of the same state with themselves.

AMENDMENT 13

1. Neither slavery nor involuntary servitude, except as a punishment for crime, whereof the party shall have been duly convicted, shall exist within the United States, or any place subject to their jurisdiction.
2. Congress shall have power to enforce this article by appropriate legislation.

AMENDMENT 14

1. All persons born or naturalized in the United States, and subject to the jurisdiction thereof, are citizens of the United Sates and of the state wherein they reside. No state shall make or enforce any law, which shall abridge the privileges or immunities of citizens of the United States; nor shall any State deprive any person of life, liberty, or property without due process of law; nor deny any person within its jurisdiction the equal protection of the laws.
2. Representatives shall be apportioned among the several states according to the respective numbers excluding Indians who are not taxed. The right to vote shall not be abridged for federal or state offices to any male, twenty-one and a citizen of the United States or in any way limited except for participation in a rebellion or other crime.
3. No person shall be a senator or representative in Congress, or elector of president and vice president, or hold office, civil or military who has engaged in insurrection or rebellion against the same or given aid or comfort to the enemies thereof.
4. The validity of the public debt of the United States authorized by law, including debts incurred for payment of pensions and bounties for services in suppressing insurrection or rebellion, shall not be questioned. But neither the United States nor any state shall assume or pay any debt or obligation incurred in the aid of insurrection or rebellion against the United States . . .
5. The Congress shall have power to enforce, by appropriate legislation, the provisions of this article.

AMENDMENT 15

1. The right of citizens of the United States to vote shall not be denied or abridged by the United States or by any state on account of race, color, or previous condition of servitude.
2. The Congress shall have power to enforce this article by appropriate legislation.

AMENDMENT 16

The Congress shall power to lay and collect taxes on incomes from whatever source derived, without apportionment among the several states and without regard to any census or enumeration.

AMENDMENT 17
The Senate of the United States shall be composed of two senators from each state, elected by the people thereof . . .

AMENDMENT 18
After one year from ratification of this article the manufacture, sale, or transportation of intoxicating liquors within, the importation thereof into or the exportation thereof from the United States and all territory subject to the jurisdiction thereof for beverage purposes is hereby prohibited . . .

AMENDMENT 19
The right of citizens of the United States to vote shall not be denied or abridged by the United States or by any state or account of sex.

AMENDMENT 20
The terms of the president and vice president shall end at noon on the twentieth day of January, and the terms of senators and representatives at noon on the third day of January, of the years in which such terms would have ended if this article had not been ratified; and terms of their successors shall then begin . . .

AMENDMENT 21
The eighteenth article of amendment to the Constitution of the United States is hereby repealed . . .

AMENDMENT 22
No person shall be elected to the office of the presidency more than twice . . .

AMENDMENT 23
The District of Columbia shall be entitled to presidential electors but not more than the least populous state.

AMENDMENT 24
The right of a citizen to vote shall not be denied or abridged by the United States or any state by reason of failure to pay any poll tax or other tax.

Congress shall have power to enforce this article by appropriate legislation.

AMENDMENT 25
In case of the removal of the president from office or of his death or resignation, the vice president shall become president.

The system of presidential succession is again amended to go from president to vice president, and another vice president is named if there is time; otherwise, the succession is to the president pro tempore of the Senate and the Speaker of the House of Representatives.

When the vice president becomes president, the president shall nominate a vice president with a majority vote of both houses of Congress.

When the president writes to tell the president pro tempore of the Senate and Speaker of the House that he is unable to conduct the office, the vice president becomes acting president until the president tells the Congress to the contrary. If the vice president and a majority of principal offices of executive department indicate that the president is unable, the vice president shall become president; Congress has four days to act.

AMENDMENT 26
Allows eighteen-year-olds to vote.

AMENDMENT 27
No law varying the compensation for the Congress shall take effect until an election of representatives shall have intervened.

1R. USE CREDIT CARDS ONLY FOR CONVENIENCE, NEVER FOR CREDIT

A credit card can be extremely convenient—buying gasoline, small items that you need as a matter of routine in your daily life. It can take the place of a "wad" of bills in your pocket and allows you to write one check at the end of the month.

This is convenience. However, because it is convenient, large balances of debts can be accumulated on a credit card for VCR, TVs, clothes. The once-convenient credit card becomes a large chain and block around your neck and can drag you down financially and emotionally.

If you keep my philosophy to live below your means in mind when you use the credit card, you will be fine.

Living within your means when using credit will protect you.

   Credit itself is something that should be avoided with a few exceptions.

Using credit to buy a home is satisfactory.

Similarly, purchasing a car also may need to be done with credit.

Combined house and car payments should be in the range of 30 percent of the take-home pay of your family.

Credit cards bring to mind the need to stress responsibilities along with rights. Spending money is easy and is a right. Without caution and the burden of actually parting with the cash, the responsibility of spending the money wisely is not fully appreciated.

Credit cards are a cash roll.
For convenience and safety to prevent a mugging,
Cards shouldn't be a tool out of control!
Restrained and unused, you will deserve a hugging.

1S. NEVER CHEAT

Never cheat; of course, never cheat. What else can be said except to never lie either?

Never cheat; it is always easier to explain why you did something than to explain why you cheated or lied. There is no way to explain cheating or lying. When you cheat or lie to others, you are cheated out of your self-respect.

So many more problems come from cheating and lying than from telling the truth.

First, if you have a lifetime commitment to not cheating or lying, your behavior will be influenced because you accept the fact that you will not be able to cheat or lie to get out of the bind. Your approach to problem solving, your approach to all of life's situations will be different if you enter into a problem-solving situation not having cheating or lying as an alternative.

Second, the character and integrity of someone who cheats is about as low as one can imagine. You know it and have to live with the burden if you cheat or lie.

Third, the person's impression of him or herself will be very low.

I would say that the large, large majority of cheats or liars are not happy and are not happy with themselves.

On the other hand, someone who achieves consistently and honestly is highly likely to be happy with themselves and with life.

Never cheat, I repeat never cheat!
Truth on our team, I must repeat.
Of all our lines I must repeat.
Never cheat, never cheat!

1T. GIVE YOURSELF A YEAR AND READ THE BIBLE COVER TO COVER

You will be enriched from the knowledge you receive from this important goal. Let me tell you what I think you should get out of this year of reading.

God is all and completely powerful. His power is beyond all understanding.

God created the heavens and the earth.

God made a promise to people that if they followed His rules, He would make everything nice—absolutely no problems, and they could live eternally trouble free. His promise of problem-free life and protection from enemies and disease was and is conditional. That condition was broken.

He made the promise again and gave the people the Ten Commandments to follow. If they—His people, followed His rules, He would protect them and provide His people with good health, wealth, and power. The people failed to follow His Rules. Again, the conditions of His promise was broken.

Ten Commandments

1. You shall have no other Gods before me.
2. You shall not make yourself an idol; nor shall you bow down to them or worship them.
3. You shall not misuse the name of the Lord your God.
4. Observe the Sabbath day by keeping it holy.
5. Honor your father and mother.
6. You shall not murder.
7. You shall not commit adultery.
8. You shall not steal.
9. You shall not give false testimony.
10. You shall not covet your neighbor's wife or his property.

He made his promise again!

Forgiveness of sins—broken rules, could be accomplished through a process of animal sacrifices and other complicated procedures. God then decided that mankind was not capable of following rules and offered a simpler way of having sins forgiven. God sent His son Jesus to earth to teach his people, then die on the cross as a once and last time when a sacrifice would be necessary for the forgiveness of sins.

If you have faith in God and Jesus and are repentant or sorry for your sins, you will be forgiven and can spend your life after death with God and Jesus in heaven.

During the period, which includes the present, when mankind is disobeying God's rules, He will not provide protection and support for His people. Prayer for things, specific acts, or general protection during this period is a waste of time and to suggest that there is power in such prayer is terribly misleading. Apparently, unanswered prayer is not a personal punishment . . . remember, God said several times that if His people are obedient to His rules, He would smooth their path and basically make them healthy, wealthy, and wise. People in general do not obey His rules, and He does not provide the health, wealth, and wisdom He conditionally promised. Ultimately, salvation, eternal life, is the important element of reading and understanding the Bible. Salvation, eternal life, is available to those who are repentant and have faith in God and Jesus.

Reading the Bible was my goal.
I can't remember how long it took.
The morning sessions took their toll . . .
When I got up early to read the book!
Salvation is its role.

1U. LEARN TO LISTEN. OPPORTUNITY SOMETIMES KNOCKS VERY SOFTLY

Listen to what others say; listen to your thoughts.

These are opportunities to be of service to another.

These are opportunities to be a friend and give support.

These are opportunities for expanding your business or professional enterprise.

Actually, I would add "observe" to the direction to listen. My advice would be to listen and observe.

Always help friends; support their needs.

Always take the high road—the compassionate road when dealing with others.

I can't say in every case—go to the nth degree to help others, but people with needs should be helped. Never contribute to a person's misery or difficulty and don't kick a person when he or she is down.

For many reasons, listen and observe for the opportunity to help others.

Of course, there are business reasons for listening. Business is service to your customers. Selling your services to your customers will always involve observing and listening.

Being at the right place, at the right time, with the right product, with the right relationship with your customer is success in business.

If you are selling a service (and this can be from the point of view of a lawyer, to an engineer, to a teacher, to a medical doctor, to insurance to computer sales to computer programming/analyst), you need to listen very carefully to the comments and conversations of others. You will identify situations for which your services are needed.

In all your dealings with others, listen and observe what they are saying very carefully. Often, more can be gained from observations than from what they say.

Listen and think about what to do.
Your career may come quietly to you!
Be your own boss should be high on your list.
Opportunity may whisper or it may not, tsk, tsk.

1V. NEVER DEPRIVE SOMEONE OF HOPE; IT MIGHT BE ALL HE OR SHE HAS

In all interactions with others, strive to create a win-win situation; each individual actually gains from the interchange.

This is much, much better than a situation in which only one person or one group of individuals is the clear winner while the other side is the clear loser.

With a win-win situation, there will be reason to continue the relationship, and both leave the interchange feeling good about themselves and the other person. Each having hope and looking forward to the future. This is what we should strive for in each of our dealings with our fellow human beings.

Hope is all some have.
But if hope is all they have . . .
What do they really have?
Not much . . . but they can build to a "have".

1W. PRAY NOT FOR THINGS, BUT FOR WISDOM AND COURAGE

Pray?

I am not going to get into a long biblical discussion here.

When God's people are obedient to His Laws and rules, He will answer the prayers of His people. He will provide for their health, wealth, wisdom, and power.

When God's people are not obedient to His laws and rules, He eventually will stop answering the prayers of His people. He will stop providing for their health, wealth, wisdom, and power.

If you pray or think about the importance of God and of Jesus's death on the cross, then you are more apt to have the faith and repentance necessary for eternal life.

But praying for things or even wisdom and courage, I sincerely believe, is a waste of time during a time when God's people are not obedient to His Laws and Rules.

Do all the right things to be healthy: diet, exercise, sleep, sound, wholesome relationships are all important.

But praying and expecting measurable results—I just do not believe are worthwhile and can result in your being frustrated and perhaps will result in the destruction of your faith in Jesus's ultimate gift. That gift being His death on the cross for the permanent forgiveness of our sins.

Praying for courage and wisdom?

That is like praying for something that is not measurable because if it is measurable, you are going to be frustrated and frustration leads to disbelief.

Courage and wisdom are desirable.

Courage is not a choice. Courage must be automatic because when you think through the choices, even when not courageous, you must be courageous because you must live with the consequences of your action or inaction.

Wisdom comes with maturity and education. When you are young, get yourself educated. Both formal and informal education are extremely important.

Newspapers, magazine, and books are all important sources of informal education. Even just reading the encyclopedia, hard copy or online, is great. Learn; learn what others did in similar situations.

That's the beginning of wisdom.

I believe wisdom is the application of knowledge; wisdom comes with experiences.

But if you have the knowledge and have opinions of your own, seasoned by your background knowledge of this opinion and have absorbed some of the wisdom of others, you yourself will have wisdom early.

Pray not for things or wisdom or courage I say.
Not that they are undeserved sins.
Pray that good will come in to play.
And we can forgive those who cheat for their wins.

1X. NEVER TAKE ACTION WHEN YOU'RE ANGRY

The general statement that you should not take action when you are angry is to keep you from making a mistake or saying something that you will regret later. It will be best to get in the habit of backing out of an angry situation. Let the situation cool and then come back the next day ready to deal with the issues.

Think about what you are going to say—perhaps write it down and—then, say it the next day.

The key is to think through what you want to say, when you are angry; then cool off before you take action.

There are other sayings that deal with the same topic of action while one is angry.

An angry boy is not too coy.

His temper royal is a real boil.

A fighting phrase will make you crazed.

Cool off first before you curse before you are cursed.

When there's an angry fire, Nautilus till you tire.

The best thing to do is to cool off first before taking action. There is no need to rush.

Angry? Who's angry not me.
I can see the forest for the lone tree.
If it anger occurs, listen to me . . .
Action requires reasoned thought you see.
So I say, think through your action . . . and let it be!

1Y. HAVE GOOD POSTURE. ENTER A ROOM WITH PURPOSE AND CONFIDENCE

Always maintain a straight-up, erect posture and hold your head up . . . same for your chin. This portrays both the appearance of pride and character and the reality of pride and character. This must be the way you live your life. An ideal companion to the appearance of pride and character is real pride and character enabled by a life consistent with these values.

Over a lifetime, this will require an emphasis on a diet and exercise program as well as an approach with life and people that will always leave you without shame and regret.

Treat people the way you would like to be treated.

With this approach to life, you will most likely always be able to walk straight up, erect, and hold your head up high.

Walk with grace, it will pay.
Stand tall, shoulders back, chest out.
Walk with an erect gait, not a sway.
Make your stance a short story of what you are all about.

1Z.   DON'T DISCUSS BUSINESS IN ELEVATORS

Don't discuss business in an elevator or when anyone else is around beyond the person to whom you are speaking.

You do not know who may overhear what you are saying. There are several corollaries:

Don't discuss business in the restroom; you don't know who is listening behind the stall door.

Similarly, do not discuss business in a restaurant or at a health club shower/changing room or at a sporting event bleachers.

The key here is the need to be aware of who is around you and the potential for them to overhear something you really would prefer them not to know or it is none of their business.

Of course, keeping your life simple enough so that it is really doesn't matter if people overhear what you are saying. This would be the best for any business, workday. There probably aren't more than two or three sentences that could not be heard by about everyone. Why not keep it simple and honest. And some of the conversations should be kept private only because they may appear to be boastful or in some way may be misunderstood and hurt someone's reputation. The elevator conversations may be more boastful or misunderstood rather than confidential.

Business and personal affairs?
Around Strangers, take the stairs.
Why involve others when you sell your wears?
Or, your business may be theirs.

1AA. NEVER PAY FOR WORK BEFORE IT'S COMPLETED

This is not intended to protect you from the honest, high-character people. It is intended to protect you from those who are dishonest and unscrupulous.

And the number of these people is getting larger and larger all the time . . . it seems.

Eventually, you will have the judgment to evaluate people and make this decision. Those who are really honest do not even expect to get paid anywhere near completely before they are totally done . . . unless they do not trust you.

So this should not be difficult to enforce as a personal policy. If a worker is installing or building something for you on a cost plus a fixed-fee basis, it would be appropriate to pay for the materials as they are delivered and for the labor at a week at a time, for example.

But if they have agreed to provide a given product for you at a given price, they would not expect you to pay them for the product until the product is done in accordance with the original agreement.

The method of payment and the delivery schedule for the finished product needs to be agreed to at the start of the project so that there is no confusion with the delivery schedule or the payment schedule. The initial agreement, written, is the key to maintaining a clear understanding of how and when payment is to be made.

People who can carry the funding of the project to the end are likely to be substantial and have experienced projects and had sufficient success to make your project successful. Deal with people whose personal practice is to try to do the right thing. Why even risk doing business with someone else with lesser values.

Make it a personal business practice . . .
To never pay early for work or for a cactus.
Cash on delivery will be a certainty.
You will be wise to take such a warranty.

1BB. BE WILLING TO LOSE A BATTLE IN ORDER TO WIN THE WAR.

Know what your objectives are.

Sometimes it may be necessary to forgo clothing expenditures in order to purchase the car. The car might be your ultimate goal, but if you aren't willing to pass up clothing or other short-range pleasures, you might not be able to afford the car. This is one battle lost compared to winning the war scenario.

Or in the case of dealing with your boss; it may not be wise to argue with him/her on every decision if your ultimate goal is to get the promotion.

These are two examples of willing wars—losing battles.

Winning a skirmish is not the ultimate objective; accomplishing your objective is the ultimate goal. Always try to deal with people in situations so that both sides, if it is that black and white, can win. Allow compromise so that your real objectives can be attained, and the other person can win and obtain satisfaction out of the interchange as well.

I remember the verbal battles resulting from a desired overnight stay. When thinking long term, that passion certainly gets in the way. Nothing, nothing should have evoked that passion, much less something as short term and meaningless. Battles over character and the tasks that are on your critical path must be the ones worth fighting and winning. Side issues, or momentary pleasures, are definitely not worth the passion and creating an adversarial relationship with peers, teammates, or loved ones.

Make sure the job is something that you enjoy doing. Find daily enjoyment in doing what you must do in the occupation you choose. That in itself can result in daily victories, or eliminating battles, for the long-term good of your career.

Know where you are going before you start!
A battle here, a skirmish there, tarnish games of the heart.
Know where you are heading or you will part.
Think long term and think wisely, control the heart to direct the cart.

1CC. DON'T GOSSIP

Don't talk about people in a negative way. If you don't have something positive to say, keep your mouth shut. Also, gossiping often breaks confidences, and that costs your credibility and the confidence of others.

If you don't have the trust of others, you don't have much.

I believe everyone gets in a situation where another person is being discussed in negative terms. You have choices: either add to the negative discussion, say nothing, or try to turn the negative discussion around by balancing the discussion with positive comments, or walk away. At least, do one of the latter two choices!

All situations are different and require different actions.

Never add to the negative; as a minimum, say nothing and try to say something positive.

To help keep this in perspective, keep in mind that anyone whom you observe saying negative things about an acquaintance or anyone else is very likely to be saying something negative about you when your back is turned.

Telling tales behind their back?
Why say it when it does not build?
Hurtful? Sure; you might as well pack.
Be a friend, tell the truth, they will be thrilled.

1DD. BEWARE OF THE PERSON WHO HAS NOTHING TO LOSE

All interchanges with people should end with a win-win situation.

Both parties should get something out of the interchange—both should win.

Dealing with someone with nothing to lose may not be typical when dealing with another person. Since they have nothing to lose, they might risk the whole thing and try for a "they win—you lose" deal. I don't think you should or want to come out of any situation where you feel that you lost and did not accomplish anything toward your ultimate objective.

Also, someone with nothing to lose may be vicious and ruthless.

Someone with an old clunker car may be less careful when they park or open their door in a parking lot—avoid parking by them.

Thieves are the best example of someone without something to lose. They can take something, even with force, and not risk a personal loss. Of course, they could be imprisoned, but thieves typically do not believe that imprisonment will occur.

Passionless people also fit into the category of an ideal thief. Without passion toward a topic, they have nothing to lose when they snip at your vision.

There are trade-offs in life, don't you agree.
More often than not, you can get what you want and so can he.
Without something to trade, you can see.
He won't get it unless it's free.

1EE. WHEN FACING A DIFFICULT TASK, ACT AS THOUGH IT IS IMPOSSIBLE TO FAIL. IF YOU ARE GOING AFTER MOBY DICK, TAKE ALONG THE TARTAR SAUCE.

Approach tasks with confidence. The implication here is a bit of a stretch though. Even blind faith of impending success is too much and beyond what I am suggesting.

When approaching a project, plan it out—step by step. You can even bring the "tartar sauce."

But it is critical that adequate planning takes place. The potential and planning for success needs to be assessed before the project is started.

Don't go after Moby Dick in a row boat with an eight feet long harpoon and a five-gallon bucket of tartar sauce. A five-gallon bucket of tartar sauce would be OK with a three-hundred-feet long ship, a cannon-fired harpoon, and one thousand feet of cable might be more appropriate.

Take a realistic assessment of potential success. Then if the chances look reasonable to you, go for it. The assessment must be realistic; then if you have a chance in your mind, go for it aggressively.

Any action you take do so with vigor.
Expect to win, count on the best.
Go for it with gusto, go with rigor.
Count on the win, count on the best.
Win the contest.

1FF. DON'T SPREAD YOURSELF TOO THIN. LEARN TO SAY NO POLITELY AND QUICKLY.

There must be a balance between doing, or trying to do too much, and not agreeing to do much at all.

Busy people get the most done.

I believe family should be top priority. Biblical teachings should guide your relationship with your family.

Then your job, seasoned with what you learned at church and from the Bible, should be your second priority.

Then church and church activities should be next.

Any one activity could be a source of overload so that nothing is done well.

Set priorities, know what your obligations are in each of your priorities, and agree to accept new items only consistent with your priorities and current workload.

Being too busy increases stress, decreases your pleasantness, and reduces the quality of what you do in life.

Base your yesses and nos on what you accept on your priorities list. Family is the first responsibility, then children, then spouse, and then parents, and so on in the family. Basic needs must be worked for and provided. Future education for children is important, but keep the abundance of your time on family. Life is a series of compromises and decisions, so keep a balance and error on the side of time for family.

Too busy to say anything but *no?*
Too busy to not say "I'm spread too thin".
There is always something to do, somewhere to go.
But then . . . you will begin to chase where you have been.

1GG. EXPECT LIFE TO BE FAIR. NEVER UNDERESTIMATE THE POWER OF FORGIVENESS. INSTEAD OF USING THE WORD "PROBLEM," TRY SUBSTITUTING THE WORD "OPPORTUNITY."

Yes, expect life to be fair. Good and bad things can and do happen to good as well as to bad people. No matter how good you are, bad, seemingly unfair events can happen to you.

Life is fair because everyone is subject to the same, seemingly random events.

There are some people who will not treat you right or fair no matter how well you treat them. That is not a statement on the fairness of life. That is a statement as to the fairness of that individual and an opportunity to choose the people with whom you associate.

Problems with people or other situations can be opportunities for you and many others to present solutions.

The way you live your life, the way you act, affects the way you are impacted by events. Accidents following an evening of drinking might not seem fair but they are certainly predictable.

What's totally not fair is the person that gets killed or injured by a driver who had been drinking. Certainly, that is not fair; but since all families may be impacted this way, fairness is not the issue. Being at the wrong place at the wrong time is a better description.

Poor health may not be fair but is totally predictable in cases of a lifestyle composed of fatty foods, no exercise, and minimal of the key vitamins C, B, omega 3 fish oil, beta-carotene, and certain minerals as magnesium, potassium, zinc, and selenium to name a few.

This type of lifestyle will result in poor health eventually; that's certain if not fair.

What is fair, you expect them to play by the rules.
But envy makes success out of sight.
Opportunity to achieve to develop the tools . . .
Should be a first and will refine your might.

1HH. NEVER WALK OUT ON A QUARREL WITH YOUR WIFE (UNLESS ONE OR BOTH OF YOU ARE ANGRY; IF ONE OR BOTH OF YOU ARE ANGRY, WALK OUT AND FINISH THE DISCUSSION WHEN YOU HAVE COOLED OFF).

Basically—that was his rule . . . my rule . . . what should have been my rule is always walk out on a quarrel with your wife/spouse.

You won't win it, and even if you "win," . . . you actually won't win; and if you think you won it, . . . I can tell you for sure you actually lost the quarrel.

A quarrel implies being angry, and if you are angry—cool off first.

Then later, before you have both escalated the situation to a totally more-serious problem than the original problem, talk it out. Talk in out later . . . much later!

By walking away, there is less of a chance to escalate the disagreement far beyond the original problem. Eventually, deal with the issue of the quarrel; but do not pursue the problem and solution while you are still angry.

An earlier philosophy charged you with never taking action when you are angry. This follows in that same theme. If you are angry, always walk out on a quarrel; cool off and come back later. Ninety-nine times out of a hundred, the problem is much less than it earlier appeared.

The activities of the day, the disappointments, the frustrations, the other interactions you may have had influence you and could result in a short temper and a quarrel. A minor issue resulting from a minor difference of opinion can escalate to a major flap.

Walk out! Go work out; go for a walk; then later resolve the issue if it still needs to be resolved.

What timely advice from one who knows.
Nothing will be won standing toes to toes.
He's and she's are not always in jest.
Continue when you are cool . . . I now know best.

1II. REGARDING FURNITURE AND CLOTHES, IF YOU THINK YOU'LL BE USING THEM FIVE YEARS OR LONGER, BUY THE BEST YOU CAN AFFORD.

Buy clothes carefully; watch for sales, discounts, etc., never buy anything anywhere near the normal retail price. Always buy quality though.

Quality, more than price. Study first and know what quality is before you buy. But when you know what constitutes quality, then search for the best price, far below retail. Lead stores in malls and other quality clothing stores often have sales where they drastically mark down merchandise so much you will be able to purchase quality clothing for 20 to 30 percent of retail.

Buy housing location relative to present and future uses of the neighborhood, values and character of the neighbors, appearance of the neighborhood, schools, shopping, police protection, overhead air traffic, power lines in the vicinity, and vehicle traffic.

Buy a car based on the *Consumer Reports* rating, style to your liking, larger than seemingly necessary engine, slightly used, like a demonstrator; buy nicer more costly cars and keep them longer; warrantees probably make you feel better than they are a value. Lean toward extending warrantees.

Actually, this is about what I do . . . except I generally don't pay attention to *Consumer Reports* . . . I usually buy cars based on style, efficiency, and other tips.

Always buy quality clothing. The best brands on sale or at outlet stores would be the best . . . my wife does the quality clothes buying. Me . . . I buy the everyday, rough and ready clothes at Walmart or Meijers . . . another large department store out of Michigan.

Choose shoes, much the same as clothing. Buy the best and they will wear longer. Avoid leather soles. Leather just does not wear well and is not worth the extra price you pay for leather soles. Me . . . I buy black or white Nike walking shoes for winter or summer off the Internet . . . It is hard to find size 14 shoes in stores. Internet shopping is very handy, and the selection is unbelievable!

Furniture . . . buy a few pieces at a time, but buy the best or high quality. If you buy a room full of cheap furniture, it will always look like a room full of cheap furniture. Buy quality, and what you have will show your good taste, and eventually you will have a room full or what you want of all quality furniture.

Get decorating advice from a noncluttered person and do not clutter your rooms with too much furniture. Bare is better.

Buy quality when it's a must.
Quality is something you can trust.
For the long haul, or bust.
The best is a necessity, it's not a lust . . .
And will more slowly turn to dust.

1JJ. BE BOLD AND COURAGEOUS. WHEN YOU LOOK BACK ON YOUR LIFE, YOU'LL REGRET THE THINGS YOU DIDN'T DO MORE THAN THE ONES YOU DID.

The key is to know what you want to do with and during your life; plan and then proceed with your life's plan. I believe the biggest regret would be to look back over the days, the weeks, the months, and the years of your life and decide that you wasted that time and did not use it to accomplish positive things. Don't you agree? Say yes!

Your plan can be reassessed, but you must have a plan, and you must be willing to move on your plan . . . say yes. Decide your
Expected success overall;
Expected success in grade school;
Expected success in sports;
Expected success in high school;
Expected success in college;
Expected knowledge in general;
Expected knowledge of the Bible;
Expected curriculum in college;
Expected accomplishments to be achieved, such as
o have a BS by a certain date;
o other degrees by certain dates;
Expected college to attend;
Expected people to be around;
Expected type of person to marry;
Expected location as to where to live;
Expected careers;
Expected travel;
Expected books to publish;
Expected approach to dealing with other people;
Be courageous; establish a plan and boldly go after it.

You might not be able to accomplish everything when you plan it—but you will accomplish more and will be more satisfied with your life than a life without a plan!

When someone asks you to do something with them . . . be a "yes man" . . . do it with them. Sometimes you may get into a bind, and you can always back out or wind your way out of it . . . but start with a yes, and mostly good things will happen.

This will help you select friends too.
Plan first, say yes . . . then act aggressively to achieve those things that you decide are important.

What is important . . . say yes to achieve?
No matter what it is, you must believe!
Dear ones I hope you know there is worth, there is worth
In the time spent since my birth.

1KK. FORGET COMMITTEES! NEW, NOBLE, WORLD-CHANGING IDEAS ALWAYS COME FROM ONE PERSON WORKING ALONE.

Committees or work groups can and usually do make problem solving extremely complicated and lengthy because all the committee members must feel good, concur, and have their say about the outcome of their committee work product.

On the other hand, if an individual with a mind capable of developing new, noble, world-changing ideas takes over the process of determining a solution to the problem, the time required to solve the problem will be greatly reduced. Then after operational, the plan can be adjusted.

Some people and personality types work better with committees but me . . . letting a committee be in charge of solving the problem guarantees delays and meandering in the problem solving process.

Discussion, developing a consensus, arriving at a solution gives everyone on the committee a chance to share the credit, but more importantly . . . it makes no one responsible, and everyone can defer the blame to others.

Once my time starts getting short and I materially care about the outcome, I will either take over the committee and lead it to where it should go (. . . in my mind) or I will leave the committee and solve the part that materially affects me by myself.

When it gets right down to the rubber hitting the road, the pedal to the medal . . . it will be the individual who comes up with the new, noble, world-changing ideas and then implements the idea without fear of taking the blame. This person knows that he/she will solve the problem and will go on to the next issue.

One man has to take charge.
By creating, by motivating my day in the sun . . .
I can lead through the maze by and large.
We know with the one it will be done.

1LL. STREET MUSICIANS ARE A TREASURE. STOP FOR A MOMENT AND LISTEN, THEN LEAVE A SMALL DONATION.

Street musicians are offering a free service in hopes that they will get paid something for their efforts. Street musicians offer something for their requested or hoped for donations.

Beggars do not offer anything in return, and their case is different. You need not feel obligated to donate to a beggar who offers nothing in return.

Try to appreciate and reward anyone who tries and has refined a skill such as a street musician.

A street musician is definitely trying; trying to do the thing they do best—play music, to support themselves.

The point of this instruction is to be aware of and kind to those people who cross our path. Appreciate the fact that they try to accomplish something and contribute. Recognize them as important people and reward them by a contribution if they are requesting a donation.

Also try to appreciate their human dignity by stopping to appreciate their talents, as you make a contribution, if at all possible.

How humbling it would be . . .
To play a flute or base fiddle on the street.
Yet you watch, they do it with glee.
Their treat, is hard to beat.

1MM. WHEN FACED WITH A SERIOUS HEALTH PROBLEM, GET AT LEAST THREE MEDICAL OPINIONS.

OK, get three opinions when faced with a serious health threat.

Don't act too quickly—get a clear assessment of the alternatives.

Hopefully, you will not have a serious health-related risk.

The deeper meaning here is that the medical community is not always a precise science; they do make mistakes; and they might not have kept up with the latest technology or research.

Starting with an imprecise diagnosis and going to an imprecise cure can result in serious detrimental consequences to a situation that was not, for certain, serious in the beginning.

Use the Internet to research the symptoms and diagnoses as well as potential treatments.

Depending on the diagnosis and treatment, seek information to confirm both as well as seek experts across the country who have the technologies and techniques recommended as having the most success.

I wish for you eternal good health.
This comes before my wish for your wealth.
But as with any decision,
Be wise and get another opinion.

1NN. WAGE WAR AGAINST LITTERING.

Never litter!

People who litter exhibit a trait that you should avoid. They are expecting someone else to clean up their mess. They are contributing to the burden with which society must deal. They cause more service needs which society must provide.

This is a user-type person who litters; not a contributor!

I contend that we have both users and contributors in our society.

People who support liberal political causes are the users. Don't depend on yourself; let the government do it for you. You don't like the messy paper-strewn landscape? The liberal, the litterer thinks that someone else, namely the government, will take care of the problem for you.

The person who cleans up after him or herself is the respectable, hardworking type who is never a victim and tries to take care of his or her problems. Avoid people who are so disrespectful that they just toss their waste out the window for someone else to pick up, or they just trash the landscape.

War against littering is too tough . . .
But don't litter, why leave trash around?
Make sure you improve, don't add to the ruff!
The opportunities for contributions abound.

100. AFTER ENCOUNTERING INFERIOR SERVICE, FOOD, OR PRODUCTS, BRING IT TO THE ATTENTION OF THE PERSON IN CHARGE. GOOD MANAGERS WILL APPRECIATE KNOWING.

Life is a series of interactions between us as individuals and others in our society.

We may be disappointed with any of these interactions, but we do not need to always speak about someone else not meeting our expectations when they fail to live up to our standards.

Nor should we speak up every time someone doesn't meet our expectations.

There is some judgment involved here. There is a question of compassion too.

So do not be so quick to judge a service or a product as inferior.

If a worker is lying or cheating, I say the question of kindness and compassion ends. Show no mercy.

For an honest mistake, there is plenty of room for compassion and kindness. Also there almost always is an easy way to correct most situations of service in a restaurant. Give them a chance to fix the problem. They usually will be glad to correct the problem; and they will do it quickly and will be grateful and respectful to you for working with them to correct the situation with them.

In some cases, the manager can and should be told. Not at the first incident though. In the absence of lying and cheating, the employee should be given an opportunity to correct the situation before bringing the manager into the situation.

Why wait till it's too late?
It does no good after you ate!
Give them a chance . . . maybe more than one.
Then, take your seat, you have won.

1PP. DON'T PROCRASTINATE. DO WHAT NEEDS DOING WHEN IT NEEDS TO BE DONE.

Procrastination is probably the biggest obstacle to accomplishing tasks and achieving your true destiny.

If something needs to be done, then do it; if you absolutely cannot do that at the moment you identified the tasks, then make a list. Prioritize the list frequently and continually make progress on accomplishing the tasks highest on your priority list.

Do one thing at a time. Look at your list as a series of "one things"!

Avoiding the performance of a task creates anxiety in the mind of a procrastinator.

Get in the habit of doing things as soon as possible after you know the item needs to be done. This habit will serve you well in anything and everything you do.

Use a list as a reminder of what needs to be done and as a symbol of all that you have accomplished.

A list with checks indicating completed tasks can be very satisfying!

Too much work and no play . . .
Is not exactly what I was trying to say.
Hard work is certainly a desirable trait.
Why wait to start until it is too late?

1QQ. GET YOUR PRIORITIES STRAIGHT. NO ONE EVER SAID ON HIS DEATHBED, "GEE, IF I'D ONLY SPENT MORE TIME AT THE OFFICE."

Get your priorities straight. Life is a series of compromises. The important things in your life need balance. Your family, your job, your health, your church activities, your hobbies, your public service efforts, and your "mark" are all critically important to you and me.

None of these noble categories of your life can receive all of one's time and resources at any one time. Your family is probably the most important. But without health and income and some sense of vision as to where are you headed in your life, your family will suffer.

You will not be real pleasant and supportive to your family without balance. At least one pleasant experience with your family each day is ideal.

With younger children in the house, that is easy. Sports and reading are a pathway to doing many things with children. Share a story, a newspaper article, or a letter with someone in your family each day. One pleasant experience each day is important.

As far as your health goes, each person needs clear-cut goals for diet and exercise. At least thirty minutes each day of vigorous aerobic and weight trainings exercises or one hour of walking and weight training are important. A diet consisting of minimal red meat and minimal fat with lots of green, orange, blue, purple, and yellow foods and complex carbohydrates; whole grains too are very important.

It is important to spend enough time at the office, but not too much. We must have the courage and judgment to know when to give our time to the office and when to stop. It takes courage, I think, because those without this courage will not feel confident enough to limit work to eight, nine, or ten hours per day. They feel like they must give more and more and more and will not know what is enough.

How does one make any sort of mark on the world as you live your life? I do not believe there is much of a mark left by anyone when they are no longer living. Memory . . . and what is a memory . . . and memory fades fast! Even the greatest, except for say a few like Lincoln—who have grown in "mark" since his death, do not really leave much of a mark. Marks quickly fade. . What's the purpose? The real "marks" are your family!

This truly may get at the real meaning of life. The real meaning of life, as a bottom line, must be a life that guarantees an opportunity to spend eternity with God and Jesus in heaven doing about what we did here on earth with our families. Only in heaven, everyone will be *kind* and *responsible*. Have faith in God and Jesus and be repentant for your sins.

Too much work and no play . . .
Is not exactly what I was trying to say!
Hard work is certainly a good trait.
That you want to start before it's too late.

1RR. DON'T BE AFRAID TO SAY "I DON'T KNOW."

What do you say if someone asks you something and you truly don't know? You say, "I don't know."

It may sound correct; it may be correct, you think, but you don't know for sure, say "I don't know."

Either you guess and fake it and risk getting caught, or you say "I don't know."

To me, there is no choice. You tell the truth. The truth is the only credible choice.

Sure, it may take courage, but that is the only choice you have as a credible person. And if you don't know, offer to do some research and find the answer. This way, you have an opportunity to learn and an opportunity to be helpful to someone else.

If they want your best guess, give them your best guess . . . but tell them that is your best guess but not something you know for sure, and that you will gladly help do the research to obtain the correct answer.

Saying "I don't know" is the thing to do.
When you don't know what I say to you . . .
Admit the truth then commit to look,
And find the answer on the net or in a book.

1SS. DON'T BE AFRAID TO SAY "I'M SORRY."

There are, at least, four kinds of "sorry" that come to mind.

One occurs after you accidently bump into someone, and another is when you truly make a small mistake or do something small that clearly was wrong and a mistake. In this case, you say you are sorry and mean it.

Saying "I am sorry" in this simple mistake example means, "I am sorry, my mistake, no biggie, my bad . . ." to use a current teenager phrase . . . "I hope you took it that way, excuse me please, and I wish I had not done that."

The third kind of sorry comes after an argument or heated difference of opinion.

This more serious "I am sorry" may come when you may be sorry the argument occurred, but you definitely do not think you were wrong in the situation. You are sorry for the argument but not the reason because the other person was the cause of the problem.

In the third example, perhaps if you avoid acting when you are angry and walk away from a quarrel with our wife when you are angry, there will be fewer things you will be "sorry" for.

The most serious "sorry," one I hope you don't have to use very often, is when you just flat out blew it, and you were wrong and made the mistake and were the whole cause for the situation. If this was the case, and you recognize that you should not have argued because you now believe you were actually wrong and you should have avoided the argument in the first place . . . apologize, say you were sorry, and will not take that position again with the person.

Never disagree for the sake of disagreeing. Don't bluff or fake a disagreement.

Saying you are sorry without an honest attempt to avoid the behavior is not sincere and not what a person with character would do. Avoid putting yourself in a situation in which you need to apologize!

What I Would Have Said . . .

Never be so proud,
Whether alone or in a crowd,
To not say you are sorry for a mistake!
Apologize and give yourself a break.

1TT. MAKE A LIST OF TWENTY-FIVE THINGS YOU WANT TO EXPERIENCE BEFORE YOU DIE. CARRY IT IN YOUR WALLET AND REFER TO IT OFTEN.

Without a goal or dream, your life will be purposeless. How do you measure success?

That is a beautiful part of life as a human being.

Humans, people get to decide what they want to do and can define how to value their personal success.

If I set lifetime goals and expect accomplishments of say X, Y, and Z, I should consider myself successful if I accomplish all three. As we pass through life, X could be changed to X', and Y to Y', etc. and still have a successful life. We get to decide what we want to do and what we actually do with our lives.

Early goals can be revised or deleted in favor of others.

The younger you are when you set your goal, the more choices you have, the more you can dream.

That does not mean the goal setting will be any more fun and exciting than dreams later in life. You just can have more choices and can be less practical. Early life goals can be more dreamy, whereas later goals will logically be more practical.

Perhaps lifetime success is not necessarily measured by what one does. Perhaps lifetime success is measured by how we positively impact other people in our life and others in general. Do we qualify for eternal life with God and Jesus.

We can have an entry on our list of things we want to do reflecting our desire to always have a positive impact on others.

You have to be willing to work for what you put on your list.

Just putting something on your list won't make it happen. Making a list is not easy, but not the hard part either. The hard part is making the items happen. This will be fun if that is what you want to do.

Also, even though I am sure more things will be accomplished in your lifetime with a list than you would have without a list, having a list without many items accomplished can result in a sense of failure.

Know and stretch your reach!
Now twenty-five could be a bit much.
But long enough to serve to teach . . .
An exciting and fruitful life will be yours to touch.

Try these:

TWENTY-FIVE THINGS I WANT TO DO!

1. Read the Bible totally through.
2. Get a BS degree.
3. Get a MS degree.
4. Play a college sport.
5. Get married and have children.
6. Celebrate a thirtieth wedding anniversary.
7. Publish a book.
8. Publish a second book.
9. Publish a third book.
10. Take a two hundred-mile bike trip.
11. Take a longer bike trip.
12. Drive across the country on back roads from DC to Seattle.
13. Drive from New England to Florida.
14. Have grandchildren.
15. Be worth a million dollars.
16. Do something good or helpful to someone every day.
17. Always live by the Golden Rule.
18. Read the U.S. Constitution.
19. Read the Federalist papers.
20. Own a Corvette.
21. Own a motor home.
22. Publish the book on poetry.
23. Tour with family in a motor home.
24. Roam.
25. And I didn't even mention owning and riding a motorcycle!

1UU. CALL YOUR MOTHER.

Of course call your mother. There is no one in the world who loves you more than your mother.

Reflecting back on the instruction relating to reading the Bible through and the importance of the Ten Commandments: honor your father and mother.

Calling them is a way to honor them; call them at least weekly.

It shows respect, and they need that.

Mothers need more attention than fathers, but fathers need some attention too.

Call your mom and dad at least once a week. Not for long drawn-out conversations, but do call. If you live close by, a weekly joint visit to church for example and dinner afterward would be nice. Keep in touch. You all will be richer for it.

Your mother will appreciate your call.
Winter, spring, summer or fall . . .
Reach out and touch your mom.
Dad will know and will support you with his calm.

2

"How To Pursue Happiness" By Adair Lara, *Reader's Digest*, P. 155, June 1993.

This title, "How to Pursue Happiness," was considered for inclusion in this book because I saw the title and the main theme as being particularly relevant. So many people struggle with the pursuit of happiness. Life, in the TV sitcoms, is totally focused on the pursuit of happiness. We feel like failures if we are not happy all the time. This title and theme tell us to pursue happiness by clearly defining what it will take for us to be happy.

DEFINE YOUR HAPPINESS

People are not required to be happy all the time. Happiness is a reasonable goal. You do not have to feel deprived if you have times when you experience something less than total happiness.

Decide early in life what experiences you enjoy by defining situations in which you are happy. Remember, you are responsible for making yourself happy.

Couples should discuss and agree on how they will relate to one another . . . and if they relate to one another as they agreed, they will have defined their happiness.

They should discuss and agree on what they both enjoy and what it will take for each to be happy. There will be things they enjoy doing together, and there will be things they don't like but the other does. Accept from the first of their relationship that each has things they enjoy but the other person doesn't enjoy. There is no need—there is nothing to be gained by forcing the other person to do what you want. They may eventually change—come around to your point of view—but there is no need to force it. It will be counterproductive to force the other to do what you want.

Enjoy what you can do together. Seek early agreement on where your time and money will be spent. Hopefully, there will be more activities that you enjoy doing together than you don't. Enjoy the good times—embrace happiness, and get through the times that are less pleasant.

Happiness, in general, though can be achieved by defining what it will take to make you happy and then designing enough of the things you enjoy into your life's activities. You are incharge of your own happiness.

Doing things that you are good at and enjoy are critical to the issue of happiness. And, it is difficult to know which comes first—the enjoyment or the being good at something, skills are programmed by natural inherited genes as well as programming through childhood experiences. The key is to identify activities that you both enjoy and are good at. That is the combination for living a life of happiness. Do things you enjoy and are good at—perfect skills and move on leaving a path of good deeds, favors, and compliments as you move through life.

Set forth what it will take
It says happiness is something you can make!
Happiness may be a skill one can teach.
Without inner peace, happiness will be out of reach.

3

"Do Unto Others As You Would Have Them Do Unto You. The Golden Rule Is Where It All Begins And Ends..." By James R. Fisher Jr., *Reader's Digest*, P. 130, June 1993.

The next nine headings are from a *Reader's Digest* article by James R Fisher Jr. The chapter headings were and are particularly meaningful to me. I want to indicate why I think the chapter headings have special meaning and value to be worth passing on as part of my personal philosophy.

3A. THE GOLDEN RULE IS WHERE IT ALL BEGINS AND ENDS

The Golden rule—Do unto others as you would have them do unto you. This, along with the Ten Commandments, is as good a basis for one's life as we might imagine.

Society is rapidly moving to one with no rules or standards against which to judge our performance. People are being taught from every direction that whatever feels good, do it. Whatever we do, it really isn't our fault that we did something; we are doing it because of something that our parents did or said to us or because our income is below the poverty level or because of something that was done to our ancestors decades or centuries ago or because of what someone said or did to us.

The reason is not important. The important fact, which seems to be present today, is that there is a reason why people commit some terrible act, or even a small but inappropriate act, to another person. Supposedly, it isn't our or their fault.

Similarly, we often hear that it is not the fault of the person committing the crime. It is never the fault of the person who beats another over the head with the stick. It never is the fault of the person who kills a baby about to be born. It never is the fault of the protester or a plant manager who puts thousands of workers out of job and out of a dignified way to support their families. It never is the fault of a kid who doesn't do his or her homework and makes poor grades in school; and it never is a parent's fault that the child doesn't learn. And it never is the fault of the person committing the act.

The fact of the matter is, we are responsible for our actions, and there are basic and simple rules against which all of our actions must be judged. I am offering these rules, which are from the Ten Commandments plus one. Other religions . . . perhaps except Muslims, have similar rules, which may be used to set the standards of conduct for all the world's people:

1. No matter who you are, you are ultimately accountable for your own actions and will eventually have to answer for your wrongful deeds against others. (You shall have no other gods before me.)
2. You must not focus your attention on things. You are accountable for your actions, and that responsibility will overshadow any short-term

pleasure you receive from an object of pleasure collected at the expense of another. (You shall not make yourself an idol in the form of anything in heaven or on earth.)
3. You shall not use fowl and inappropriate language. (You shall not misuse the name of the Lord your God.)
4. Weekly, observe a day of rest to reflect on your relationship with your fellow human beings; refocus your life on the importance of these rules; and the importance of keeping the number of unrepentant violations of these rules at zero. (Observe the Sabbath day by keeping it holy.)
5. Honor your father and your mother.
6. You shall not murder.
7. You shall not have sex outside of marriage. (You shall not commit adultery.)
8. You shall not steal.
9. You shall not tell a lie. (You shall not give false testimony against your neighbor.)
10. You shall not wish for your neighbor's wife, house, land, workers, or farm animals; if you want something, go out and earn your own, not someone else's. (You shall not covet your neighbor's wife, your neighbor's house, land, workers, ox, or anything that belongs to your neighbor.)
11. Treat others the way you wish to be treated.

These are broad, universally known, and accepted rules or standards of acceptable performance. Other people may offer modifications; however, these rules or standards will be among the final version. This entire text is intended to offer a father's suggestions for all aspects of life, from affection to zany behavior. The Golden Rule, though, offers the simplest, all-encompassing rule, however. If we want to have courtesies and respect shown to us, we should show courtesy and respect to others. If we would expect others to work hard and effectively for us, we should work hard and effectively for our supervisor/managers. We usually know what we expect from others; consequently, we should know what others expect of us.

Do unto others as you would have them to do unto you. Treat others the way you would want to be treated.

The Golden Rule keeps it simple.
You don't have to make it so mental.
Picture in your mind's eye . . .
How unto others you will try?

The Golden Rule appears again.
You can do less but that would be a sin.
All need attention when you begin.
And too, later on especially in the end.

3B. TO HAVE A FRIEND, YOU MUST BE A FRIEND, STARTING WITH YOURSELF. "DO UNTO OTHERS . . ." BY JAMES R. FISHER JR., *READER'S DIGEST*, P. 130, JUNE 1993.

It is very difficult to be pleasant and positive with others if you are not happy with yourself . . . that is, if you don't consider yourself a friend. To be happy with yourself and consider yourself a friend, you must believe you can do at least one thing well and are better at that one thing than some.

First, it is impossible to do everything best and better than all others. However, it is possible to do one thing best or well. Maybe you can do several things best; that may be possible—but everything cannot be done the best.

You can consider yourself a friend—you can like yourself if you are satisfied with your abilities or your looks or your physique or your accomplishments. This is the concept that is often misused—"know yourself."

It is easier to be a friend to others if you are satisfied with your abilities and yourself.

What do you expect of yourself and others? A friend cannot be demanded to be a friend.

What do you expect of yourself and others? You would like to receive acceptance—everyone needs acceptance. Everyone has an ego, and everyone needs to feel good about themselves. Your wisdom will help you quickly appreciate the source of people's actions and will enable you to appreciate them quickly.

There are some responsibilities, though. You must be there when your friend needs you. I don't know—that's pretty trite—probably trite but true. Also, your focus should be on what you can do for your friends—not what your friends can do for you. And that can be the answer to many of the emotional and depression-type maladies from which people suffer. Focus on doing the things that help others.

Accept yourself—be good at something and support your friends. Be interested in your friends' activity, their wins, their losses.

What I Would Have Said . . .

To be a friend
You must be there in the beginning and in the end.
A friend is there when things go well.
And a friend too is there when the tears swell.
Someone once said that a friend of mine . . .
Must be willing to give me time.
And dividing that valuable commodity.
Between family and others, it's plain to see,
That a friend is a jewel . . . and for sure not free.

3C. THE GREATEST VIRTUE IS KINDNESS. YOU CAN'T LOVE EVERYONE, BUT YOU CAN BE KIND TO EVERYONE. "DO UNTO OTHERS..." BY JAMES R. FISHER JR., *READER'S DIGEST*, P. 130, JUNE 1993.

The greatest virtue is kindness. You should always be kind to people in your life. It's easy to be kind to those who are kind and nice to you.

But what about those who are not kind to you. Agreed, it is not possible to love everyone. I say first of all, you have an obligation to be kind to those who are kind to you—and be kind to those who are neutral to you in terms of how they treat you. What to do with those people who are not kind to you. Try, try to be kind to them, no retribution, but get away from them.

This is not a study of the various forms of love—are there three or whatever—that's not important.

The important point there is that . . . love or affection for everyone is not possible. That's a feeling—and not as easy to turn off or turn on. What you can do however is to act kindly to the people you deal with and help as many people in a day's time as possible.

Treat others kindly, through what you say to them and what you can do for them when they need help. What you say or don't say to others about them are acts of kindness as well. What you say in their behalf should be positive and reinforce their personhood. There are many, many ways to be kind to other people.

There is no cost to being kind.
Why not be kind, it's how you set your mind.
Most see kindness as a style to find.
Somewhere. Being kind will not put you in a bind.

3D. BE ENTHUSIASTIC. NOTHING OF CONSEQUENCE WAS EVER BEEN ACHIEVED WITHOUT ENTHUSIASM. "DO UNTO OTHERS . . ." BY JAMES R. FISHER JR., *READER'S DIGEST*, P. 130, JUNE 1993.

Be enthusiastic, exude energy, pep, and excitement.

Act as though you really enjoy what you are doing whether you do or not.

That energy and positive attitude is catching—it will spread. Others around you will exhibit the same high energy approach to life. Set your mind to the fact that the high energy level is catching and is something you can catch too.

The key thought is that enthusiasm gives the appearance of an adjusted, happy person who enjoys what he or she is doing. You should know that this is the type of personality most people are attracted to.

Go the extra mile; don't be satisfied with just enough; go further, longer, faster, harder than just enough. Do this with a high energy level, be enthusiastic, and have a happy approach to life. Cheerfully exceed the expectations of people with whom you work with and work for. Attack problems and seek correction aggressively. Maturity will bring sufficient analysis before action. Preparation and vision are equally important to enthusiasm for action success.

Be enthusiastic if you can . . .
A ball of energy in the land.
Focus on your vision, it's in your hand.
A targeted force . . . you will be in demand.

3E. BE POSITIVE. POSITIVE PEOPLE ATTRACT OTHERS, WHILE NEGATIVE PEOPLE REPEL. "DO UNTO OTHERS . . ." BY JAMES R. FISHER JR., *READER'S DIGEST*, P. 130, JUNE 1993.

Be a positive, possibility thinker. Most things are possible if you truly want them to occur and you start early enough. The more time spent waiting and procrastinating, the more the target or goal could become distant and difficult.

I do not believe that all things happen for a good cause, but the creative, positive individual can achieve a useful purpose out of every event.

Even in defeat or in the face of a major disappointment, it is best to portray a positive front. Try to learn something from every event, good or bad. Accomplish something positive every day.

People are repelled by a negative person who has nothing good to say about anybody or anything.

Most negative people show their negativism by saying negative—bad things about other people—backbiting negative gossip.

And I believe it certainly is true if they are talking negative about someone behind their back, they will be talking negatively about you when you are not around. What they say about others in front of you will be said about you when you are not around.

Try to find something good to say, and if you can't, keep your mouth shut in most situations.

Positive people achieve, while negative people talk about you and then wait for events to confirm why something can't be done.

I once had a work associate say, "A pessimist is an informed optimist." Nothing could make him change from that position. He was a unique individual in that he would sincerely think and try to accomplish tasks either assigned to him or to his group. When things got hectic, he would say, "Things are better now than they ever will be again." Harold was one of a kind, and his can-do spirit was much better than his little sayings . . . probably the only "negative" person I ever enjoyed working with.

I believe the positive person has to assess the current situation, must believe and act as though he or she can and will make a difference and will make the situation better.

Find a way to win.
A positive search is what it takes.
If you wonder where to begin,
A positive start makes the breaks.

3F. GOSSIP CHEAPENS THE ONE WHO GOSSIPS MORE THAN THE ONE GOSSIPED ABOUT. "DO UNTO OTHERS..." BY JAMES R. FISHER JR., *READER'S DIGEST*, P. 130, JUNE 1993.

Sure, in theory, gossip cheapens the gossiper because anyone with any sense at all would realize that a gossiper will gossip about anyone not present.

Gossip is negative comments about someone, statements in which the person is made to look less than their best.

Positive statements, statements intended and which effectively build up a person, are not gossip. It is perfectly fine in my mind to compliment people behind their back... hopefully someone will pass it on to the person being complimented. Positive statements are compliments; "someone spoke well of you" type comments. Positive statements spoken about you are OK of course whether you hear them or not.

Gossip, negative comments, may be intended to build yourself up at the expense of another; however, the gossip usually just takes away from the gossiper's character image and may or may not actually hurt the one being gossiped about.

Knowing the low regard people have about gossipers might make you feel better. However, it doesn't correct the damage that might, unnecessarily, be done to the person being gossiped about by a person who speaks negatively about them. Gossip is often unprovoked and causes unnecessary ill will and damage to another. Don't gossip... and do confront those who do gossip.

Gossip cheapens the source.
You watch in normal discourse...
Negative comments can be on or off course.
You will, in the end, show remorse.

3G. COMMUNICATE CHEERFULNESS. "DO UNTO OTHERS..." BY JAMES R. FISHER JR., *READER'S DIGEST*, P. 130, JUNE 1993.

What do you leave when you leave a room? Do you leave a glum, downcast, and sad feeling? I hope not . . . concentrate on communicating, in everything you do, cheerfulness.

That's the goal; no one is perfect.

There are times when it is not appropriate to be outwardly cheerful—pleasant but not bubbly cheerful. For example, just after someone has just received bad news or the person is dealing with a sad, family situation. Nothing bubbly . . . be pleasant, friendly, but not bubbly.

Overall, it is best to be cheerful and make others feel good about themselves. That is one of the most important things we can do for ourselves, as a person and for others—to try to cause them to feel good about themselves.

How hard is it to approach every conversation, every interchange, with another person trying to make sure the other person leaves the conversation feeling good about themselves? It is not hard! That is what we should set as a goal.

So many people (myself included) often see an interchange between themselves and another person as an opportunity to make themselves look good. I really have to avoid self-aggrandizing. This is not necessarily at the expense of another—but often the other person does not feel cheerful, better, or any way better off as a result of the conversation.

Approach almost every conversation or interaction with others as an opportunity to make them feel good about themselves. Try to never talk about yourself or your situation. When you are with someone and you have to choose between talking about yourself or them, talk about them or their family. Choose them rather than yourself or your family. This is a reminder for me, and I believe others in our family . . . because it is difficult sometimes resisting talking about my family in these situations, and I should resist.

Just merely acting cheerful may be a misleading suggestion because one can be cheerful and still not accomplish the purpose of making the person feel good about himself or herself. Try to leave the other person lifted up by the conversation so that they will truly feel better about themselves.

People have little use for a black cloud . . .
That follows them around.
Good cheer can brighten a crowd.
Laughter is beautiful sound!

3H. IF YOU ARE GIVEN TO MAKE FUN OF SOMEONE, BE SURE IT IS OF YOURSELF. "DO UNTO OTHERS . . ." BY JAMES R. FISHER JR., *READER'S DIGEST*, P. 130, JUNE 1993.

Often a person, usually in a power situation over the victim, makes fun of or pokes fun at another. Notice that I said that the person making fun of another in a power situation over the victim. This action is no less a bullying tactic than the school yard bully most everyone has experienced in their life. A little self-deprecating humor—making fun of oneself, will not hurt anyone and often aids in the relationships between people.

Also, while I certainly would not recommend it—but if you insist on making fun of someone else—make fun of someone in a power situation over you. Make fun of your boss, the school bully, the macho man on the street or bar or wherever.

Hopefully that will satisfy your need to make fun of another and will contribute to curing you of making fun of another person.

It can serve no useful purpose to make fun of another person. Most people have memory scars of being on the receiving end of being made fun of. That is no fun; do not cause another person to be hurt by the needless making fun of them.

Making fun of another . . .
Is not to be done to a brother.
But you have an urge and you have druthers,
You are the one ridicule will smother.

31. A SMILE DOESN'T COST ANYTHING AND PAYS BIG DIVIDENDS. NOT ONLY DOES IT MAKE YOU FEEL GOOD, BUT IT MAKES EVERYONE ELSE BE BETTER TOO. "DO UNTO OTHERS . . ." BY JAMES R. FISHER JR., *READER'S DIGEST*, P. 130, JUNE 1993.

Similar to being positive, enthusiastic, and kind, it is so easy to give people a little smile and a personalized greeting.

It doesn't cost anything to smile, and it pays dividends insofar as making the other person feel OK about themselves, and a smiling personality is healthful for you as well.

Additionally, concentrating on being pleasant and smiling will be beneficial to you because of the development of a good habit and better interpersonal skills. Being concerned with the feeling of other people will no doubt be helpful to you . . . another great life's lesson.

The sense of friendliness projected by smiling and recognizing the other person will build a bond between people of good will.

The smile is an outward sign of what's on the inside. Forcing yourself to smile will remind you to keep the smile on the inside too. See people for what they are . . . all trying to find some level of happiness and seeking to be recognized for some positive aspect of their being.

Give others a smile or extend a vehicle driving courtesy, open a door, hold open a door . . . all will reaffirm the other person and help them to feel good about themselves.

A smile of affirmation goes a long way . . .
To help you make your day.
And the others will notice and say . . .
Friend, this is going to be OK!

4

"Trust In God But Lock Your Car," From *Life's Little Instruction Book*, Vol. II. H. Jackson Brown Jr.

4A. NEVER LAUGH AT ANYONE'S DREAMS, FROM *LIFE'S LITTLE INSTRUCTION BOOK*, VOL. II, H. JACKSON BROWN JR.

Without looking at *Webster*, the type of dream referenced herein is a thought or written vision, or plan for the future, which the individual develops with excitement in anticipation of implementation.

A laugh pokes fun at and belittles a dream, a hope, that a person has. Sometimes that is all they have is a dream or hope.

In others, a laugh will stifle creativity because the person may not have the personal conviction to dream in the face of apparent ridicule as a laugh will present.

Dreams, even if apparently misguided, are evidence of thought and anticipation of the future.

Dreams must first be understood, then supported.

The dream of a child is so positive it shows a passion and excitement for life rather than a dreary, bleak, day-in-and-day-out existence. Dreams are evidence of and for passion.

And really, the same applies to teenagers, young adults, middle-age adults, and yes . . . even senior adults. A person who has dreams has to be a more-adjusted and contributing person than an individual who sets around and just watches TV or even less.

A person who dreams is using his or her brain in a proactive way, while a person who doesn't . . . becomes a totally reactive type person waiting for the next event to overtake them.

I believe a no dreamer type person has the potential of mental-health problems. Dreaming is a healthy activity, don't discourage dreaming by laughing at others.

Why would you ever laugh aloud . . .
At another's dreams while standing in the crowd?
It is a given . . . a laugh at a dream is cruel.
To do so puts you in the class of a mule.

4B. BELIEVE IN LOVE AT FIRST SIGHT, FROM *LIFE'S LITTLE INSTRUCTION BOOK*, VOL. II, H. JACKSON BROWN JR.

Love at first sight is possible but not always.

When a mother first sees her newborn son or daughter, that is love at first sight!

When the teenage boy sees the bikini-clad model, the boy thinks that is love at first sight too. When a single thirty-year-old adult male and a single thirty-year-old adult female see each other from across the dance floor, and they are attracted to each other, that probably would be called love at first sight as well . . . but it isn't.

True, these probably are widely considered examples of "love at first sight," but they are not exactly the intended purpose of this chapter.

The thesis is, when a young man who legitimately is an eligible candidate for marriage sees a young single woman who legitimately is an eligible candidate for marriage, they see each other and immediately fall in love.

Sure this is possible, but it is the type of love described in the same variety as the teenage boy seeing the bikini-clad model and thinking that he is falling in love.

This is only proof of the fact that males of the human species are attracted to a female of the human species, but not necessarily for a long-term relationship of love and respect.

This instantaneous love is more a confirmation of sex appeal than it is a confirmation of a long-term relationship of love and mutual respect.

Of course, it is possible for some of the "sex appeal" loves to eventually develop into a long-term relationship of love and respect. The likelihood of this occurring is remote if the passion is spent before the understanding and respect are achieved. It (the love) will probably end as the passion dwindles. A sex-appeal love and not true love built on respect and understanding will certainly dwindle.

Love at first sight is a dream.
What is love, it's not what it seems!
Passion at first sight may make your heart flutter and teem.
But true love, true love is not to be seen.

4C. REMEMBER THAT NO TIME SPENT WITH YOUR CHILDREN IS EVER WASTED. TIME IS A COMMODITY—WE ALL HAVE SOME OF, SOME MORE; SOME LESS THAN OTHERS, FROM *LIFE'S LITTLE INSTRUCTION BOOK*, VOL. II, H. JACKSON BROWN JR.

Time is used in everything we do. Ask me twenty years from now if I have ever felt like the time I spent with our children was wasted.

To not have been wasted, the time spent must have resulted in some discernable good. And the "discernable good" test was going to be difficult to verify how well things would turn out. We have time and over five, ten, twenty years; we have lots of time. If we don't spend the time with our children, we will do something else with it. We can spend the leftover time on our job being the best we can be and exceeding management's expectations of us or just keeping our job. We could contribute time to feeding the poor or building houses for the poor. We could do committee work at church or travel or go to the local, state, or professional sport team events—or we could write a book.

How necessary is sport? How necessary is a tucked-in shirt, or how necessary is setting vitamins on the table—when the vitamins are not taken unless they are pushed hard?

I believe some time spent is wasted for an "ungrateful know it all type" child/person . . . hopefully, not totally. Eventually, they will/may come around and be a normal appreciative person—and at that point, time spent with them would be worthwhile. Until then, out of a duty to be a responsible parent, certain parenting things must be done. Enjoy the experience and make the most out of the experiences you can.

There will be times when it will be clearly worthwhile. However, for the most part, the value of the time spent will need to be assessed several years into the future.

Unreasonable expectations of what should be done with time are important before deciding whether time is wasted.

Time wasted, while trying to change what you have no control over, should be no surprise. Decide that you will not try. Seek to change only what you have potential to change. Enjoy what you are doing and accomplish one significant thing each day.

Wasted time can be measured hour by hour.
Side-by-side TV watching will go sour.
Some time TV is better than another.
Being with kids should be your druther.

4D. WHEN TRAVELING, TAKE TWO BIG SAFETY PINS SO YOU CAN PIN THE MOTEL DRAPES SHUT, FROM *LIFE'S LITTLE INSTRUCTION BOOK*, VOL. II, H. JACKSON BROWN JR.

When traveling, be prepared; not just for the motel drapes, which gap, but for other situations. Just about anything one could mention would be as microplanning as the two pins.

From an earplug for your portable radio, to a thermos, to extra batteries for the camera—be prepared!

When you are driving, always be aware of everything around the car. The faster you are going, the further away you should anticipate emergencies. In a hotel room, be prepared to pin the drapes closed, or you could tape them closed. Lock the door using all choices available. Anticipate the interstate highway turn long before the clover leaf comes up. When walking at night, always be aware of what and who is around you. If you want to be treated as a mature adult, act like one. Anticipate the situations, and your road will be less bumpy.

So why is it so important to bring the pins? It isn't . . . any more than bringing a trunk full of things one might need regardless of the situation . . . no matter how remote the possibility is, plan for emergencies and be flexible in your approach to unanticipated situations.

Like a good scout, be prepared and take a pin.
Dozens of other things could help you win . . .
The day when a tear appears on your garment rear end.
Take out your pin and repair the tear with a grin.

4E. ACCEPT A BREATH MINT IF SOMEONE OFFERS YOU ONE, FROM *LIFE'S LITTLE INSTRUCTION BOOK*, VOL. II, H. JACKSON BROWN JR.

Before you get into a close conversation, do something to make sure your breath is acceptable. Waiting until you are in a close conversation with another person before you consider your need for a breath mint is poor planning . . . and often can result in putting you in a potentially embarrassing, if not uncomfortable, situation.

It would be so easy to anticipate in advance and eat/chew on a breath mint before the conversation starts.

Most of the time during a close conversation, a person feels Self-conscious about his or her breath and takes out gum or a mint for him or herself. Then, with the mint out, this person feels obligated to offer the other person a mint. The other person accepts of course. But the accepting person never knows whether his or her breath was so bad that the person offered the mint or the offering person had the problem and was just being nice.

Such detailed advice you don't need.
Nevertheless, if it occurs, you should take heed.
Trusting me at the right time . . .
Could be better than this rhyme.

4F. KEEP THE PORCH LIGHT ON UNTIL ALL THE FAMILY IS IN FOR THE NIGHT, FROM *LIFE'S LITTLE INSTRUCTION BOOK*, VOL. II, H. JACKSON BROWN JR.

Every family member is important, and that needs to be reinforced at every possibility.

It is a special reinforcement to every family member to be told in a small and subtle way that they are important by leaving the outside lights on to show the way home.

The reverse—turning the outside lights off before the last family member is in—is a subtle reminder that their later arrival was not worth a few cents of electricity needed to show the way home.

The late-arriving family member has a responsibility too—turn off the lights after he or she arrives home and inside. That too is a small courtesy the person owes to the remainder of the family.

Know when all are expected to be in for the night. Ask, before they leave, when they will return home, and then leave the porch light on.

The light on and light off are both small, subtle courtesies that can be expressed between family members. Both are important.

Turn the light out at the end of the day.
All is well when they come back your way.
Your team is home . . . all is OK!
A light is a welcome sight, I must say.

4G. REHEARSE A JOKE BEFORE TELLING IT, FROM *LIFE'S LITTLE INSTRUCTION BOOK*, VOL. II, H. JACKSON BROWN JR.

Always rehearse a joke or any other presentation before you tell or give it.

First, the presentation is an important part of the joke, and especially remember the punch line.

Rehearsing can just be silently going over the words in your mind rather than out loud to smaller group. Remember the set up and especially the punch line.

More importantly, the suitability of the words and theme in the joke should be assessed before your actual presentation. Are they appropriate for the audience? Is the joke in good taste? Does the joke enhance or tear down the image you want to create for yourself?

First, think through the joke; think about the words; think about the punch line; then decide if the joke is appropriate for the audience, and does the joke build or detract from your personal image.

Most important on this topic is, if it is important to practice merely a joke to do it well, just think how important it is to practice other significant tasks in your life. Practice presentations and speeches much more.

Another point is, practice the skill at a level so that your skills are improving on the topic. Don't practice carelessly or half speed. Your skill will not improve unless you practice at a level comparative to the excellence you must deliver under a competitive and realistic situation.

Practice, practice whatever you do.
No matter what it is, practice will pay off for you ...
From jokes to about anything you can construe.
Be your best, it's just a joke but it's still true.

4H. ALWAYS TRY THE HOUSE DRESSING, FROM *LIFE'S LITTLE INSTRUCTION BOOK*, VOL. II, H. JACKSON BROWN JR.

In a new restaurant, always try the house dressing, perhaps on the side in a separate bowl; but try it.

It shows, in your character, as being willing to take a little risk and being a little curious. In small ways, your confidence in the waitress or waiter is affirmed.

Try it; it may be a new and important discovery for your life—be it small.

You can always finish your salad with "the old standby" salad dressing after having added a new pleasure and discovery to your life.

Risk-taking character, but not wildly so, is a positive tribute to be applauded. You are willing to take a chance, maybe a small chance, but a chance. You would be willing to steal the base in baseball, go for the pin in wrestling, or a tackle in football. You would be willing to try for something more than just the most conservative stock for great gain. Being a risk taker, to a point, is a desirable personality trait that is to be applauded.

Trying the house dressing also shows your willingness to affirm the accomplishments of another person. It is a great gesture of confidence to your fellow "man." Affirm the people you deal with by showing confidence in their abilities.

Trying the house dressing is a small example of discovery, but it is, and additional growth can always occur when you are willing to reach out to discover new things and situations.

Be open to a change of pace.
Change around when you are in their place.
Salad dressing is something to sample.
Try something new . . . set an example!

41. DON'T LET A LITTLE DISPUTE INJURE A GREAT FRIENDSHIP, FROM *LIFE'S LITTLE INSTRUCTION BOOK*, VOL. II, H. JACKSON BROWN JR.

Life and relationships with other people are a series of decisions and hopefully compromises. Everyone who isn't brain dead has opinions about events that occur and need to occur in life.

If you spend your time with a person or persons with values similar to your own, the opportunity for conflict or even a little dispute is reduced.

Aside from life's major decisions—say, the level of the Ten Commandments and the Golden Rule—there are many situations of possible dispute between people.

I don't know why, but some people, some of the time, can find something to dispute about unless you do absolutely everything they say or suggest. It is unavoidable. They can dispute about anything. Don't wear that hat; come with me; come in with me; do this; do that; why not? Is this the way you are always going to be, and on and on, etc.

What can I say?

The point is even God would not be able to avoid a conflict with such a person . . . if God had any thoughts whatsoever on His own . . . and He does.

How can we remain great friends with such a person? It's tough, but the only answer can be is that they are not always that way, and you are not always around them. Their other qualities and attributes must counterbalance these traits.

People's reaction to events, which could initiate little disputes, are very much influenced by the way they feel, other relationships that they maintain and other events in their life that influences the way they feel about themselves and think. Any unusual or out-of-character reaction should be assessed based on other issues in the past and which may be still occurring in their life.

There isn't much that is worth a friend.
Maybe they come and go—Is there a trend?
More than a dispute . . . time dwindles them away.
A friend is there for golf and every day.
A friend takes time to work and play.
For me, family is the friend I chose.
Life and time will tell whether I win or lose.

4J. ONCE IN A WHILE, INVITE THE PERSON IN LINE BEHIND YOU TO GO AHEAD OF YOU, FROM *LIFE'S LITTLE INSTRUCTION BOOK*, VOL. II, H. JACKSON BROWN JR.

This is an excellent opportunity to go forth and perform an unsolicited act of kindness. One of the easiest is to let a person, with a small number of items in the grocery store checkout line, to go ahead of you. It is such an easy way to be kind to another person and makes so much sense.

Another way to exhibit an act of kindness occurs when you are walking up to a counter to purchase an item at the same time as another person. Don't make that subtle speed up to beat them. Let them go forward and be waited on first.

The same for the parking place nearest to the door of a supermarket. Take the courteous approach and be kind to the person that arrives at the place the same time or even after you do. Give them a break; it may be the only break the person gets all that day.

In any case, always, let the person with one or two items ahead of you in the grocery store line.

In a similar situation, when you are behind someone in line, just as the store opens another line, thereby giving you an opportunity to move into the new line and ahead of the other person, give the person who had been in the line the longest an opportunity to move into the new line first. This should be done whether the person has only a few items or many items; this is simply a fair thing to do.

Always let one with one go ahead.
Usually, to one with two, I am after you.
Most of the time to one with three, you instead.
Never let one with a full cart play through.

4K. SEND YOUR MOTHER-IN-LAW FLOWERS ON YOUR SPOUSE'S BIRTHDAY, FROM *LIFE'S LITTLE INSTRUCTION BOOK*, VOL. II, H. JACKSON BROWN JR.

This is a great idea and tradition. I have never heard of this or even given this a thought before.

I endorse the idea or tradition and will start it up my next opportunity in December. OK, so I am not perfect, but I still think this is a good idea.

There are spouses, and then there are spouses. A spouse who gets up in your face and demands her rights and her way will not garner many flowers nor will her mother get many flowers.

A spouse who loves you and acts like it by considering your wants and desires needs to be cherished and cared for; not the least of which is this consideration of the occasional flowers for her and her mother.

This "in-your-face demander of the best of every consideration and treatment" person should never be abused verbally or physically or any other way. They should be treated as a very equal partner. Always be fair and considerate of her feelings.

A lady who takes, sneeringly, what she thinks she deserves and needs will get a lot of what she wants but will come up short on the gift of birthday flowers for herself and her mother.

Flowers are such a treat!
No matter who she is, it's such a thrill.
Your lady's mom will worship at your feet.
She will, she will, I know they will.

4L. BUY LADDERS, EXTENSION CORDS, AND GARDEN HOSES LONGER THAN YOU THINK YOU'LL NEED, FROM *LIFE'S LITTLE INSTRUCTION BOOK*, VOL. II, H. JACKSON BROWN JR.

Nothing profound here except to say that there is no way to add extra height or length to a ladder or extension cord once you bring it home . . . except perhaps by standing too close to the top of the ladder and putting yourself in a very dangerous situation.

Whereas, if the ladder or cord is too long, you do not have to use the whole thing.

Don't climb to the top of the ladder.

Leave some slack in the extension cord. Pulling the extension cord too tight will eventually weaken the plug connection and short out the electrical connection.

There are other similar topics of advice that may be offered, such as

Plan ahead: Think ahead of where you are on the page, floor, trip, story, letter . . . so that a portion of your work won't have to be redone . . . like going to the second line?

Practice makes perfect: Redo the thought pattern so that under stress, the outcome is predictable.

Read the map before leaving: Know the exact route so there will be no missed turns and extra driving.

Know where you are going: Again, no missed turns or extra driving.

Don't take any wooden nickels: Don't take any fake currency as payment or as change.

You can always use a half, but you can't use one and a half without a second: A half of a written line will only take one line of space, but if you write one and half lines, you will take two lines.

Or a **stitch in time saves nine:** Make repairs early before the tear gets much worse and needs nine times the stitches to make the repair.

All are based on perfect logic, and more could be written for each.

Buy ladders extra long or tall.
Just a little thought that's all.
You can't reach it when it is too short as I recall,
A short ladder may result in a fall.

4M. NEVER BE THE FIRST TO BREAK A FAMILY TRADITION, FROM *LIFE'S LITTLE INSTRUCTION BOOK*, VOL. II, H. JACKSON BROWN JR.

Never be the first to break a family tradition! Better still, never break a family tradition. Family traditions are important!

What "family traditions" to which am I referring?

Christmas: Traditions surrounding Christmas are most important. All family members need to be in place on the twenty-third of December so that the Christmas Eve walks, Christmas light drives, breakfasts, shopping trips, and meals can all take place as planned as in the past. Then on Christmas morning, gift openings at the appropriate places. Dinner at the appropriate places and later, other gift openings at other places as traditions dictates.

Family gatherings at Thanksgiving are also a very important. Thanksgiving and Christmas are the holidays with the strongest family traditions of being together.

Family traditions also should be kept around Mother's Day, Father's Day, birthdays, births, baptisms, weddings. These, to name a few, are events around which traditions should be continued.

Selecting a mate can be the single most important factor in determining whether someone will break family traditions. Different religions, different areas of the country, different races, even spouses with potentially similar traditions will force changes.

All can be important in determining whether family traditions will be broken. Once a tradition-breaking decision is made, such as marrying someone outside the immediate geographical area where your family is/was located, the family traditions will be broken.

There should be no surprise or heartache later when the tradition break occurs. It will happen when there is a wide geographical area difference or a family background different from your own!

Primarily, it shows a lack of priority of family traditions. Why be surprised when the traditions are broken when educations, jobs, mates, etc. are chosen regardless of the impact on traditions?

What about traditions of gift exchanges around Christmas? Rather than each family buying a separate gift for each person, each family member participating should put their name in hat and draw names. Each person could buy a, say, $50 gift for the person whose name the person drew or was assigned if not able to be present for the drawing.

Family traditions must be kept.
Tradition is the glue that binds.
Parent's wisdom keeps us adept.
But tradition leads us to be wise and kind.

4N. STEER CLEAR OF ANY PLACE WITH A "LADIES WELCOME" SIGN IN THE WINDOW, FROM *LIFE'S LITTLE INSTRUCTION BOOK*, VOL. II, H. JACKSON BROWN JR.

This is not going to be one of life's big suggestions. It will come under the heading of well-meaning suggestions aimed at saving the young man or lady the potential of trouble.

What kind of place might have such a sign in the window? From my experience, such a place might be a bar that is trying to bring in lots of heavy drinking and rowdy young males by encouraging and perhaps offering free admission to young women.

Young single guys will be attracted to such a place. My perception is that these young single guys will be a rowdy bunch and will be more apt to fights and other acts of aggression than other places where there is a better chance of having an equal mix of men and women and don't advertise for young women.

And why would a young lady with any degree of self-respect want to go into a place where they are obviously trying to attract young men with her? It makes no sense. Stay away, young lady or any lady. Stay away from the bars advertising "ladies welcome."

Why risk it? Go to the places where there is more-formal family-type entertainment or there is more certainty of a friendlier and less-rowdy clientele.

Steer clear of places where there are added risks.
Signs posted will give you clues . . .
When ladies are solicited, trouble ensues.
Such signs are clues which should grease your shoes.

40. DON'T STOP THE PARADE TO PICK UP A DIME, FROM *LIFE'S LITTLE INSTRUCTION BOOK*, VOL. II, H. JACKSON BROWN JR.

Keep life's decisions in perspective. Use the appropriate response to life's issues.

Picture a one-hundred-unit parade marching down the street, and all of a sudden, someone drops a dime in the middle of the street. You spot that incident and stop the whole parade to allow the person to pick up the dime. That would not make much sense, and the stopping-the-parade response would not be appropriate to the issue.

In response to any situation, think the issue involved through and decide upon a response in relative proportion to the incident.

Don't overreact and don't underreact; try to come up with an appropriate response to the issue. For example, a dropped dime would not be worth stopping a parade. Run across between units to pick up the dime or wait until the parade has passed or forget about the dime. All might be appropriate responses—stopping the parade would not be appropriate.

Many of life's decisions are not black and white. There is judgment involved and may be made with the benefit of many of the suggestions put for in these pages.

So judgments on life's issues are not always easy.

Everyone wants to do the right thing, but they do not always know the best way to respond. Inconvenience the fewest people with your decision.

Don't make decisions that result in you or others getting injured. Think before you act!

Don't stop to pick up a dime.
Keep priorities in order . . . all the time.
Know where you are heading; find the range.
Keep actions in sync to make a change.

4P. ASK ANYONE GIVING DIRECTIONS TO REPEAT THEM AT LEAST TWICE, FROM *LIFE'S LITTLE INSTRUCTION BOOK*, VOL. II, H. JACKSON BROWN JR.

Always make sure that you clearly understand what people tell you.

Faulty communication is often the root of people's problems. So what better advice than to make sure you accurately hear any directions that are given to you, especially if what you do with those directions is important.

A technique that I have seen some, who I consider to be particularly skillful in communications, use is to listen what the other person giving directions or communicating has to say . . . then try to say it back to them to confirm that you understood what they had to say.

Then let them repeat it back to you so you are again clear as to what they had to say.

This is an excellent communication process. They tell you directions or their position. You repeat it back to them to show them that you were listening. Then let them repeat it or acknowledge that you heard them correctly.

Also, be selective in whom you ask for directions, advice, or answers to your questions. There are some who it really would not matter whether you heard them or not; they do not know what they are talking about. Police, mail carriers, bus drivers would be expected to know enough about the area to give sound directions.

Parents, of course, are well equipped with children's interest in mind to give sound advice to a young person. Their advice is much more than you would get from just the casual observer. They will offer loving and well-thought-out advice totally aimed at the good of the young person.

Similarly, ask people for advice or directions who might reasonably be expected to know something about the topic in question. It is better to get no advice and use your own instincts than to get advice from a person you believe knows nothing about the topic or from a person whom you do not trust.

Employment situations offer challenges as to whose advice and counsel you really value and need to succeed. Generally, use these listening techniques discussed above for all business conversations. It will be a valuable learning experience.

Until you gain experience, the quality of your decisions will definitely be influenced by the quality of the person you ask for advice.

Seek a clear exchange when directions you need.
The message is sometimes tough—take heed.
But directions are so important for you to take the lead.
Ask for a repeat just to be sure you will succeed.

4Q. DON'T WASH A CAR, MOW A YARD, OR SELECT A CHRISTMAS TREE AFTER DARK, FROM *LIFE'S LITTLE INSTRUCTION BOOK*, VOL. II, H. JACKSON BROWN JR.

Don't wash a car, mow a lawn, or select a Christmas tree after dark if you care what they look like when you are finished and it matters what the ultimate job looks like.

Usually, if the "job is worth doing, it is worth doing well." Therefore, if you are setting out to complete a task, set up a situation that will allow you to do your best.

If your car is splotched with dirt and road soil after you wash your car, you certainly won't be asked to wash their car. Nor will you be asked to do work for them no matter what their activity. If you do a sloppy job on one thing, you are likely, they will think you do a sloppy job on other tasks. Exceed normal expectations when you complete a task for yourself or others.

You should realize that people's opinion of you will be guided by how they see you perform in every situation. Whether you realize it or not, it is very important to do your best at every opportunity.

If your car always looks perfect and the lawns that you mow always look perfectly manicured, people will look at you and will see that you actually care and want to do a good job.

Future jobs and other positions will be dependent on what you have done and what people believe you will do in the future based on what you have done in the past.

When you complete a task, step back and look at the job that you did as the customer would look at the complete task. Would they see stripes of grass still needing to be mowed? Will they see strips of grass around all or some trees and around the house and taller grass still on one end of the yard? If they do, you will not be called back as a first choice. Stand back and look at your completed task and check it out. Then go back and do that extra to exceed their expectations based on how the completed job looks.

Do your best and design the effort such that you have the maximum opportunity to do your best.

Sometimes it is absolutely necessary to try to accomplish something and the conditions are not the best. Cars can often be washed at night if there is plenty of light. Analyze the circumstances and make the conditions positive as you can make them to give you the best odds of achieving the best job.

There is a time and a place . . .
For all facets of the race.
Being out of phase . . .
Will make you a little crazed.

4R.   HOLD YOUR CHILD'S HAND EVERY CHANCE YOU GET. THE TIME WILL COME WHEN HE OR SHE WON'T LET YOU, FROM *LIFE'S LITTLE INSTRUCTION BOOK*, VOL. II, H. JACKSON BROWN JR.

Holding your child's or your grandchild's hand is such a small and fleeting event.

Holding the hand is symbolic of establishing a bond with that child that transcends just the hand holding. Establishing the bond is the existence of mutual warmth of feelings and love.

There is no basis for the confidence that the other will always be there when needed . . . well . . . maybe just a flicker of hope, and you can convey a temporary degree of confidence to the youngster. It is a very warm feeling to hold that little hand.

There are no absolutes with raising children. You do your best to establish a bond between parent and child or grandchild, but there are certainly no guarantees in life or with relationships. The parent does the hand holding and all other nurturing because that is what parents do (should do), and that is the limit.

Parents should do the best job they can with the nurturing process, and that is the limit of the guarantee. Know that you have done the very best you can do! Everything you do with the children and grandchildren is a teaching experience.

Live the life that you teach. Your actions should be consistent with what you say so that you can always hold up your head . . . and make sure your behavior is the very best model for teaching.

Think through how this relates to holding your child's hand. It relates because it is part of doing the very best in nurturing the child and protecting them as they grow older. Not because of what will come to you as a payback in years to come . . . but you do it because you want and need to know that you did the very best you could to prepare the child for the next phase of their life.

And then, when the child is grown, you will be able to look that person in the face and know that you did your best . . . whether you see them daily or yearly or somewhere in between.

Whatever you do and whoever you are with, do your best. Your family will appreciate you, and you will be recognized for being an excellent example. Doing your best will always be worth the effort and will be a basis for confidence and satisfaction for the whole family.

Hold that little hand.
There's no greater feeling in the land!
Time passes so fast.
Store them up so they will last.

4S. OWN A HAMMOCK, FROM *LIFE'S LITTLE INSTRUCTION BOOK*, VOL. II, H. JACKSON BROWN JR.

Own a hammock? The concept here is to be able to relax and have a way to relax.

You don't really have to own a hammock to relax. You can relax on the couch; you can relax at the health club; you can relax in your own bed; you can relax on an air mattress out in the yard where there are no trees on which to hang a hammock; or you can relax going for long walks.

Balance is important. People need to establish an appropriate balance between work and play . . . a balance between duties and this and that and relaxation. The hammock represents the relaxation.

The normal tendency of people, absent outside stimulation, is to relax. They seem to have the relaxation mastered. The real obstacle to overcome is to get up and out of the hammock . . . cut the relaxation short . . . and accomplish something every day.

With a vision of the future and sense of how to get to your vision, develop a plan. You probably want happy, healthy, and employed children and want your spouse to be happy and healthy and share your vision for the future. With a vision of the future and a plan for achieving your vision, you will feel more able to relax. Enjoy your achievements and keep a sense of balance between an achievement and time to relax to enjoy your successes.

A hammock, a symbol of rest . . .
It's a chance to regain your zest.
Life must be challenged with all your might.
An occasional pause will assure your flight.

4T. NEVER BE PHOTOGRAPHED HOLDING A COCKTAIL GLASS, FROM *LIFE'S LITTLE INSTRUCTION BOOK*, VOL. II, H. JACKSON BROWN JR.

A photograph showing you holding a cocktail drink will forever give the impression that you are a drinker. No matter if the glass contained water or ginger ale; people who see the picture will always wonder how many drinks you have had at best or assume that you are a heavy drinker and always have a drink in your hand. And with the Internet, Facebook, YouTube, etc . . . once a picture is out there, it will last forever.

Perception makes a difference. What people think when they think of you may be important. Or it may not be important to you. That is a personal choice you must make . . . but remember, once a picture is on one of the social websites, the picture will live forever. You may wish for your image to change as you move through life, and that may be more difficult when there are pictures of you out there doing something you are not particularly proud of. The first person you must satisfy is yourself. If your overall performance is satisfactory to you, that is the major task. Being satisfied with your own performance is very important. Then if what others think of you is important too, you must deal with issues such as being photographed in situations appearing to reflect less than your best.

Then if the perception of others is important, don't be photographed holding any glass.

To eliminate any question of what caption someone would put under your picture, do not allow yourself to be photographed holding a cocktail glass.

Today with friends you enjoy a glass of tea.
Flash, that scene is captured for eternity.
Once that innocent picture is out . . .
You have no say in what they portray you to be about.

4U. GIVE PEOPLE MORE THAN THEY EXPECT, AND DO IT CHEERFULLY, FROM *LIFE'S LITTLE INSTRUCTION BOOK*, VOL. II, H. JACKSON BROWN JR.

People will always be looking at you as an example of how to behave. Don't let them down.

Give people a shade (or more) more than what they expect, and they will be satisfied.

Give people a shade (or less) less than what they expect, and they will be disappointed.

There may be very little difference between slightly more than what they expect and slightly less than what others expect. The difference in the perception of the received action will potentially be drastic because the one receiving more will be a satisfied customer, while the one who receives less will not be a satisfied customer . . . a big difference.

Why risk disappointing your spouse, customer, associate, coach, parent, and the like . . . provide more than what people expect of you. Carefully assess expectations and exceed that. There should never be any question . . . exceed their expectations cheerfully.

Always make it a point to know what your customers or people you deal with are expecting from you and exceed it.

The one hundred and twenty percent guy . . .
You should appear to be in their mind's eye.
The slightly less guy will no doubt be . . .
A victim and will accomplish less than you and me!

4V. SOMEONE WILL ALWAYS BE LOOKING AT YOU AS AN EXAMPLE OF HOW TO BEHAVE. DON'T LET THEM DOWN, FROM *LIFE'S LITTLE INSTRUCTION BOOK*, VOL. II, H. JACKSON BROWN JR.

No matter where you are and how far you are away from home, someone will always see both the good and the bad that you do. And you can bet that they will be more likely to pass it on to someone who might wish to know, if what you did makes you look less than your best.

Always act as though you believe that your moves are being televised for national television viewing. Again, with Internet, traffic cameras, Facebook, and YouTube, having your actions televised is very real. From your driving, to your dealing with store clerks, to how well you do on a math test, to your performance in a football game . . . smile . . . you may be on TV.

People observe and make judgments about your performance. And once something gets out that is less than your best, there is no way to retract that performance.

The people especially molded by your good and poor behavior will be the young. Use every opportunity to go forth and do good; you will feel better, and our society as a whole will be improved by the quality performances of just one person like you. Each of us can be that one.

Once you do some activity for which you are not proud, there will be someone who is watching and ready to make a note or photographic record. They will see your less-than-proud moments and will be glad to share them with the very person you do not want to know.

Make a note to check out of the corner of your eye.
Someone will see your mistakes and sigh.
So act like you expect to show . . .
Those younger and simpler . . . the way to go.

4W. DO YOUR HOMEWORK AND KNOW YOUR FACTS, BUT REMEMBER IT'S PASSION THAT PERSUADES, FROM *LIFE'S LITTLE INSTRUCTION BOOK*, VOL. II, H. JACKSON BROWN JR.

Prepare, practice, study, get your mind and body ready for the challenges, the specifics of life's challenges we know to be ahead.

Life's challenges are out there! Whether the challenge is next week's sporting event or a major sales presentation or a major exam to assess your competence to get into one professional school or another, there are real challenges you will need to prepare for to succeed.

Preparation is a must; the world's most gifted scholars and athletes all must input the knowledge and skills into their bodies in order to have the ability when the time comes to perform.

At the time for the performance, the skill produced by the practice and other homework needs to be delivered with the passion and intensity of character. It is passion that carries the day between two of equal abilities and equal preparation.

Today there is so much talent around; the difference between teams and athletes and sales representative and scientist will ultimately be passion. The passion of one team or athlete will carry the day. Passion is today the ultimate "last straw" that makes the difference for the victor to carry the day.

Even more so, it is passion that motivates one to be prepared. Natural skills and preparation soon fall short when there is no passion.

Preparation is a key.
Research and study are a must.
Success is never free.
Without passion, you will be a bust.

4X. BE AS FRIENDLY TO THE JANITOR AS YOU ARE TO THE CHAIRMAN OF THE BOARD, FROM *LIFE'S LITTLE INSTRUCTION BOOK*, VOL. II, H. JACKSON BROWN JR.

It is important to be friendly to everyone. Obviously, some deserve your friendliness more so than some of the others. Social status or wealth is not a basis to withhold a friendly gesture here or there or a hello.

I believe there is a basis for granting a person more honor and respect if they have advanced to the point of being chairman of the board or some similar . . . high position. While everyone should be friendly with all people who cross your path . . . everyone including the janitor. Some deserve the respect more than others as a result of their hard work and achievement. But treat everyone as you wish to be treated.

There are certain basic dignities each person should be given. Everyone should receive respect. Respect their dignity as a person, as a human being. Each person deserves a basic level of respect.

The issue here is the hypocritical act of being respectful and extra nice to the person of authority over you just because that person is in a higher position than you in your organization.

Be friendly and nice to others regardless of where they are in the organization. Being friendly just because they can be nice to you and can grant you favors is not the measure of the quality person I am trying to portray in these writings.

Kindness must be a way of life.
From people to pets—all want to be free of strife.
From doorman to CEO—be kind.
Perhaps they will catch kindness as a state of mind.
More than just to influence their behavior.
Kindness could be their savior.

4Y. WHEN SOMEONE ASKS YOU A QUESTION YOU DON'T WANT TO ANSWER, SMILE AND SAY, "WHY DO YOU WANT TO KNOW?" FROM *LIFE'S LITTLE INSTRUCTION BOOK*, VOL. II, H. JACKSON BROWN JR.

Occasionally, you will be in a position where you get asked a question . . . something to the effect "have you stopped beating your wife and kids?"

If you say yes, that implies that you were beating your wife and kids, but you have stopped.

If you say no, that means you are still beating your wife and kids.

Now, in all likelihood, you have never beaten your wife and kids, but the person is just trying to put you on the spot by asking you an embarrassing question.

This is not your friend asking you such a question.

Respond, "Why do you want to know?" The nonfriend questioner probably will not even respond, showing their true colors. Or they will say what they really wanted to know.

Smile coolly and ask them, "Why did they really want to know?"

Smiling coolly and asking the questioner why they really wanted to know is not the way you should act around people with whom you normally associate . . . friends and family. The people I hope you are fortunate to associate with would not ask you an embarrassing question; they would already know the answer to their question or you would have no problem telling your family and friends. Friends and family should have a warm and supportive relationship and not teeming with undercurrents of tension.

Across a few feet of space . . .
What is the look on his face?
Why do they want to know?
There is a belief I have that continues to grow,
Most ask questions out of true concern.
There is no need for a slow burn.
Keep your life simple and pure.
There is no need for a "why do you want to know?" cure.

4Z. OVERESTIMATE TRAVEL TIME BY 15 PERCENT, FROM *LIFE'S LITTLE INSTRUCTION BOOK*, VOL. II, H. JACKSON BROWN JR.

The key is to arrive on time. Often, unpredictable events occur en route and will cause you to be late if you don't leave early.

By overestimating travel time, you will leave early and have a better chance of arriving on time.

Arriving on time is a sign of respect for the people you are meeting with; arriving late is a sign of disrespect for the people with whom you are meeting.

This is another of the "treat others as you wish to be treated" actions that routinely come up in life. Having others arriving on time when they are meeting you is a common courtesy that you would appreciate and is something you should strive to attain in return.

Just like being well groomed or being in good physical shape, arriving on time is a symbol of being confident in one's self. It shows that you are in charge and not a victim of the traffic light or the train crossing or the accident en route causing a traffic jam.

It also shows that you are dependable and totally capable of delivering what you say you will deliver. You are a person of your word, and that is important to establish in every aspect of your life.

And if it looks like you truly will be unavoidably late, everyone has cell phone, use yours to let the person expecting you what your amended time of arrival is.

Travel time is a variable which we can adjust.
The others are not so—I trust.
To be there on time . . . leave early or go fast.
With the latter, you may not last.
If all else fails, your cell is a must.

4AA. NEVER WEAR A WHITE BATHING SUIT, FROM *LIFE'S LITTLE INSTRUCTION BOOK*, VOL. II, H. JACKSON BROWN JR.

Of course, when it gets wet, you can see through it, and that certainly defeats the purpose of the swimming suit.

This is one of the many clothing recommendation I can make.

Don't wear a dark shirt on a hot, sunny day.

Always tuck in your shirt.

Don't wear the same color shirt as pants.

Don't mix stripes and checks.

If you are chubby, don't wear horizontal stripes.

Make sure the language on your shirt is clean.

Wear your baseball cap right.

Wear a belt or suspenders.

Don't wear white socks with dress shoes . . . wear dark socks.

The admonition to not wear white . . .
When swimming; white becomes more of a window . . .
And less of a shade that stops a line of sight.
A white of anything when wet is a show.

4BB. DON'T DISMISS ANY GOOD IDEA REGARDLESS OF THE SOURCE, FROM *LIFE'S LITTLE INSTRUCTION BOOK*, VOL. II, H. JACKSON BROWN JR.

Sharing ideas is a difficult topic.

I have not found many people prone to accepting ideas from others, especially uninvited ideas . . . thus the topic of this book . . . "What I Would Have Said . . ."

Someone offering you an idea that you did not ask for . . . basically offering their opinion when you did not ask for it . . . is sometimes difficult to deal with given you must stop, think . . . compare their idea to your existing thoughts, and then either reject their idea or incorporate their idea as part of your own.

Then if they are an "idea crusader" and keep pushing their idea . . . over and over . . . what do you do and still be polite? And for sure, don't you be an "idea crusader" yourself!

If someone asks for your opinion . . . give it if you wish. Give them your idea once.

Even then, the likelihood of them accepting your idea is small. Since they asked, it won't be because you forced your idea on them to cause them not to accept your idea. It won't be personal.

The reason will be that they have their own idea, and more than likely, they have developed their idea based on their background, and naturally, they like their ideal best. As I said, this is not personal . . . people just do not take other people's ideas very well.

I question, why waste your time and energy and never offer an unsolicited opinion about something that doesn't impact you insofar as the outcome of the situation? If you are impacted and you believe the issue is worth the confrontation . . . abandon the committee approach and handle the issue the way you think best.

For you personally, it is wise to have your own idea on how to do things. But listen to the ideas of others and try to incorporate their ideas into the overall plan. Don't reject an idea just because it has a source other than your own mind!

Listen, consider and analyze every idea offered to you. Otherwise, they will stop offering ideas, and you will be without the thinking of others concerning issues and the problems of the day.

How you treat people is at issue here.
Do unto others . . . be of good cheer . . .
The lowest on the pole.
Should be treated as if he has the highest role.

4CC. WHEN YOU SAY "I'M SORRY," LOOK THE PERSON IN THE EYE. WHEN YOU SAY YOU ARE SORRY, MAKE SURE YOU MEAN IT, FROM *LIFE'S LITTLE INSTRUCTION BOOK*, VOL. II, H. JACKSON BROWN JR.

Any time you can't or won't look someone in the eye when you are speaking to them, they are likely not going to believe you. An apology will come off totally insincere unless you look them in the eye and say that you are sorry for . . . very slowly and clearly.

Our society calls for you, in order to be believable, to look someone straight in to the eye when you are speaking to them.

Again, when you apologize, in order to be believable and sincere, look the person straight in the eye and say that you are sorry.

However, if you have to apologize to the same person, for the same or similar event in the future, they are not likely to believe that you are truly sorry the second time . . . regardless of whether you look them in the eye or not.

You don't get many, usually not more than one, opportunity to maintain your credibility with a person. They may forgive you once, if that, but you must never ever do again what you are apologizing for to maintain any semblance of credibility to your apology.

How to act . . . what to do?
Will always be a dilemma to me and you.
Always look the person in the eye.
Think before you act and you won't have to say why.
Take charge; treat them as you would be.
And you won't have to apologize . . . you'll see.

4DD. PUT THE STRAP AROUND YOUR NECK BEFORE LOOKING THROUGH THE BINOCULARS, FROM *LIFE'S LITTLE INSTRUCTION BOOK*, VOL. II, H. JACKSON BROWN JR.

Anticipate accidents; the binoculars are expensive and are a delicate piece of equipment. To avoid an accidental slippage of the binoculars out of your hands and falling to the floor, put the strap around your neck first before looking through the binoculars.

There are many other similar sayings or suggestions that we might think up.

Put your seat belt on before you start driving the car.

Put the dog's leash on before you start the walk.

Brush your teeth before you go to bed.

Look before crossing the street.

In Little League, put your helmet on before stepping up to the plate.

The same for riding your cycle . . . put your helmet on before leaving the curb.

All are safety precautions, which are advisable before taking an action.

Put your seat belt on before you start.
Look both ways before you cross.
Read the label directions you know by heart.
Being safe prevents a loss.

4EE. TRUST IN GOD BUT LOCK YOUR CAR, FROM *LIFE'S LITTLE INSTRUCTION BOOK*, VOL. II, H. JACKSON BROWN JR.

Trust in God for what?

Trust in God . . . to keep thieves from stealing your car, or stealing the valuables from your car.

Not really!

Trust in God to forgive your sins and admit you to heaven if you have faith in God and Jesus and are repentant of your sins.

Trusting in God to protect you and your possessions is misplaced energy and confidence.

There are many people around today without the character to respect the rights of others. Therefore, the basis for universally trusting our fellowman is a bit of a stretch.

Protect yourself from those without character and those undeserving of trust. Lock your door!

Trust in God for Salvation, not day-to-day protection.

Trust in God . . . will he respond?
But lock your car.
This appears to limit those who would abscond.
It is merely a limit on how far . . .
God is willing, for now, to let us link our star.

Trust in God to do what you say?
Protect your car . . . in your own way?
You can hope . . . but God will not protect you by night or day.
But . . . He will give you eternal life...hooray!

4FF. NEVER SAY ANYTHING UNCOMPLIMENTARY ABOUT YOUR WIFE OR YOUR CHILDREN IN THE PRESENCE OF OTHERS, FROM *LIFE'S LITTLE INSTRUCTION BOOK*, VOL. II, H. JACKSON BROWN JR.

Never say anything uncomplimentary about your wife, your children, or your mother or father in the presence of others.

If you can't depend on family to protect you and your name, you can't depend on anyone.

Of course this is an ideal statement.

As the head of a family, an occasional internal family counseling session may be necessary to maintain family standards. These sessions should be as private as possible and include people just within the family.

Family members must be loyal and respectful to each other.

Mutual trust is important; don't second-guess and do not check up on everything the other family members do.

People need to know they are trusted by the other family members. Accept the other family members but remind them initially they have to earn that trust by being honest with the other family members and meet their responsibilities. There should be certain minimal standards for behavior and dress. These should be clear.

There are limits to where and what you say.
Unless they are perfect, nothing is OK!
Nothing to humiliate or a confidence to betray . . .
You need to be able to discuss events that come your way.

4GG. NO MATTER HOW OLD YOU GET, HUG AND KISS YOUR MOTHER WHENEVER YOU GREET HER, FROM *LIFE'S LITTLE INSTRUCTION BOOK*, VOL. II, H. JACKSON BROWN JR.

Yes, no matter how old you get, hug your mother (and father) when you greet her (and him). Reestablish that bond each time. It takes so little of a child's initiative and love to make a parent happy. Do it often. If there is distance, hug by phone. Just as an "in-person hug," an occasional call continues the connection and bond between child and parents.

That parental, motherly connection between mother and child is always there and should always be very close.

To a slightly less degree, between father and child, that relationship will always be close too. The father, less so only because fathers tend to be a little less expressive and needs less attention than does the mom. Father may be a little more gruff but still deeply care about their children.

Mothers especially are sensitive to the proper greeting and thrive on all the affection from her children.

Men don't show that so much, but their feelings are there, just about the same as the mother.

A little time and respect are the fuel of parents. That keeps them cheered and secure with their relationship with their child. Then they can be freed up to do the other of life's rich opportunities. Show your respect for the near unconditional love they have for you.

A hug and kiss on the cheek anyway is the proper way to greet most family members.

No matter where or who's there.
A hug and a kiss for Mom is due.
You must be aware!
Mom expects a hug and kiss and so does Dad too.

4HH. PRAY. THERE'S IMMEASURABLE POWER IN IT, FROM *LIFE'S LITTLE INSTRUCTION BOOK*, VOL. II, H. JACKSON BROWN JR.

Pray for what? Power for what? Power to do what?

When you pray, what kind of power do you expect?

If you pray expecting God to grant you health, wealth, or power, you are wasting your time and energy! I believe that prayer may give you the power of positive thinking and the will to overcome the adversity that is concerning you.

Based on what, you say?

Because mankind is so sinful, I do not believe God is answering those prayers.

As I said, spending your time praying for God's help in giving you good health, wealth, and power is a waste of time. Prayer may give you additional hope and will to overcome your adversities.

Prayer can be a time of reflection and communication. Reflect on your thoughts, issues, and questions that come up regarding everyday life as well as what God and Jesus say in the Bible about the topics that you deal with in life.

The confusion regarding praying for God's protective intervention is caused by the fact that so few people believe the literal or any interpretation of the Bible. In brief, God said several times in the Bible that as long as His people followed His teachings/instructions, He would protect them and cure their diseases. He finally gave up hoping that His people would behave . . . so He sent Jesus who died on the cross as a sacrificial lamb so that our sins would be forgiven and we could enter heaven upon our death *if* we were repentant of our sins and believe in Jesus and God.

Please don't rely on prayer for health, wealth, or power.

Do the best you can with education, hard work, and your vision of the future. Your lifestyle is important too. Make informed, healthy decisions regarding your future lifestyle.

Rather than pray for God's intervention, you must be repentant of your sins and have faith that God and Jesus will provide for eternal life.

In terms of health, wealth, and power, if you seek them, they must be a lifelong strategy and lifestyle that you work for and earn.

Health must be a lifestyle of informed diet and exercise.

If you get sick, fight the disease by picturing yourself well, eat foods that are known to strengthen your immune system, and act like you are well. No depressed moping around.

A diet focused on fruits and vegetables, complex carbohydrates, and minimal meat or milk fat products will offer you the strongest chances to avoid serious sickness. Enhance your natural foods with vitamin supplements. Take a good multivitamin plus beta-carotene, vitamins Bs, C, Omega 3, Mg and potassium.

There are no guarantees in life that you will remain healthy; but these are positive steps you can take to maximize the possibility of good health.

Wealth is also something that I believe must come with a lifelong plan and lifestyle. If at any time accumulating wealth becomes a primary goal in life, you are heading in the wrong direction. The plan . . . your financial plan . . . must be set in motion and then carried out; it shouldn't be something that occupies significant portions of your waking hours.

Accumulation of wealth must be part of a long-term financial plan. Continual savings in the stock market and stock-based mutual funds are my recommendation to young people just starting out.

Praying for power will just not get it. Everyone needs to have some power over the factors that control their life, but not through prayer. You gain power and influence by being good at what you are doing. You become good by hard work, education, and your vision of where you are headed and how you want to get there. Rely on God and Jesus for eternal life by being repentant of your sins and having faith in God and Jesus.

Thomas R. Wallin

It is often said to those who are well.
That there is power in prayer, its swell.
And . . . there may be, but I am not the one to tell.
Faith and a repentant heart may power you but surely will save you from hell.

4II. BRUSH YOUR TEETH BEFORE PUTTING ON YOUR TIE, FROM *LIFE'S LITTLE INSTRUCTION BOOK*, VOL. II, H. JACKSON BROWN JR.

Common sense . . . it is almost impossible to brush your teeth without getting toothpaste on your tie.

Plan ahead; think about what you are doing and expect things to happen; these little things need to be anticipated.

There are numerous suggestions that are similar to this one.

Don't wear clothing that you care about while you are painting the house.

Don't drive on a freshly oiled road.

Mow the lawn wearing old shoes.

Don't eat spaghetti with red sauce with a white shirt on; preferably wear a red shirt.

Keep a bath towel with you if you eat while you drive . . . use it as a bib.

These are just common sense little thoughts that come with experience or with a little anticipation.

It seems insulting to give advice about such low-level issues such as these. Yet most of life's decisions can actually be so minimal and elementary. Think through decisions made and anticipate the consequences of their impact. In life, it's the secondary impacts of your decisions that will "get" you.

Anticipate events before they occur.
Brush before adding your tie.
The white drop may only be a blur.
But it will leave its mark . . . you sigh . . .
And they all will know why.

4JJ. NEVER ASK A BARBER IF YOU NEED A HAIRCUT, FROM *LIFE'S LITTLE INSTRUCTION BOOK*, VOL. II, H. JACKSON BROWN JR.

(And never ask someone who may be affected by your decision for advice.)

The theory is . . . they can't always separate the advice for you and the impact on them. However, who else could better determine whether you need a haircut, and whether a hair cut would do you any good? You don't have to take their advice anyway! No kidding!

I suppose, bottom line, you need to find a barber that you trust and then ask them for advice. Some people go to a barber every two weeks so they don't have to think about it every time. If two weeks are too often, go once a month.

Similarly, find the insurance sales person you trust and ask for advice about insurance; find the car dealer you trust and ask him/her for advice.

The advice must not be accepted without thought. You have the possibility of discussing the topic with others or just ignoring the advice.

But you absolutely should be able to ask the experts for advice.

People are different; two barbers may have different opinions. Two people will have different opinions even; no matter whether they sell the product or not.

People are different and have different ideas about the same thing.

Because of the wide range of people, barbers are in contact with other barbers who have a broad range of ideas, which they can comingle into their own. Also from the barbers, I know and have known, they all seem to be clear thinking and honest. Also, for a $10 haircut, why question their judgment?

There is no one else in the country selling you something so important to your looks, at such a low price, as your barber. Ease up on barbers; question the car salesman, the real-estate salesperson, the clothing salesman, and the jeweler person but not the barber.

Why pick on the barber to avoid . . . for advice?
It should be just as true . . .
As an insurance rep and much lower in price!
If you have a question, oh, go ahead, ask a barber or two.

4KK. PHONE HOME IF YOU'RE GOING TO BE MORE THAN TWENTY MINUTES LATE, FROM *LIFE'S LITTLE INSTRUCTION BOOK*, VOL. II, H. JACKSON BROWN JR.

Common courtesy, to a point, that is all it is.

Of course, with so many sinister and evil people in the world, always make sure someone is expecting you to be somewhere. If you don't show up reasonably on time, either you call or your family should come looking for you. Beyond dealing with dangers of life, the twenty-minutes-late call is a courtesy and a well-advised one at that. If everyone would remember the little common courtesies . . . what a wonderful world it would be.

There are many common courtesies in life that represent the way you would want to be treated yourself.

Remember the Golden Rule here: Treat others as you would want to be treated. There are so many of these. The phoning if you are going to be late is just one.

Don't stuff the trash pail full and leave it for someone else to take out; if it's full when you put the last item in it, take the trash out yourself.

Don't take someone's parking place just before they pull in to it.

Don't put your dirty dishes into the sink without washing them; wash them or place them in the dishwasher . . . one or the other . . . no exceptions!

Don't park in the middle of the drive!

Don't kick your shoes off and leave more than one pair of shoes by the back door. Put the rest in the rack where they belong.

If you borrow something or use something of others, put it back . . . ask permission first too.

If you drink the last, or nearly so, of the juice, make more or get more out of storage.

Don't complain if you are asked to walk the dog; do it without asking.

Phone home is one courtesy . . .
We would want to see.
Hold the door open for another to pass . . .
Be nice to every lad and lass.

4LL. REMEMBER THAT EVERYONE IS INFLUENCED BY KINDNESS, FROM *LIFE'S LITTLE INSTRUCTION BOOK*, VOL. II, H. JACKSON BROWN JR.

I believe character, ethics, responsibility and morality are prerequisite to appreciating kindness.

Without character, ethics, responsibility, and morality, kindness is perceived as a weakness, and the person is not necessarily positively influenced by kindness.

The primary rule is to treat others the way you would want to be treated.

If you want respect, treat others with respect. Try this once or twice—maybe even three times.

But if they don't return the respectful treatment at that point, avoid them and don't go beyond that.

Kindness won't help either if the respect you showed them didn't cause them to show you respect. Kindness certainly won't help them either.

Unprovoked acts of kindness to people as you pass through the day will be appreciated by people. Many people will be touched by your acts of kindness, and they will not be in a position to return that to you. And you will not expect it. Who knows, some of them may even deserve it. And I believe you'll observe that unprovoked acts of kindness will generate unprovoked acts of kindness from your recipients to others as they pass through their day.

You will know, after a while, about the people around you. Some deserve your kindness, and some just deserve your civility.

Kindness must be a way of life.
From people to pets ... all want to be free of strife.
From doorman to CEO ... be kind.
Perhaps they will catch kindness as a state of mind.
More than just to influence their behavior.
Kindness could be their savior.

4MM. OVERPAY GOOD BABY-SITTERS, FROM *LIFE'S LITTLE INSTRUCTION BOOK*, VOL. II, H. JACKSON BROWN JR.

Just as with any business arrangement, it is a good practice, if we are speaking of a salaried position, to pay the better performers at a higher rate.

Reward those who perform the best at a higher rate than those who perform less well. The quality workers will strive to do better as well as work harder and smarter to improve themselves.

A baby-sitter is an individual performer, usually working alone.

Reward the sitter whom you believe does the best job.

The sitter should be given a list of child care or game duties along with instructions, to play games if they have time. Also they should clean up messes, which originate during the current baby-sitter's visit. Additionally, you may ask them to clean up possible messes time permitting, such as dirty dishes, from the family meal just before the baby-sitter arrival and just before the parents' departure to their social event. The good baby-sitter will take care of the children and keep them safe and clean as well as a few extra chores.

Hopefully, a better baby-sitter will do that plus will clean up all messes that originate while the parents are away.

The best baby-sitter will take good care of the child, play a game or a few games with the child, clean up all messes, which originate while the parents are away, and will clean up messes, dirty dishes, and the like, which originate before the sitter arrives. In this latter case, the baby-sitter exceeds expectations and should be rewarded.

Pay the baby-sitter fairly—based on the prevailing neighborhood and area wages for sitters. Pay the better sitters as a bonus of at least 25 percent more than the prevailing sitter's wages. Pay the best sitters a bonus of at least 50 percent more.

As you pass through life, you will need the services of numerous people, from baby-sitters to doctors to mechanics to carpenters to electricians to plumbers. When you develop a relationships with people of quality, keep those resources and reward them with bonuses if they continue to exceed your expectations.

Good help is hard to find.
Especially to have peace of mind,
With treasures of your soul.
Dig a little deeper into your roll.

4NN. IF YOU'RE AWAY FROM HOME AND HEAR CHURCH BELLS, THINK OF THREE PEOPLE WHO LOVE YOU! FROM *LIFE'S LITTLE INSTRUCTION BOOK*, VOL. II, H. JACKSON BROWN JR.

Count your blessings when you hear the church bells.

The church bells are just a reminder.

You could just as well count those blessings . . . when you hear a train's horn or a siren or some other sound. Really, any reminder would do.

A church bell is good; there are lots of them, and the symbolism of a church bell and love is excellent.

Most people have someone or a few people who love them. Your mother and your dad are good examples of people who love you.

Your spouse will love you, maybe. Your children will love you, maybe. Your parents' love is unconditional. If you have been married for any time at all and your spouse still truly loves you, that is a blessing.

The blessing of a way to earn a living, to earn money, is another valuable blessing. Appreciate that for sure. Good health is a major, major blessing!

Use each day to appreciate your blessings, and do not be a little rain cloud as you spend and pass through each day. Cheer people up! Don't cast any cloud on their happiness. Each day will be a blessing to you, and you will be a blessing to others.

Count among your blessings your family, your health, your job, your home.

Use the bell as a reminder of your blessings . . . appreciate what you have.

Spend time, given a choice, appreciating what you have rather than longing for more.

Church bells are as good as any.
Just one example of many.
Loved ones are a passing treasure.
Enjoy them, cherish them with great measure.

400. LEAVE A QUARTER WHERE A CHILD CAN FIND IT, FROM *LIFE'S LITTLE INSTRUCTION BOOK*, VOL. II, H. JACKSON BROWN JR.

Children need dreams; positive dreams for them to build on in their future. They need fairy tales where everything always works out right. They need Santa Claus, the Easter Bunny; they need to believe they will have good luck and that they are in charge; well, some of the time.

By leaving a quarter out, here and there where the child can find it, you will encourage the child's dreams. Perhaps the good fairy left the quarter. Perhaps the Easter Bunny or Santa Claus made one last pass through the area to perform the gift giving.

Now, of course, this good fairy, Easter Bunny, or Santa Claus stuff isn't the only thing we should be teaching that child.

Morality, character, truth, hard work, honesty, all topics that should be taught, shown, and lived for the child to observe as he or she matures.

There is, however, nothing wrong with teaching the child to expect a little good luck, and the quarter will help.

This comes under the heading of going around and committing unprovoked acts of kindness. Kindness to the child is an excellent example, but there are many others; some are highlighted in this book. Treat others as you would wish to be treated. Always do what you would want others to do to you.

The joy of a child is easy to bring out.
Simple surprises . . . a quarter here and there . . . inspire a sweet little shout.
Enjoy their childish hope . . .
That sometimes slackens the rope.

4PP. WHEN IT COMES TO WORRYING OR PAINTING A PICTURE, KNOW WHEN TO STOP, FROM *LIFE'S LITTLE INSTRUCTION BOOK*, VOL. II, H. JACKSON BROWN JR.

Worry about something while you can still make a difference. Once it is too late to do anything about the problem or situation, move on to something you can do something about. Your health, your wife or husband, your children, your financial security, your job, your home, your car all need attention.

Deal with problems and think through your strategies for dealing with each now—present tense. In a sense, deal with, not worry about, these elements now while you can do something about the issues.

Don't wait until they are out of your control or beyond something that you can do something about. Worry or deal with the issues now—later it may be too late.

I use "worry" here as a sense of doing something or thinking about the situation.

With my limited experience as a painter/artist, both as a home-improvement painter or an artist, it is hard to know how and what advice to give.

Even with the home-improvement variety of painting, at the right time, if you quit, the surface material is covered; the paint is smooth, and that is great. If you don't quit then and add more paint, the paint will run, the surface will be full of bumps, and the resulting product will not be what you wanted.

Painting as an artist has to be about the same thing; you work on the colors, the layout, the perfection of the areas where you want people to focus. If you don't stop at the right time, the final product will be cluttered, and the area of focus will be fuzzy.

Don't worry; act on what you can do something about; act early enough to give you an opportunity to make a difference. Worrying is just a wasteful consumption of brain capacity and energy. Brain capacity and energy should be utilized by planning and anticipating situations you can still do something about.

It is difficult to know the difference between situations that you can still have a positive impact and situations which are too late.

Worrying is such a waste; it decays.
By then, effort has been delayed.
Anticipate, plan . . . be visionary all your days.
Before the fact, success can be portrayed.

4QQ. AVOID USING THE WORD "IMPACTED" UNLESS YOU'RE DESCRIBING WISDOM TEETH, FROM *LIFE'S LITTLE INSTRUCTION BOOK*, VOL. II, H. JACKSON BROWN JR.

There are some words, "impacted" is an example, that are overused and frequently used by people that are the bureaucratic talkers and not necessary doers of our time.

Here are some examples of similar words to "impacted," which should be avoided. Some examples of these are:

Multicultural
Diversity
TQM
Disadvantaged
Coordinate
Relationship
Integrated

Also avoid the F word, the N word, or the H word.

Words that are frequently used by bureaucrats and talkers that describe their jargon will often cause people's eyes to glaze over and lose focus on what they are saying.

Some words must be avoided because people, at least the writer, gets tired of certain popular words in use today. Their use and meaning seems to bind action people in knots and hinders true success. The warning here is to avoid the popular buzzwords of the day. People just get tired of them, and they show an absence of creativity by the user.

Some words are used too much.
Impacted came into view.
Oft used words vary . . . they are a crutch.
Thinking less is a symptom too.

4RR. BE BOLD. PROVIDENCE LOVES BOLDNESS AND WILL ASSIST YOU IN WAYS YOU WOULDN'T IMAGINE. PROVIDENCE IS A NONENTITY, FROM *LIFE'S LITTLE INSTRUCTION BOOK*, VOL. II, H. JACKSON BROWN JR.

Be bold, and with your character, your ethics, your morals, your intelligence, you are many more times more likely to be successful.

Without action, nothing will happen, that's obvious!

Action will produce results, some good and some bad.

As stated before, with your character, ethics, morals, and intelligence, your actions will be mostly successful.

Boldness has generated all the great events of mankind.

Boldness also created all the great disasters of mankind.

Of course, natural events and disasters are not included in this statement. I am writing of the man-made variety of events. Boldness therefore is responsible for the great man-made events of our time.

If properly conceived and with the right purpose, an action will result in a positive significant event.

Providence does not exist; hard work will generate results. Hard work with character, ethics, morals will produce positive results.

Providence is used to explain events and the way things happen that we don't understand. God's will is another way of explaining providence. Mankind does not understand God's will. I say this only because much of mankind claims to believe the Bible but does not believe the Bible when it says that God will turn His back on His people if they are grossly disobedient. His people are grossly disobedient. With God's back tuned on His people, things happen, which we cannot explain: both good and bad. Thus, the word "providence," or "fate," seems to mean uncontrolled events. Your success then will depend on your character, ethics, morality, intelligence, hard work, and boldness!

Be bold and aggressive . . . success will follow.
Not a gift or providence, that's hollow.
Working to succeed is the message I tell.
Take charge, stretch, till you hear the bell.

4SS. NEVER ORDER CHICKEN FRIED STEAK IN A PLACE THAT DOESN'T HAVE A JUKEBOX, FROM *LIFE'S LITTLE INSTRUCTION BOOK*, VOL. II, H. JACKSON BROWN JR.

Chicken fried steak is greasy and is probably full of preservatives and other nonnutritive items. If you aren't being benefitted by the atmosphere of a jukebox and other amenities, avoid the chicken fried steak.

This points out that life is full of trade-offs and choices.

Don't settle for anything less than the best unless it is a rational decision and there are legitimate trade-offs. Decide that the bonus benefits that you receive are worth the reduction in quality you are accepting.

Set your goals, your vision, and stay on a track unless the distractions are rationally worth modifying your direction. Without a plan, a vision, the distractions will be overwhelming because you will have no basis for deciding against the easy and pleasurable distractions with very short-term appeal. And there are some distractions, such as the gravy on chicken fried steak, which are not worth it no matter what the situation is.

Chicken fried steak is just the focus of this point. Chicken fried steak especially with gravy, the way it is normally served, is not a healthy food. There must be some redeeming features of chicken fried steak or the restaurant or don't eat it. Order it without the gravy no matter where you get it.

Life has its choices to be made by us.
To be worth the grease there must be a plus.
The jukebox and the memories are a help.
Have the country fried steak but go heavy on the fibers and kelp.

4TT. GO ON A BLIND DATE; THAT'S HOW I MET YOUR MOTHER, FROM *LIFE'S LITTLE INSTRUCTION BOOK*, VOL. II, H. JACKSON BROWN JR.

Not really! Nor do I think that this is an especially appealing way to find a spouse.

Dating can and should be a long, fun, enjoyable process, which, after a year or two, can give you enough experience and wisdom when dealing with the opposite sex on which to base a decision about a lifelong partner and friend.

Going on a blind date without knowing the other person is one way to meet people. A blind date is totally for a group activity and in no way should be considered as a way to meet a spouse unless it is recognized to be the beginning of a very lengthy dating process.

There are too many crazy people in the world to risk being alone with someone you really don't know and don't know about their character, ethics, morality, and health.

This saying is another way to be inquisitive; meeting people this way can be fun. There are other ways to meet people as well.

I didn't meet your mom on a blind date.
She is cute and there was chemistry first rate.
A blind date through a friend is OK but don't berate.
A church friend for a start would be great.

4UU. CALL YOUR DAD, FROM *LIFE'S LITTLE INSTRUCTION BOOK*, VOL. II, H. JACKSON BROWN JR.

Of course, call your Dad. Call your Mom; together or separately. They both appreciate the attention and are more interested in what you are doing than anyone else in this world.

Earlier in this saga of essays, I wrote of the need to call your mom. Call your mom and give her all the details, even minute details of your life. She is interested and wants to listen. She enjoys the attention. She enjoys the details.

Your dad is interested but more so in the broad generalities without lots and lots of details.

He wants to know that you are happy and healthy and will offer advice if requested. But you can skip the details if you wish.

Call your dad too!
He likes to hear from you.
Dad can be loud and to him, stories are hard to sell.
But he certainly enjoys hearing from you through . . . "Ma Bell."

5

"Win With Your Strengths" By Donald O. Clifton And Paula Nelson, *Reader's Digest*, P. 74, May 1993.

5A. PICK AT LEAST ONE STRENGTH TO USE AND TO PURSUE FOR SUCCESS.

"Win with your strengths." If you are to succeed, you must win with what you have; you must win with the abilities, the strengths, that you have—not the abilities you wish you had or would like to have or would have had if you had not been white or black or bald or poor or living in a rural area.

You must make your successes with the abilities that you have.

To be successful, you must satisfy yourself. And to satisfy yourself, you must be good at, at least one thing or activity. Decide what your strengths are and then perfect your skills in that area.

Look honestly; it will be obvious to you what your strengths are.

There are untold numbers of people who have accomplished much, but because their definition of success is either poorly defined or not existent, they never become satisfied with themselves. That is unfortunate.

And if you develop your strengths to the point that you are very good, that fact will be confidence building enough to inspire you to great achievement.

Your strength may be some academic topic, such as math, science, history, or writing.

It may be some sports activity.

Your strength may be a skill in dealing with people or situations.

There are many situations in which a strength can be identified and used.

Recognizing and developing strengths can be great confidence builders and can be stepping stones for your life's work.

"Win with your strengths" is a great place to start!
Using the tools you have . . . makes sense if you are smart.
Why waste time when you have the heart?
Assess where you are and from there depart.

5B. "EXERCISE YOUR STRENGTH DAILY" BY DONALD O. CLIFTON AND PAULA NELSON, *READER'S DIGEST*, P. 74, MAY 1993.

Exercise your strength daily. Win with your strengths . . . sure, but the old standby—practice needs to be stressed!

Practice does not make perfect, but practice and practice at a level equivalent to the best quality performance you wish to achieve will give you the confidence that you have worked very hard and have done your best. That too helps program your body to make the right moves automatically.

Armed with that knowledge that you have done your best, then no matter what the outcome, you will know you have done your best.

Without the knowledge that you "exercise your strength daily," you physically or mentally will not be prepared for the events of life.

Also, keep in mind that you cannot be just a single discipline person.

It just takes one category . . . music, sports, academics, scholastics, etc . . . to excel to be justifiably confident in yourself and have the confidence to deal with people and issues from a position of strength.

But you cannot be just a single discipline person in the daily routine of life. For example, with any avocation, other than business, you must couple your strength with a business sense to be able to take care of your own affairs. Additionally, you must have some nominal skill in communication, both verbal and written, to be able to fully take advantage of your strength.

Your main emphasis should be on the main skill that you use to earn your living or that you put forth as your personal statement. But there are numerous skills or related qualities that must be nurtured or acquired in order to succeed to your satisfaction.

Exercise your strength daily, I say.
Practice, practice hard is not play.
Today's strength is not here to stay!
Without work, it will go away.

5C. "IGNORE WEAKNESSES THAT DON'T HINDER YOU," BY DONALD O. CLIFTON AND PAULA NELSON, *READER'S DIGEST*, P. 74, MAY 1993.

There has been, perhaps, only one perfect human being, and that was not you or me. Ignore weaknesses that don't keep you from achieving your goals. Select goals, which are a stretch beyond what you might conservatively believe you could achieve, but are realistic too. Don't set your direction toward weaknesses . . . set your vision and direction toward your strengths and skills.

There are two levels of thought here.

First, consider the perspective of having certain skills that you develop as overall confidence builders. Confidence is the first level. The second level is relative to lifetime success. Here on this higher, second level, it takes several skills meshed to put a personal lifetime strategy together. Scholastics, sports, and business for example all must be meshed into a single plan.

It is on the first level where you can ignore weaknesses that don't hinder you. From the perspective of having certain skills that you develop as overall confidence builders, it is recommended for you to ignore your weaknesses. Focus on your strengths and enjoy the confidence built by knowing that you are truly good at your strength . . . maybe only one item. Remember, you really only have to be good at one skill to truly deserve to be proud of yourself, and you should be confident.

On the second level, weakness must be dealt with to make sure it doesn't hinder you. Remember, everyone has weaknesses, which they must overcome. As I indicated, it takes several skills combined to form a personal lifetime success strategy. Scholastics, sports, and business for example all must be meshed into a single plan for you to be successful in sports, business, or professional school during the five or ten years after high school. Beyond that, scholastics, business, social skills (speaking, writing, and selling), and perhaps parenting must be meshed into a single plan for the next five to ten years.

It is in this second level . . . really just living your life . . . where the weaknesses must be identified and mitigated if not mastered. Issues, such as alcohol, video games, drugs, friends, which detract from your life plan and vision, are the type of weaknesses that you must overcome to keep your lifetime vision and happiness secure.

A weaknesses that doesn't hinder you . . .
May be one that certainly hurts too!
The confidence from being great...
Will help you carry life's freight.

5D. "LOOK FOR COMPLEMENTARY PARTNERS" BY DONALD O. CLIFTON AND PAULA NELSON, *READER'S DIGEST*, P. 74, MAY 1993.

Know your strengths and refine them dutifully—a topic already covered. With respect to building your ego and self-concept, ignore your weaknesses and focus on the perfection of your strengths. Work hard and be confident that you are prepared to deal with the issues of the day. In short, be great, know you are great and have a lot to offer and enjoy it.

Insofar as the mechanics of moving through and being a success in life, look for complementary partners. Life and business weakness must be identified and dealt with as best as possible to minimize the weakness they cause. The road to success certainly will be softer if your associates or partners have strengths in the area(s) of your weaknesses and at the same time share in your core beliefs and values.

Whether the partner is a spouse, a teammate, an actual business partner, the partner should be carefully chosen so that they possess the skills, talents, and attributes in areas in which you are weakest. They must come with similar values and ethics . . . character. Character is important!

In families, as with most other situations in sports or business, there must be a division of labor in which partners, regardless of whether they number two or more, have responsibilities in their area of expertise. It will be more satisfying and probably successful if the abilities of all the partners contribute to portions of the entity's success.

The partnership with shared activities and complementary abilities and talents takes the pressure off individuals for having to "know it all." And complementary skills take away the likelihood of conflicts between the partners as a result of them stepping on each other's "toes."

Partners with complementary skills can then excel in their area of expertise for the good of the team.

You don't have to carry the whole load.
Picking your partner must be done with care.
Success for you will be decided down the road.
A complementary match will guide how you fare.

5E. "DEVELOP A SUPPORT SYSTEM" BY DONALD O. CLIFTON AND PAULA NELSON, *READER'S DIGEST*, P. 74, MAY 1993.

Starting out, whom do you trust; whom can you depend to be there when you need them? Society today is so complex; it is hard to know whom to trust and on whom you can depend.

Start with your parents and grandparents for sure. Family members such as older brothers and sisters if they are there.

A few, maybe one or two, and if you are lucky, three at the most may have your interest as any semblance of a priority to them. The most loyal will be parents for sure.

Later you can begin to branch out to others that you can trust.

An occasional teacher will pop into view. A Sunday school teacher may be another one you can trust as well. Then a coach or two can be added to your circle of trusted associates. Friends come and go; but a few will be with you all along.

Later, service people such as mechanics, carpenters, electricians, plumbers, computer technicians, all will be identified, one at a time, as parts of your support system of trusted associates and service providers.

All are necessary for you to be most successful and have a happy, smooth life. A successful parent, spouse, teammate, student all need a support system to accomplish various aspects of the tasks of life and business.

Keep in mind that the support system components are added one at a time . . . to your little black book. They don't just miraculously appear and you have all the support you need. Aside from parents, the rest of your support network comes after hard work and mutual support, in return, to them.

The support network is not just one way. There will be mutual support; you will need to support others and be part of their support network at the same time, if not before, you can hope to gain their support on your activities of life.

In return for the significant effort of your support network, be loyal to them as well.

Develop a support system; listen to this word.
They will be so numerous, they will look like a herd . . .
So beyond you closest, pick others who with you will contend . . .
And will be with you till the end.

6

"What Winners Know," *Reader's Digest*, March 1994, And Condensed From *The Winner Within: A Life Plan For Team Players* By Pat Riley.

Pat Riley currently is retired as a coach of the Miami Heat of the National Basketball Association in 2008. He has been the very successful coach of the New York Knicks. His teams, if it hadn't been for Michael Jordan and the Chicago Bulls, would have been NBA champs several times.

Pat Riley has been a very successful coach and has a lot to say worth listening to regarding success and especially, successful team sport play.

Pat Riley was recently identified as being number three in popularity when it comes to motivational speakers. Lou Holt, Rick Patino, and then Pat Riley were the top three in popularity. Each of these speakers charge in the range of $10,000 or more for personal appearance to deliver a motivational and inspirational speech.

The following pages are borrowed titles (only) from chapters of his article in *Reader's Digest* and are included for additional discussion in this book.

Riley has won with the Knicks.
His team called the HEAT certainly clicks.
Listen, search out what he has to say.
His advice is to the point even when you don't pay.

6A. **"BE A TEAM PLAYER,"** *READER'S DIGEST*, MARCH 1994, AND CONDENSED FROM *THE WINNER WITHIN: A LIFE PLAN FOR TEAM PLAYERS* BY PAT RILEY.

Many of life's activities come with teams. Families, sports, and businesses are good examples of situations where successful team play has much to say about our overall success.

First, to be part of a successful team, each team member must refine his or her personal skills. Each teammate must be prepared to deliver when the time comes for his or her skill to be expended.

Families, school project groups, sports teams, office groups, small companies, and military action groups are all teams.

First and foremost, families must internally have love, respect, and support for the others within the family. Love, respect, and support between family members are essential, but love is the essential difference between the family team and the other variety of teams. Love is the special bond. Without internal love, respect, and support, the family that argues, bickers, and fights will destroy itself from the inside.

All teams need to have a source of income to sustain its activities and to provide shelter. Bringing in this income may be a joint effort or the role of just one or more of the family. Regardless of the sources, the need to bring in the income must be recognized and adequately addressed and appreciated by all members.

Couples, before beginning to have children, must personally prepare so that they will be able to support and sustain the family over the long term.

All team members must focus on the others and encourage them to do their best as well. Cheerleading or encouraging teammates on to do their best is an important team player activity. This is more than just a casual "way to go"—it is to really excitedly encourage; it means to pep up, to be a rah-rah person to instill some enthusiasm in the behavior of the others of the team. It is not just your responsibility for the team's success. You all have a responsibility, and all are responsible for the picking up and encouraging the others when they are down.

If you are prepared, you will have the confidence of knowing and believing that you can do the job when called on to perform.

The overall long-term success of the team . . .
Will certainly depend on, it does seem,
Teammates willing to give and take.
Allow others, perhaps, to get a break!

6B. "WELCOME CHANGE," *READER'S DIGEST*, MARCH 1994, AND CONDENSED FROM *THE WINNER WITHIN: A LIFE PLAN FOR TEAM PLAYERS* BY PAT RILEY.

Welcome change, but . . . change just for the sake of change is not what is being pushed. Change within the context of your team achieving its long-term vision is the kind of change being recommended.

Even when things or the situation all seem to be going about as well as can be expected, look to make change consistent with the long-term improvement necessary to achieve the vision of the team, family, business, or club . . . as examples.

Without positive change, the organization, the team will become stagnant, and the rate of improvement will diminish, and eventually, the change will be forced by indecision . . . in the negative direction.

Welcome change is another way of saying "seek continual improvement." With your vision of the future firmly in place, you can welcome change . . . even cause change, to improve your situation along the path of continuous improvement.

Personally welcome change as opposed to fearing change. Be flexible, but without an overall plan, you will not have much of a chance of getting to the vision or goal you want to achieve. Welcome change because there are innumerable factors in your environment that can cause change; expect change, welcome change, and plan on reacting positively to change.

Don't make changes for the sake of change. Changes that you originate must be part of your short—and long-term plan, strategy, or vision.

The flip side of welcoming change is to fear it or to hope that is doesn't occur. Fear of change will put you at a disadvantage. With built-in fear or dread, getting mentally up to deal with the inevitable change will certainly be difficult.

Welcome change sounds vague to me.
If the context is clear for you to see.
Your change will be controlled formally,
In the direction you want it to be.

6C. "BEWARE OF COMPLACENCY," *READER'S DIGEST*, MARCH 1994, AND CONDENSED FROM *THE WINNER WITHIN: A LIFE PLAN FOR TEAM PLAYERS* BY PAT RILEY.

Complacency assumes that the final results are a given. For a person and team that is focused on achievement, that should not be the case. As long as there is any question about the outcome of the event or activity, do not be complacent. Always stay focused on the result you want to occur until the outcome is settled.

A complacent competitor is often the loser but not by choice. The complacent competitor makes the decision to stop trying to affect the outcome, and the rest is foreordained.

There is no room for complacency in any phase of life where your desired outcome is still in doubt . . . whether this pertains to your job, your marriage, your games or your health. As long as the desired end result is in question, stay focused on your desired end result.

Beware of the "whatever" attitude. A "whatever attitude type person" is a person who believes in "whatever" when you ask them what they think. Avoid them like the plague.

Beware of complacency is a good warning especially when you want and expect to be on a winning team. Complacency is being satisfied with "whatever" happens. It is *the whatever happens attitude* and is not the attitude of a winner.

A winner needs to be focused on the effort it takes to be the best, and that is nowhere near a whatever person. Winners need to know and believe that they are in control of their own destiny and will never be a victim of circumstance.

Contrast the whatever, complacent person who lets whatever happen with the take-charge person who has a vision and equates success with working toward that vision.

Never take success for granted. Work and put forth the effort in preparation, and you will be ready when the times come. You will have confidence in yourself because you will know that you have done your best. No matter what the outcome, you will have prepared to do your best. Entering into a situation poorly prepared will have at least two negative impacts. One will be that you are not likely to be successful without adequate preparation. The second is that no matter what the outcome, you will know that you did not do your best and could not have approached the situation with confidence. Being complacent in your preparation will lead to a complacent, lackluster performance. A focused committed approach will get you to where you want to be.

Beware of complacency, a "whatever" phrase.
It will lead you to a "lackluster" craze.
A focused vision in your "Mays" . . .
Will lead to success in your "December" days.

6D. "REMEMBER, ATTITUDE IS MOTHER OF LUCK," *READER'S DIGEST*, MARCH 1994, AND CONDENSED FROM *THE WINNER WITHIN: A LIFE PLAN FOR TEAM PLAYERS* BY PAT RILEY.

Attitude is mother of luck. Attitude begets luck. Watch the people who you think are lucky. In most, most cases, these lucky people will show you that they earn their luck by hard work, persistence, and a winning attitude. Oh yes! A person who is aggressive, expectant, and has a winning attitude is likely to be "very lucky".

Avoid people who rely just on luck for their successes. In most cases, their hoped-for successes will not be there. There are many people just relying on luck, and most will be disappointed. They should not be, but they will be disappointed that they were not successful. And they certainly will not honestly be able to recognize that they absolutely did their best.

On the other hand, those people who have an attitude of hard work and thorough preparation will either be successful or will be satisfied that they have done their best and will be confident in their approach to life's challenges. Often, I have heard people say that they would rather be lucky than good—but not me. Hopefully, they are just kidding and recognize that they were lucky in the incident of reference. Anyway, they should be kidding. Luck is neither dependable nor something that others will attribute to your own skills. Luck happens, and I know everyone would rather have good luck over bad luck or no luck at all.

But a winning attitude built around skillful preparation and hard work will be much more predictable and satisfying to you for a lifetime model.

A person has little choice when choosing parents. Therefore, he or she has little control over his or her genetic abilities.

Being born with good health, considerable intellect. Say an IQ in the range of 130 plus physical attributes in the range of: six feet four inches, and 250 pounds is luck. What you do with it is the attitude point at issue in this discussion. A person can be a smart, big, fast, and handsome counterperson at McDonald's, but that is not realizing one's lifetime potential. This book is about what I think about attitude. The winning attitude can bring you success just like luck and is much, much more dependable and rewarding.

Beyond that, you can assess where you are, what your basic physical attributes are, and where you want to be. With hard work and preparation, you are liable to be very lucky and. I believe, successful. A person who is a focused hard worker will be successful . . . and some will call it luck.

Your attitude is the mother of luck.
Your attitude will lead you to, either the muck . . .
Or to the pinnacle of success.
But luck may determine whether it's more or less!

7

The 7 Habits Of Highly Effective People: Powerful Lessons In Personal Change By Stephen R. Covey.

It has been a while since I read this book, but I thought, at the time and still do, that the seven habits mentioned by Covey were extremely relevant to our family and should be relevant to all hardworking people in the world today. The following are the seven key elements of his book and are included here as a list. Later, each will be elaborated on and discussed in detail: be proactive; begin with the end in mind; put first things first; think win/win; seek first to understand, then to be understood; synergize; and sharpen the saw.

7A. BE PROACTIVE

Effective people are not victims. Effective people do not wait for events to track them down and happen to them. Effective people exhibit Covey's seven habits and act.

Effective people are proactive, and being proactive means that they begin with the end in mind; put first things first; think win/win; seek first to understand, then to be understood; synergize; and sharpen the saw.

Being proactive means that if you think something needs to be done, you do it. Being proactive means that if you want something done, you develop a plan to make sure that happens.

Being proactive means if you want better grades, you develop a plan to get better grades. Then you set out to implement your plans to receive those better grades.

If you are proactive and want to play football, you build up your strength and speed and go out for the team when the time is posted for practice to begin.

Being proactive is close to opposite of being a victim. Being proactive is assuming that you can overcome most obstacles that you are exposed to and you sincerely try to overcome those obstacles.

Don't wait for things to happen. Decide what you want and go after it.

A personality that waits for things to happen thinks like a victim. Such a person thinks he or she has no control over ones destiny.

That is being a victim. If you don't want to be a victim because of any number of reasons for failure—you must decide that you will cause things to happen toward the goal you have selected.

Always assume that the power to solve the problem or achieve the goal rests with you.

There is little value to existing unless you are proactive and attack.
The issues of this world can be taken off your back.
Be aggressive and get rid of the slack!
This is the best style to pull out of your sack.

7B. BEGIN WITH THE END IN MIND: A POWERFUL LESSONS IN PERSONAL CHANGE, BY STEPHEN R. COVEY.

Begin with your vision of the end in mind. Know where you are going and develop your plan around where you want to be. The faster you are moving down the road toward your vision, the farther out you must look to stay on course.

The key though is to know where you want to go, where do you want to be one, five, ten, and twenty years later in life. The further out you plan, the higher level of achievement will be in your potential range.

The important thing to keep in mind is that the plans can and will change, but have the plan. Assess your goal every year or so. Naturally, as you move through life, you opinion will change regarding your vision, and that is to be expected.

The end in mind can be in the form of a map of events for your life; where you want to be and what it will take to get there are all important to your end plan for the future.

Always move toward a goal. Deciding whether you are seeking to achieve a short-term or long-term goal often will be the real question.

Most people have something in their mind or in their mind's eye when they act. The ideal situation is one in which the short term goal to which you are striving also fits into your long-term plan.

Simply have a goal; set your goals—short and long range—and then set about toward achieving those goals.

Even before implementing the trait of being proactive, one should have a goal first, then be proactive to attain your goal.

Begin your life's quest . . .
With a plan, "Young man go west."
The plan can be kept close to your vest . . .
Or can be broadcast.
Who can say which is the best.

7C. PUT FIRST THINGS FIRST: POWERFUL LESSONS IN PERSONAL CHANGE, BY STEPHEN R. COVEY.

Prioritize, put first things first.
First, your education; next, your financial plan; next, your partner, your mate for life; then children and your job, your life's work are bases you will want to consider. You don't need to touch all the bases, but the ones you do touch should be generally in the order listed.

There is a natural order of events, and things generally work out best if they are taken in the proper order.

Of course there will be different opinions about what the proper order of events is. The important element here is to develop a rational order of intended events and put things first as they mesh with your value system and the value system of your family.

With your plan for achieving your goal, your strategy should include an order in which things should be attained first.

The plans should have an order of events. Before you start accomplishing tasks, you should first decide upon an order in which should occur.

With a thoughtful strategy, you will know which things to put first and which to do later.

Maintaining a sense of which things are more important and necessary to be done first is a valuable skill. Such skills can be fine tuned but still are very important.

Things will come easier I surmise . . .
If you plan and prioritize.
With the end in view I say to you . . .
The advantages to doing first things first will be true.

7D. THINK WIN/WIN: POWERFUL LESSONS IN PERSONAL CHANGE, BY STEPHEN R. COVEY.

Think win/win; no one likes to lose.

In all your interpersonal relations, figure out a way for all parties to end up with a win or something positive on which to build.

A complete and demoralizing victory over your opponent does little for you more than just a win. A devastating loss can create an enemy for life in your opponent.

Of course in sporting events, where they keep score, the object of the game is to win. A tie can occur, and that may be a win/win situation, but normally, athletic teams do not play for a tie. Therefore, one team wins, and one team loses. This does not support the case in point of this section.

In athletic events, though, there are wins, and there are *wins!* A win is a win where the winning margin might be for baseball, 6-0 maximum. A devastating *win* might be a win with the score something like 20-0. Or in the case of football, a win might be a win with the score something like

35-6 maximum, where a devastating *win* might be a win with the score in the range of 66-0.

The large margins of wins totally demoralize the opponent team and may very well create significant enemies in the future.

Give the opponents something that they can build on and allow them to have hope for the future (unless your opponent is a liberal).

In a business situation, it makes no sense to win by making your profit and totally bankrupting your competitors. Go ahead and figure out how to achieve a profit for yourself without devastating the other person. If you are both selling the same product or offering the same service, a win/win situation may be difficult but possible.

The other person, seeing that you are willing to grant them a reasonable win or position, also is going to be much more agreeable to grant you what you need or deserve. A win/win-oriented person is not selfish. No matter if it is doing the chores or driving down the highway or passing on the street or giving the people you deal with or come even remotely in contact with some small victory in each exchange . . . you will be better off. And you will make them feel good about the exchange; it will make you feel good and will make life much easier for both you and the other person.

A win/win game is hard to play . . .
When the largest score wins the day.
A tie is not a win most will say.
But if their loss can be a win, the message, will be . . . OK.

7E. *SEEK FIRST TO UNDERSTAND, THEN TO BE UNDERSTOOD: POWERFUL LESSONS IN PERSONAL CHANGE,* BY STEPHEN R. COVEY.

This is advice to try to understand what the other person is doing and why they are doing it before you let loose with your opinion. Often, when someone else does something, you instantaneously believe you know what and why they do it. True? I bet it is. And there is a whole spectrum of correctness to your presumption. You actually may be totally right or totally wrong or somewhere in between.

That is why it is best if you first seek to understand why the other person acts the way they do. Ask a question something like "Why did you do that?" or "Help me to understand why you did that."

Try to be as nonjudgmental or challenging when you ask your question trying to better understand why the other person did or said that point under discussion.

If they ask why you want to know, just tell the truth. You are not sure you understood why they did something, and in order to know how to react to what they did, you want to clearly understand why they did what they did. Only then is it necessary and essential to make sure they understand you and only if that clarification into the question adds to your communication process.

If you have a negative reaction to something that someone else says, by asking them why they did something or asking them to help you to understand why they did something . . . most of the time, I believe, the miscommunication will be cleared up. Then if it is resolved, nothing further will need to be said on the topic. If a problem remains, then you can seek to be understood.

When dealing with others and an exchange of ideas or a clash of will occurs, before pursuing further explanation of your position, try to understand where the other person is coming from. Try to understand them before further explaining what you want.

Attempt to state in your words what their position is. This shows that you are trying to understand their position and will confirm fairly quickly and easily whether you do in fact understand what they are trying to say and their position. This will show the other person that you are trying to understand their position by stating what you understand them to be saying in your own words.

Then after you clearly understand what they're saying or wanting . . . you can try to further explain your position. Then after both positions are clearly understood, arrive at a conclusion where both achieve a win—a win/win situation.

First, seek to understand the whys and what fors.
Then let that sink in.
Maybe, even do a few chores.
Before completing your "understandin'" . . .

7F. SYNERGIZE: POWERFUL LESSONS IN PERSONAL CHANGE, BY STEPHEN R. COVEY.

Synergize, synergize, synergize. What in the world does that mean?

The *Thorndike-Barnhart World Book Dictionary* defines "synergize" as "to cooperate with and enforce the activity of" or "the combined action of different agents or organs producing a greater effect than the sum of the various individual actions as in a medicine composed of several drugs."

By combining your efforts with the efforts of your teammates, office peers, or family members, your combined effort can and will be greater than the sum of the various individual actions or parts.

This is important in teamwork. Teamwork should be obvious in certain team sports, such as basketball, baseball, or football. In these sports, there is a great deal of teammate interaction, which must take place if the team is to be successful. This opinion is also true for activities, which may not seem so important for team work, such as cross-country running. Teams train together year round. During races, they run together as a group. Team work here is important because they encourage one another during the long training sessions, as well as during competition.

The team has no chance in winning unless all teammates try their best and do well. Individuals can win without the rest, but often the best times are from runners who have been spurred on throughout a race by their teammates.

Gain strength from your interaction with others. Support others in their endeavors.

People naturally focus on their own problems and situation. Trying to focus on others will be healthy and will improve your image in their opinion as well. There may be others with strengths in areas you don't have. Working with and supporting them would be helpful to them, and in turn, the relationship would be helpful to you.

What does it mean to synergize?
If you know, you are really wise.
If you know what it means to synergize . . .
By working together you can maximize . . .
Your products, your score; it is never too late to realize.
So my young friend, don't compromise!

7G. SHARPEN THE SAW: POWERFUL LESSONS IN PERSONAL CHANGE, BY STEPHEN R. COVEY.

A sharper saw cuts best, and to have a sharper saw, the saw must be sharpened. In other words . . . your success habits must be perfected.

We all agree on this point, "The more you are willing to sharpen your skills at whatever field you have selected, the better off you will be at performing the skill."

FAMILY
In the family setting, the sharpening may not be quite as clear. A sharpened saw in the family setting is the taking care of family responsibilities and personal fitness, day after day, before the time they absolutely have to be done. Perfect your family support skills.

The routine responsibilities are taken care of with minimal interference from the outside and early. When the togetherness, the fun things of family life are to be done, they can be enjoyed by everyone. The routine duties of the family are mostly done anyway. When the partner procrastinates, delays, talks to others outside of the family, time is taken from the fun things of life that the family members can do as a team. Some of the individual unstructured activity is and must be acceptable. However, it must be kept in perspective because that's just the kind of activity that takes away from the fun family togetherness activities.

When the children are young, the family can then do the fun things together. When the children are grown, the sharpened saw, the perfected success habits, will give the husband and wife time to do fun things together.

SPORTS TEAM
Sharpening the saw means to practice the individual skills necessary to perform with the team when in competition. Sharpening the saw means physical conditioning yourself so that your body will deliver when the team needs you in the competition. And sharpening the saw means getting the nutrition and rest that your body needs for you to be your best when the physical exertion calls for vigorous effort on your part.

WORK/BUSINESS SETTING

Sharpening the saw means being prepared for any situation you work or business job demands. This means to be mentally and physically prepared for the task at hand. From closing the big insurance deal to teaching the class in a daily upbeat and high-energy style, you must always be mentally alert and ready to deliver. Never allow yourself to enter into a business situation with the aftereffects of too much partying the night before.

Improve yourself; improve your skills, learn more about everything.

Synergize . . . practice and perfect the first six attitudes of Covey's book. You should practice being aggressive, identifying targets, and going after your goals. Practice knowing what your goals are; know what you stand for and be proactive in setting priorities and going for them. Be proactive when striving to set up situations that allow both people to win and achieve something out of the interchange. Be proactive to understand others first before you insist on others understanding you. Be proactive when working with others and contributing your strength. Allow others to contribute their stronger attributes . . . and practice, practice, practice!

Sharpening the saw means your family will be primed.
Sharpening the saw means being loyal, courteous, and kind.
Sharpening the saw means practicing without being timed.
Sharpening the saw means being prepared of the mind.
Sharpening the saw means doing without needing "the remind."
Sharpening the saw means you are effective, but it isn't rhymed.

8

"People Need Trouble—A Little Frustration To Sharpen The Spirit On, Toughen It..." By William Faulkner, *Reader's Digest*, March 1994.

It is not that people need trouble, a little frustration to sharpen the spirit on, and toughen it. Trouble and frustration do come into people's lives. When they do, people, you, can decide whether you want to be beaten by the adversity or you want to consider the adversity a learning experience. If you choose to be beaten by the adversity, you will be and will set the direction for your life.

If you choose to use the adversity to sharpen your spirit and toughen it, then you will be better off in the long run.

"Sharpen your spirit" means to me in this context... you are developing within your own personhood the will to win. This is your developing a winning attitude within your personality, which will carry you far. A winning attitude is not developed or discovered when things always go smoothly or the way you originally plan your life. Overcoming the trouble, which will come, can be a tremendous learning experience.

Eventually, you will be able to decide whether you want to make an effort to plan and design your approach to life to minimize trouble. That is a choice. However, no matter how hard and how cleverly you plan, trouble will sneak in. Minimizing the trouble is about as far as you can go. It is important to me to minimize trouble.

Trouble, and the frustration, which will accompany the trouble, will sharpen your winning and creative spirit and will toughen your personality. Don't go looking for trouble . . . it will find you; it will certainly find you. As with almost everything, you get better by practicing that skill. Dealing with problems is no different. If you pay attention and try to learn from each experience, dealing with a problem, which occurs, will sharpen your skills and will sharpen your problem-solving talent.

Dealing with frustration will teach you and will prepare you to deal with other issues of life. Look past the current frustration and your solution of it. Learn to see the bigger picture. This learning experience will toughen your spirit to deal with and overcome adversity. The positive thing to keep in mind . . . don't go looking for frustrating experiences to solve; don't look for trouble. They will come into every person's life.

When frustrating moments arrive—expect them and learn from how you deal with them and how to prevent that particular event from happening again. Try to turn trouble, frustrating moments, into opportunities. Make something good out of every frustrating or troubling experience . . . even if it is only how to keep it from happening again.

Trouble comes for sure, but not with glee.
The use is made when it ventures in and it will be . . .
A learning opportunity . . . you will see!
Choose to toughen the spirit, a choice too for you, not just for me.

9

"It Says Something About The Capacity Of Government To Manage The Health Care System When A Private Publisher Had A 192-Page Summary Of The Clinton Health Plan In Bookstores For More Than A Month While Only A Thirty-Two-Page Summary Was Available From The Government printing Office . . ." By Malcolm S. Forbes Jr., *Reader's Digest*, March 1994.

The federal government should do only those activities assigned to it by the U.S. Constitution or what are absolutely necessary because there is no chance that the private sector can perform those functions. The health care system in the United States is already the best in the world.

The major problems with the health care system in the U.S. are related to and are probably caused by government. They will not be solved by more government action. The biggest problems with our health care system are the fact that many people cannot afford health care and costs are inflating more quickly than other goods and services of our economy.

People that can't afford health care are provided health care via some government program, such as Medicaid or hospital-provided care because the hospital administration feels obligated to provide the health care. Getting jobs and getting off welfare will put many more people in the position of being able to afford health care or health care is provided as a perk to their employment.

The costs for health care will moderate when more and more people must make their medical care decisions based on what it costs them. People will make decisions to force the costs down when the decision affects them in the pocket book. With insurance picking up the tab for all health care costs for some people, the people do not care how much the costs are. If their health care funds were to go into a medical health savings account and they could financially benefit if anything were left in the account at the end of the year, the people would strive to get medical care at the lowest possible costs. That would drive medical care down for everyone.

To some extent, the ability or the capacity of government to manage any problem is exemplified in the situation of the health care system: a private publisher had a 192-page summary of the Clinton health plan in bookstores for more than a month, while only a thirty-two-page summary was available from the government.

As Pres. Ronald Reagan said, "(In most, most cases), the government is the problem, not part of the solution." The role of government beyond the absolute tasks assigned to the government by the U.S. Constitution must be limited to those functions that people cannot do for themselves. And government must enforce the laws that we do have. By saying "cannot do for themselves," I am saying absolutely situations in which people cannot "do it for themselves."

Always when the taker wants something more . . .
They look to the government to serve as the store.
Government should provide our defense, our police and our adjudicator.
But health care is best left to the private sector.

10

"Hope Is Not The Same As Joy . . ." By Vaclav Havel, *Reader's Digest*, March 1994.

Hope is not the same as joy.

You have joy when things are going well enough for you to feel happy about events.

We must challenge ourselves to find joy in everything that we do; we should seek to achieve joy in each of our days. Every one of our days should include joy. It is our responsibility to find joy in our life!

Hope is our investing in enterprises that are apparently headed for success, and we are willing to continue working for the project to succeed. We believe it will be successful. Maybe, we even think that the endeavor will be successful. This is hope! Hoping that something will be successful expresses a desire that something will occur. Hope is not the knowledge that something will turn out well, but hope is that you want it to turn out well.

Hope is the anticipation that something will occur. Joy is a state of mind, of happiness.

Hope is not the same as joy . . . when things are going well, or willingness to invest in enterprises that are obviously headed for early success. Hope is not the certainty that something will turn out well, but rather an ability to work for something to succeed. Hope not certainty that something will turn out well but our want that something makes sense regardless of how it turns out.

Hope to me meant a somewhat unproven belief that something will turn out the way you want. Hope to me means something close to wishing something is true. The word "hope" refers to a desired outcome—not an expected result from a correct process.

We can hope for many events to occur in our life. We can hope that we and our families are healthy. We can hope that we will be successful in any undertaking that we choose to proceed with. If we want something to occur, we must do more than just hope. We must take action based on, for example, the personal traits or attitudes of highly effective people. Hoping without careful planning and hard work is a shallow concept. Plan, assess, evaluate, and then implement all must go into achieving a goal—not just hope that the event occurs.

Hope, my dear one, you will see . . .
Must be something that you take with thee.
Joy should be a daily find.
It is a gift of your mind.

11

"The Sight Of A Gravestone, Weighty Not Only In Its Granite, Allows Us Perspective On Problems As Pressing As Burnt Toast, Taxes, And Hay Fever..." By Donald Hall, *Reader's Digest*, March 1994.

The sight of a gravestone, especially one without your name on it, should put situations of life into perspective. The same can be said of the daily obituary column in the newspaper. If your name is not there, things are going pretty well. You can always regain joy if you are down.

Death is very final, and the gravestone and obituary are symbolic of the end of your chances to improve things here on earth. All your affairs, including your relationship with Jesus and God, better be in order before your name appears in the obituary column or on a gravestone.

That is important. Life and death must be kept in perspective and taken seriously. On the other hand, problems like burnt toast and hay fever really are not much to worry about and should not occupy much of our time.

Compare death and the name of a loved one on a tombstone to a verbal slight by a peer. The verbal slight may make you feel upset for a short while but hardly worthwhile when compared to death and the name of a loved one on a tombstone.

The sight of a gravestone allows us perspective. There are so many events in life that we must face, big problems and little problems.

Death is a big problem; burnt toast is not. There is a wide-range of emotion between burnt toast and death!

Try to control or influence the situations that you can do something about. Change your behavior to stop the little problems—don't burn the toast. You can influence those decisions by not letting them occur.

Death too can be influenced. Don't take unnecessary risk of injury; drive defensively; watch out for the other person.

Eat the right foods; don't smoke. Exercise and keep your weight under control.

Deal logically, using what you know to avoid problems. But . . . not all problems can be anticipated. If an undesirable event occurs, try to learn something from it and go on; don't second-guess yourself. Do the best you can, but do your best! Kidding yourself that something is your best without giving that extra 110 percent effort is just kidding yourself.

Nothing can be more final than a loved one under a cold stone.
Compare death to burnt toast or a fallen ice cream cone.
It doesn't make much sense to anguish over what's lost.
A cup of pleasure; the ice cream was a minimal cost!

12

"Genius Is A Bend In The Creek Where Bright Water Has Gathered, And Which Mirrors The Trees, The Sky And The Banks," By Edgar Lee Masters, *Reader's Digest*, March 1994.

It would have taken a genius to create a scene as beautiful as these . . . a bend in the creek where bright water has gathered and mirrors the trees, the sky, and the banks . . .

Picture a lazy clear stream rounding a wide, still bend. The still water resembles a glass, a perfect mirror. The double view of the trees right side up and right side down in perfect symmetry . . . the view is breathtaking.

It would take a genius to set up a picture as pretty as might be created by nature through the reflection off a bend in the creek where smooth, bright water has gathered. Can you picture in your mind's eye a scene in which the creek widens and stills at the bend downstream?

The sun is behind the trees and beginning to set on the far side of the bend. The water is smooth and reflects the image of the trees, the flowers near the bank, the three deer and two rabbits on the water's edge. The evening is coming on, and there is a hint of chill in the warm spring air.

There are at least five different varieties of trees with most of them being majestic oaks, some maples, willows, blue spruce, and red bud.

The pink blossom of the red bud provides most of the color farther out in the water because they are actually higher up, off the ground. There is a hint of green on the limbs of the oaks, maples, and willows. The dignified blue spruce has its full array of bluish-green spikes totally ready to soak up all the warm spring sunlight. Everything can be seen by twos. Take a photograph, and you would be able to turn it upside down and see the same picture setting.

Is the genius of this setting coming through?

Appreciate the simple things in life and nature.

The reflections off a pool of water can be so inspirational, so beautiful.

It would take a genius to set up a scene and still never equal the beauty and symmetry of the natural setting. Appreciate the healing beauty of nature. Seek out such a scene and setting. Take your problems there, and armed with a problem and a pad of paper and a pen, do some creative problems solving and develop an action plan to deal with the problems you are facing. Answers will come.

Genius is a bend in the creek where bright water reflects.
Natures beauty has gathered two copies . . . they come in sets.
Some pointing up and some point down.
The picture is the same whether you turn it up or around.

13

"Snobs Talk As If They Had Begotten Their Own Ancestors," By Herbert Agar, *Reader's Digest*, March 1994.

Be careful thinking that you begot your own ancestors. There are various degrees of personality traits operable here.

First, there is pride in the accomplishments of one's ancestors. There is nothing wrong either with a little pride of your ancestors. Give people a little slack when they show pride. There should always be clarity that the ancestor's accomplishments are what they did and are separate from those of the living people today. They deserve no credit for what their ancestors did . . . but can dream that they also have the ability within themselves to, perhaps, accomplish something similar to what their ancestors did.

Second, the individuals who act like they are superior to you because of the accomplishments of their ancestors are the ones who "talk" as if they raised and taught their own ancestors. And obviously, that is not the case, and they deserve absolutely no credit for what their ancestors accomplished.

A snobbish behavior is not something to copy and generally is a personality trait to avoid. Never make people think that you believe you are better than they are. Every person has value and needs to feel, from you, that they are important. It is more important that you deliver what you are through your own actions than it is to tell people what you are.

Rely on what you are, not what your family has been. Each person is what they have become, not what their family has been. Your family can help you become what you want to be. There can be family standards and family resources, but you must want something and then go ahead to accomplish your vision.

Ancestors are important if they achieved notable accomplishments in their lifetime. They serve as a marker beyond which you should strive to attain. If there were no notable ancestors that you know of, pick someone else to be the standard beyond which you wish to attain. The best ball player, the best engineer, the best banker, the best teacher, the best doctor, and the best stock broker are goals to set as examples.

Regardless of the standard, your accomplishments, your friends, your compassion are and should be the basis of how people assess you . . . not your ancestors.

With their nose held high.
You can watch them cruise by.
The snob trips over the fence . . .
Before any friendship can commence.

14

"Self-Esteem Cannot Be Sought As An End In Itself But Must Come As A By-Product Of Meeting Standards Of Excellence, Taking Pride In Work, Supporting A Family, Bringing Up Decent Children, Learning About Life And Imparting That Wisdom" By Aaron Wildavsky, *Reader's Digest*, March 1994.

It is accurate to point out that self-esteem is a by-product of meeting standards of excellence and taking pride in work, supporting family, bringing up decent children. All the while, you are learning about life and imparting that wisdom to your children, spouse, peers, and other with whom you come into contact during your day-to-day activities.

You can take charge of your personal self-esteem by working at what your responsibilities are so that you are very good at what you do. Whether the activity is sports or business or being a parent or being just about anything, it is not difficult to know what the overall standards of performance are. If you practice hard and become very good at what you do, you will know it. You will have an elevated self-esteem and will feel good about yourself.

Baseless compliments from your parents and family will be clear and will, after a while, serve no purpose whatsoever except, perhaps, make the parent or family believe they are doing some good. But you will not trust anything they say because you know their compliments are baseless, and you do not deserve them. Seek to be the best at what you choose to do, and the self-esteem and confidence will come.

So many people seek self-esteem. Probably thousands of books are written about self-esteem and how to attain it. How to be self-confident? How to be this or how to be that? Books are written to help people achieve self-esteem. Self-esteem comes from being good at something and knowing that you are good. Know when you study, do homework lessons, and practice . . . these are the only ways to achieve excellence. Being excellent at something is the only way to achieve higher self-esteem.

The real lesson that needs to be taught is . . . for you to achieve high self-esteem, do what it takes to achieve excellence; practice and study. Prepare your mind for the future. Prepare your body for the future. Practice! Study!

Some people today try to get the recognition and then connect that recognition with self-esteem through their dress, their tattoos, their antisocial language, and their antisocial actions. They are not getting the respect and admiration of society. Some people may get the admiration of a degenerate few in society but not society in general. Achievements must be in scholastic, athletic, and real-life endeavors and must be recognizable. Self-esteem evolves from recognizable accomplishments.

Self-esteem is not something you go out and do.
Self-esteem will come to you.
Achieve excellence . . . does self-esteem come into your mind's view?
Confidence will come, and self-esteem will too.

15

"This Grand Show Is Eternal. It Is Always Sunrise Somewhere, The Dew Is Never All Dried At Once; A Shower Is Forever Falling . . ." By John Muir, *Reader's Digest*, March 1994.

There are always jewels of nature worth observing as a treasure of life.

Nothing is as spectacular as a sunrise over water, amber waves of grain, or purple mountain majesty. The red ball of the early morning sun is always spectacular and a relief for the sun to be coming up again to start a new day. Day after day, the sun rises and the sun sets . . . both occurrences are beautiful.

The early morning grass and flowers are moistened by the water drawn from the morning air by the coolness of the predawn. Such a magical process of draining water out of our air warrants your/our full appreciation.

And then, the life-giving moisture from the air is falling somewhere . . . somewhere in the United States. Have you watched the national weather station on TV? You will recall that you can always see some raining somewhere in the country. The national radar map on TV will show that it is always raining somewhere . . . and it is always bright and sunny somewhere too.

The beautiful sunrise continues across the U.S., across the Pacific Ocean, across China, across the old USSR, across India, across the Middle East, across Europe, across the Atlantic Ocean, and back across the U.S.

Life goes on; the big picture is under control. Enjoy the basics in life, the beauty, the peace. The sunrises were here before us and will be here after us. Life is too short to have any of it taken away over nothing—petty squabbles. Remember, your squabbles can also be petty!

Enjoy beauty; seek the peace of mind that is accomplished by finding something you enjoy and then doing it. Seek out and be around people who enjoy doing the things you enjoy.

You will not and should not be able to change people's behavior. Find the right mix.

Life and nature are precious. Often, sadly, neither are truly enjoyed until life itself is in the balance. Then life is enjoyed minute by minute, day by day; sunrise by sunrise.

The grand show is eternal.
But if not appreciated, rain can be dismal.
The little things must mean a lot.
More than the sun will make us hot.
We must find joy or life will be abysmal.

16

"It Doesn't Matter If You Win Or Lose, Until You Lose" By Angie Papdikis, *Reader's Digest*, March 1994.

How often have you heard, "It doesn't matter whether you win or lose but how you played the game"? Or have you heard, "It doesn't matter whether you win or lose but whether you had fun"?

We have all heard these . . . and does anyone believe them? I don't think so. Do you know why? They keep score. As long as they keep score, winning is important. People take walks for fun or to start some minimal exercise program. Then when they start keeping track of the time and distance they traveled, it may still be fun, but they strive for ten thousand steps per day or walking 5 miles. The whole experience will be fun as long as you believe it is fun.

But let a minor injury come up with the result being you can't walk as fast and as far as before, then it is not quite as much fun. The same goes for team sports: it is great to have fun, but how much fun is it for your team to play the game and the score favoring the other team is totally one sided?

It is absolutely no fun to lose. Practice and find a sport that you enjoy doing and then learn to do it well enough so that your skills are significant, and you will contribute to a winning score.

Nothing is more ridiculous than a mother asking their child, are you having fun? when the score is 10-0, favoring the other soccer team. They usually don't really care about anything other than they feel compelled by some deep-down motherly and a nonathletic value system in their being to choose at that time to make the point that the important thing is to have fun . . . not to win.

If they keep score, you will have more fun if you win. If they don't keep score, then the activity can be considered a practice. But if you practice sloppy and half speed, then your performance when it counts will be sloppy and half speed.

Once you have tried winning, you won't care for losing. Other than sports, it is important to strive for putting yourself into a position for a win but also to give your opponent something of a win too. In sports, a win is a win, and there is little long-term benefit to you to devastate your opponent. Get your win and move on.

As long as they keep score in the sport, you must play to win. In order to play to win, you must practice. If you are not willing to practice to achieve excellence enough to win, play or participate in activities that a score is not kept, try running; for example, where only your personal best is the only score you must keep in mind.

Some would say that a win is a sin.
Others insist that it is a sin if you don't win.
If you are playing for fun and that is OK . . .
Don't keep score and keep the numbers away.
But if there is someone around putting the numbers down,
Then go full speed ahead to be able to earn the crown.

17

Are We Demanding Enough Of Our Kids? By Edwin Kiester Jr. And Sally Valente Kiester.

The truthful answer is no doubt . . . some are
and some aren't . . . searching for that star.
Kids need to be nurtured without a scar . . .
And directed toward excellence or on par.
Kids need to feel loved without a grouchy czar . . .
And have proper nutrition and rest to exceed the bar.
Who knows for sure . . . wait till their memoir!

17A. REMEMBER WHO'S WHO, *ARE WE DEMANDING ENOUGH OF OUR KIDS?* BY EDWIN KIESTER JR. AND SALLY VALENTE KIESTER.

Kids need to understand that they are the child and the parent is the parent. The kids are not in charge. They should have a say; they should be listened to, but they should understand who is the parent and who is the child.

A child is not expected to have the mature judgment that comes with years of experience. I do not want to pretend that adults always have the ultimate answer for every situation either.

The thing that a parent, the adult, brings to the relationship is that in most, most cases, the parent, adult loves the child more than anything else and sincerely is thinking about the good of the child in every decision the adult, parent, makes relative to the child.

The child might be thinking about having a good time and fun with his or her friends, but the parent almost always will be making decisions for the good of the child.

The child needs to be reminded, with love, that as long as the child is accepting support from the parent, the child will be expected to follow the rules of the adult, parent. The child will often not make the connection of support to being able to make the rules. This may cause the child to believe the parent is not being fair. Nevertheless, the parent who provides the support must be in charge and set the ground rules for the home.

Remember who's who when you are dealing with a child.
The "who" who makes the rules may be too mild.
The important fact here is to clearly say . . .
The parent is the boss come what may.

17B. DON'T LET THEM QUIT, FROM *ARE WE DEMANDING ENOUGH OF OUR KIDS?* BY EDWIN KIESTER JR. AND SALLY VALENTE KIESTER.

Children often come upon a tough situation, and from their perspective, the best choice would be for them to quit. Quitting when the going gets tough is definitely learned behavior. Quitting once makes quitting the next time even easier.

Always encourage them; if they start something, insist that they finish it. If they come up against something tough and ask for advice or at least seem willing to listen to advice, don't encourage them in any way to quit at anything. Stress the need and importance to finish. It is too easy to get in the habit of quitting. Finish what they start. Finishing those difficult situations build character and develop that mental and physical toughness necessary for success in life.

Older children are difficult, sometimes, to convince to do anything, much less something they do not want to do. Remind them that they must finish what they start. In these situations, the parent must be willing to use whatever tools they have at their disposal to encourage the child to finish the project. Taking away privileges seems to be a leading technique to convince a recalcitrant teenager to take an action they might not wish to take.

Driving privilege will always be a key to use to deal with teenager behavior, such as quitting, staying out late, back talking parents, or not making grades sufficient to receive the good driver discount offered to students with an overall B average.

The key to keep in mind here is that quitting becomes easier the more they or anyone does it. Quitting on a class in high school will get easier, and when they want to quit the next class, the decision will be easier. Then in college, when they think they should quit a class, the decision will be easier. Later, when they get out in the workplace and the going gets tough, they will find the decision to quit easier. Before they know it, they will have gone through two or three careers with no longevity in any place. All this . . . "quitting" . . . because they did not learn to stick with something back in grade or high school and college.

This same mental toughness is necessary for happiness in life. Happiness comes from the confidence that you can finish what you start and can stick with something. Kids need to know that quitting is never the preferred choice. Kids may believe the choice is between doing something that might be difficult or something that is very easy or doing nothing at all. The parent should make the choice for the child to be between doing something that might be difficult and something else that might be equally difficult or rigorous. Kids should never be allowed to choose between a difficult activity at school and doing nothing but playing video games after school. The choice would be between difficult school/scholastic activity and a job immediately after school or homework later, and so on.

It is easy to say but hard to do . . .
Don't let them quit, I am reminding you.
Play hard ball with the youth in your home.
Teach a sure lesson or they are sure to roam.

17C. GIVE THEM CHORES, FROM *ARE WE DEMANDING ENOUGH OF OUR KIDS?* BY EDWIN KIESTER JR. AND SALLY VALENTE KIESTER.

Children need to understand that their effort is connected to their own personal success. During the school season, the combination of actual chores, homework, and participation in school-sponsored school events (e.g., plays, musicals, clubs, and athletic teams) should add up to a minimum of twenty hours per week. This, coupled with school attendance during the day, will be roughly equivalent to a full-time job.

During the summer, when the teenagers are not going to school, actual chores, participation on athletic teams should add up to a minimum of fifty hours per week. This should be equivalent to a full-time job plus some home-maintenance work.

Even if you get to a point in life with your teenager, and the habit of chores has not been stressed enough, take the topic on and initiate the chore responsibility. The key is to recognize that when they are in school, school time and preparation should fairly be counted as chores in the hourly totals listed above.

Success in school, or in a school event or activity, or on an athletic team will be brought about by hard work. Similarly, success in life results from hard work. The earlier that lesson is learned, the earlier the child will be on a course toward success in life.

Kids need to help the family with the necessary duties of the household. They need to know that they need to join in with these duties. They need to be aware that there are certain responsibilities that come with their rights as family members.

Duty and service are taught through these household chores. Chores, like jobs later in life, need to be factored into one's life. The kids need to learn that fact too. Giving the kids chores early in life helps to teach them this.

Keep the tasks quantifiable so that they can see the task clearly and that there can be life after chores as long as they complete the chore. They can go on with other things that they might prefer. Ideally, the chore will match what they're most interested in. But this doesn't have to be the case.

Kids especially need to be able to see beyond the task at hand and do not add additional things on top of the assignment they are performing. Set limits so that they can finish the chore and move on.

Quality can also be taught through this training by insisting that the job be performed correctly before they are set free to go on to other activities that they might prefer.

Children need to learn, that is their role.
Learning chores is a skill you must bestow.
What a tragedy it would be . . . the toll.
Where many of the lessons of life are not just blow.

17D. BUILD SCAFFOLDING, FROM *ARE WE DEMANDING ENOUGH OF OUR KIDS?* BY EDWIN KIESTER JR. AND SALLY VALENTE KIESTER.

Challenge your kids; be demanding of them; expect a lot from them; push them.

All are excellent admonishments for setting high expectations for our children. While setting high expectations, set up a support structure to make sure they don't fall and hurt themselves while they are growing.

The scaffolding portrays the image of a supportive network structure propping up the work under construction until the project has acquired sufficient strength to support itself.

Here, we are not speaking of a permanent auxiliary support structure but merely a temporary support structure, such as the steel tubing scaffolding.

Kids need to learn by doing. They will make mistakes, and a support system or "scaffold" must be set up to help them. Scaffolding during the construction, building phase, provides support for the object of the building—the kid.

Scaffolding provides a structure on which the attendant can work with the project, again the maturing child.

Care should be given that during all this building/construction phase, the kid is protected to the maximum extent possible from injury . . . meaning both physical injury and injury to their ego or their psyche. Preserve their health and their confidence/self-concept.

The cold steel, it is all Spartan and bare . . .
To help hold the object we are building in the air.
Easy together, and easier apart.
The scaffolding, for a while, must hold up our young piece of "art".

17E. HANDS OFF THE ANSWER SHEET, FROM *ARE WE DEMANDING ENOUGH OF OUR KIDS?* BY EDWIN KIESTER JR. AND SALLY VALENTE KIESTER

Challenge the kids, your children, with situations and give them opportunities to solve their own problems. It is not appropriate for parents to immediately solve their children's problems. This takes a true learning experience away from the kids.

Childhood serves a useful purpose; much more so than just the time spent waiting for the child to become old enough to move out on their own. Childhood should be a learning experience. For the parent, it should be an opportunity to teach and observe, teach and observe the child moving through many of life's experiences.

When you are teaching and observing, don't immediately solve or supply the answer to the child moving through these experiences. Let them search and solve their own problems as often as possible. Get involved when their safety and long-term health are at risk. Also, get involved when they could be doing something illegal.

Also, if they could be getting involved with something immoral according to your own standards, your involvement would be important at these times as well. The Ten Commandments plus would be an excellent basis for setting and teaching personal standards of behavior.

Let them know what you think. And to the best of your ability and reasonable initiative, do not let them do things that are illegal or immoral or likely to injure their health. For the rest of their young life's learning experience, let them try and fail and try and solve the predicament before you supply the answer.

It is not adequate for you to tell your child to "do as I say, not as I do." That is hypocrisy; they will see through hypocrisy immediately.

Let the kids solve their own problems and answer their own questions. Offering answers either before their questions come or at the same time limits their leaning how to be a problem-solving person.

This is difficult for a parent! Time is short often, and accepting the need to let the kid solve his or her problems is difficult.

Nevertheless, hold back, observe patiently. Protect them from serious injury or hurts, but let the kid experience some of the mistakes to serve as a powerful lesson for preparing them for the challenges of life.

The young child lives at home to grow.
The young child lives to know.
A parent must resist the urge to quickly show . . .
And lets the child stub his toe.

17F. ENCOURAGE WORTHWHILE FUN, FROM *ARE WE DEMANDING ENOUGH OF OUR KIDS?* BY EDWIN KIESTER JR. AND SALLY VALENTE KIESTER

Encourage worthwhile fun. But what is worthwhile fun? Who gets to say and at what time in life was the particular activity fun?

It must be for every age, there is worthwhile fun, and there is, or must be from the implication, nonworthwhile fun. From this knowledge, I am saying the worthwhile fun is both legal and does not violate the Ten Commandments plus. That will be the test used here. The fun must be both legal and does not violate the Ten Commandments, nor does the fun violate the Golden rule of "do unto others as you would have them do unto you."

Then after passing my test, worthwhile fun must be OK. Fun does not have to be productive, although that could be a test of worthwhile ... work. I think enjoy would be a better target for worthwhile than just fun. People picture fun as situations where the participants are laughing and giggling when that is not always the case. Fun can just be a situation that people enjoy doing. It could be playing horseshoes; fun could be playing checkers or watching a movie or doing about anything that you enjoy. Fun is in the eye of the beholder and is acceptable as long as the Ten Commandments, or a law, or the Golden Rule are not violated.

The key then, along with encouraging all the work-ethic type characteristics and traits, it is important for all of us to enjoy a certain amount of leisure time. A life directed by a lifetime vision will have plenty of time of enjoyment because there will be direction. There will be a sense of direction brought about by being in charge of your destiny and not a victim of events and wandering.

It is so pleasant, so satisfying, to see a bunch of young teenage boys and girls playing sport or standing/sitting around talking and laughing and enjoying each other's company.

There is nothing better as a parent to seeing your children happy and healthy and enjoying the company of their friends. This should be encouraged. Sports, group activities, such as playing games, helping others, working on projects for school or community, all should be encouraged, since the results are positive, and the kids can have fun and enjoy the activity.

Clean, wholesome fun along with other purposeful activities is what I am describing. This is not at the expense of someone or others. Everything must be positive, and no one suffers.

Worthwhile fun can be the "heehaw" variety.
Fun can vary from person to person.
Or fun can change with more or less notoriety
The key is for fun to be part of your plan, my son!

17G. DON'T SOLVE THEIR PROBLEMS, FROM *ARE WE DEMANDING ENOUGH OF OUR KIDS?* BY EDWIN KIESTER JR. AND SALLY VALENTE KIESTER

One of the hardest acts of a parent is to not solve their, your children's, problems. Tiny daily situations come up in a child's life. If the parent takes too active a role in solving the problems of their children, the child will be robbed of the experiences necessary to learn to solve the problems of life later on.

Solving the child's problems teaches the child that they do not have to be responsible for their own actions, they learn that they do not have to solve their own problems and perhaps you are implying the child cannot solve their problem.

This is much too important a lesson to take away from the child.

Without going into too much detail on this topic, letting children solve their own problems is a very important lesson. Failing to give them this opportunity robs them of so much. Let them solve their own problems.

Youth, teenage years are a period of time in a person's life in which they must learn how to deal with the world and the problems it will present.

Obviously, when they are born, they are just beginning to learn. By the time they are twenty-two, they had better be ready to deal with the world head on.

The interim is a learning period during which time they learn to solve life's problems. Solving the problems for them will take away learning experiences, which they need to enter adulthood, ready to deal with the world—head on.

The parent of a teen asks, How did I raise such an irresponsible child?
When he fibs, I fibbed for him to make his punishment not existent or mild.
When he did not do well on a test, I made excuses for him to his teach.
Then I handed things to him that were out of reach.

17H. POINT THE WAY TO THE STARS, FROM *ARE WE DEMANDING ENOUGH OF OUR KIDS?* BY EDWIN KIESTER JR. AND SALLY VALENTE KIESTER

"Point the way to the stars" might first appear to be a lesson on encouraging the young person to enter the field of astronomy or to enter the NASA astronaut program. But it is not. Pointing the way to the stars in the context of raising and working with your children refers to pushing the children to set a lifetime vision sufficiently high to give them a meaningful target for their life's work. The object of the vision can and will change over the years, but unless the target is adequately high, the effort toward lifetime accomplishment will be met too early and too easily.

Pointing to the stars equates to setting a high target or vision for one's life. The vision can and probably should cover such areas as level of education, the type of profession, where they want to live, the kind of lifestyle they wish to experience, the type of spouse they want to spend their life with, and so on.

Then armed with a plan or vision of what they want to do with their life, they will be prepared to use the other concepts of these authors, Edwin Kiester Jr. and Sally Valente Kiester, in Remember Who's Who, Don't Let Them Quit, Give Them Chores, Build Scaffolding, Hands Off the Answer Sheet, Encourage Worthwhile Fun, and Don't Solve Their Problems.

Help your children aim high. Close to anything can be achieved by a child in his or her lifetime if the child plans and starts early enough.

Help them to aim high. Help them to do something that really excites them and something that they will be happy doing and something that will make them feel good about themselves.

First, decide the lifestyle they wish to experience. Keep in mind that the way the child wishes to live will be affected by the lifetime occupation they choose. Then choose an occupation that will meet the earning or situational potential, which will allow them to enjoy the lifestyle they wish to enjoy.

The occupation or vocation that they chose should head them in the direction of how and what they want to do with their life. While the initial occupation should not initially be expected to get them exactly where they want to be as a lifetime occupation, it will start them down life's path.

Tell the children:

"Aim high, plan, work, and set your plan in motion."

Point the way to the stars.
This is more symbolic than to Jupiter or Mars.
We all have but one life's worth of time.
Armed with a vision, yours can even be more complete than mine.

18

The Book Of Virtues, By William J. Bennett, 1993, By Simon And Schuster.

William Bennett collected his book of virtues and made the points of each of them by sharing short and long stories and poems.

William Bennett wrote a book in 1993 about virtues—ten virtues. These virtues are self-discipline, compassion, responsibility, friendship, work, courage, perseverance, honesty, loyalty, and faith. I have not read the book and cannot vouch for his text, but I very strongly suspect that I would endorse what he had to say. The ten virtues he selected and wrote about are certainly virtues that I endorse for life and for me and my life as well.

Therefore, I chose to include his ten virtues in my text of philosophies. Each virtue will be defined, discussed, and interpreted with a limerick.

The virtues are not presented in priority order. In fact, I contend that there can be no set order that makes sense all the time.

The World Book Encyclopedia Dictionary defines "virtue" as "moral excellence; goodness; good quality; merit; the quality of being chaste; or purity."

Therefore, William Bennett's book on the book of virtue also could be thought of as the book of moral excellence; the book of goodness; the book of good quality; the book of merit; the book on the quality of being chaste; or the book of purity.

So often today you hear of people who do not want old men such as William Bennett or myself to expound upon definitions of behavior. They would prefer a society without standards by which behavior is judged. Theirs would be a system whereby everything and anything goes. Some would prefer that there would be no standards and the use of virtuous situations would not be applicable in their everyday discourse. Without standards, there would be no way for their behavior to be judged as unacceptable.

The writer believes that there is still room for acceptable standards of behavior, and the virtues provided by William Bennett are excellent places to start when listing these virtues or standards.

Bennett's *Book on Virtue* is a standard of moral excellence or goodness.
To possess virtue is to have merit, I make no shallow promise.
Chaste as a virtue, by all means young lad and lass.
Purity too is a virtue I say with class.

18A. SELF-DISCIPLINE, FROM *THE BOOK OF VIRTUES*, BY WILLIAM J. BENNETT, 1993, BY SIMON AND SCHUSTER

Definition: Ability to stay focused on one's objectives even when distractions occur. Self-discipline requires a goal in order to portray itself. Without a target or goal, a self-disciplined person has no meaning. With a goal, then the self-disciplined person will stay focused on the goal. The personal focus needed to stay headed for the target is . . . self discipline.

It is so easy, even when you know where your want to go, to get diverted. The weather, the time of day, reading the newspaper—just about anything can divert one's attention if one does not possess self-discipline.

Clearly know your goal! Develop a plan, including a schedule that you plan to maintain. Then set forth to achieve your goal. The virtue or personal attribute of self-discipline is a critical virtue. Without self-discipline, people will not be able to force themselves to live within a system of order.

Without self-discipline, there would be chaos in the world. No one would be able to own property or grow up or grow old without self-discipline from most of the world's inhabitants. Self-discipline is essential to live within the boundaries of rules and laws.

We must have the self-discipline to live within the rules. And so must most everyone else have self-discipline. Without accepting the rules of law and order, none of the things we possess or people whom we hold dear would be safe. Self-discipline is essential just to adhere to the rules of law of our society.

Further, self-discipline is even more essential for us to prepare to excel in this world. There are many, many people who are more than willing to take what we have. They are willing to either work for or take without working what we have or what we are working for.

No matter whether we are in business and are trying to make our business grow and become more and more successful and profitable or just a student in a classroom or a student athlete, unless we have self-discipline, others will be more than happy to outwork us and outhustle us to take over the fruits of our labor and our customers.

Similarly if one is speaking about a football quarterback as another example. There are other members of the team and other players on other teams who, if given a chance, would be glad to take your position as quarterback. Unless you have self-discipline, you will be sitting on the bench, and they will be playing.

Self-discipline is critical to a successful and happy life.

Self means you have to do it yourself.
No . . . success does not depend on the good elf.
Take charge, you are the one who must perform.
Excel, never run with or compete for just the norm!

18B. COMPASSION, FROM *THE BOOK OF VIRTUES* BY WILLIAM J. BENNETT

"Compassion" is defined in *Webster's New World Dictionary*, third edition, as "to feel pity, to suffer, sorrow for the sufferings or trouble of another or others, accompanied by an urge to help; deep sympathy, pity."

The World Book Encyclopedia dictionary defines "virtue" as "moral excellence; goodness; good quality; merit; the quality of being chaste; or purity."

The premise of the combined assertion of Bennett and the definitions is that the moral excellent thing to do is to feel pity or to suffer sorrow for the sufferings or trouble of another when they are experiencing problems, accompanied by an urge to help. The sorrow or pity can be for a person or animal.

Compassion is especially evident for a wounded bird, perhaps injured by a passing automobile or by a hunter. There is nothing more pitiful than a wounded bird fluttering around unable to fly and expecting full well that very soon a cat will come by and consider the bird to be a choice meal.

What about compassion for a tiny child having to be taken away from its parents every day to go to a baby sitter? Or what about a child that has to spend his or her time in fear not knowing what will happen next? There are innumerable opportunities to feel compassion about situations we are exposed to in a day's time.

Every single person has to deal with little or big setbacks in a day's time. No one escapes the big or little setbacks and are candidates for compassion. What to do about it is always tough.

Picking up hitchhikers beside the road used to be commonplace. In 1965, I occasionally hitchhiked from SIU, Carbondale, to Marion. I had a weekend job in Marion and would catch a ride over to work the job. My mom or dad would take me back. The point is, hitchhiking used to be common. Today, I will almost never pick up a hitchhiker.

Knowing what to do following an urge to be compassionate just is not always easy. In the future, I would never pick up a hitchhiker. The risks outweigh the potential good you can do. Compassion for a weaker opponent in a sporting event is another topic. Beat them, but show mercy by not running up the score.

Achieve, strive, but be sensitive to the position of others. That's compassion. Compassion is an attitude of concern for other people, places, and things, which we deal with in our society. There is no need to take away from someone in order to achieve your desires. There is room in this country for everyone to succeed and to have success.

It is compassionate to be concerned.
Compassion is something you must have learned.
To avoid joining the life of the spurned . . .
Go beyond compassion or you'll be burned.

18C. RESPONSIBILITY, FROM *THE BOOK OF VIRTUES* BY WILLIAM J. BENNETT

"Responsibility" is defined in *Webster's New World Dictionary*, third edition, as "condition, quality; fact or instance of being responsible; obligation, accountability dependability, etc."

So many times in today's society, people expect their rights but forget about this key virtue. Protecting rights without responsibility in return is meaningless. "I have a right to do this" or "I have a right to be this or get that"; all are common utterances today. The simple fact of the matter is, sure you, we have rights, but we definitely have a responsibility to do our fair share in every aspect of our society in which we enjoy rights.

We have rights to opportunity equal to everyone else in our society. Sure, we have rights, but we definitely have a responsibility to work very, very hard to take advantage of our rights. There is a difference between a right to an equal opportunity and a right to an equal result. Results are based on our effectiveness as well as many other factors; many are out of our control as well as the control of many who are around us.

We have the responsibility to always do our very best and try to be successful. We have an obligation to be responsible in order to make our society work. Our society will not work if people are walking, moving around with their hand out, asking for their rights when they should be working to achieve wants in a responsible manner.

You, are responsible for your actions. You must take responsibility for achieving your goals. Self-discipline is a tool that the responsible parties use to stay focused on their goals. A responsible person is compassionately sensitively to the situation of others.

Someone must be responsible for every goal-oriented activity undertaken. Someone must be in charge; that person is responsible for the undertaking. If someone is in charge, the likelihood of success is enhanced.

And we often hear in this country that people have rights—the bill of rights; rights to do this right or that. It must not be forgotten that they also have responsibilities and must be responsible for their actions. They must be responsible for the overall impact of what they are claiming rights to. For example, if someone is claiming a right to say something, they also must be responsible for what they say if their statements cause some injury to another person or to our country.

Responsible behavior makes your breaks.
Demanding a right isn't what it takes.
You are not owed to be among the great!
You must take charge of your fate.

18D. FRIENDSHIP, FROM *THE BOOK OF VIRTUES* BY WILLIAM J. BENNETT

"Friendship" is defined in *Webster's New World Dictionary*, third edition, as "the state of being friends; attachment between friends."

Friendship is an important virtue because, after it is all said and done, here on earth, the relationship you have had with your friends and family and what you have done for your friends and family may very well be the most important accomplishments of your life.

Friendship is the state of being friends. Your treatment of your friend is similar to the Boy Scout oath modified to be an oath to your friend and to your family: "On my honor, I will do my best to do my duty to my friend; to help my friend at any and all times; to keep myself physically strong, mentally awake, and morally straight, and to use the Ten Commandments Plus as a guide. To be a friend, you must be trustworthy, loyal, helpful, cordial, courteous, kind, cooperative, cheerful, thrifty, brave, clean, and reverent."

Yes, to be a friend, it is virtuous and is worthy of elevation to the status warranting special attention. People know dozens to hundreds to perhaps thousands of people. You know the students you go to school with, students you have gone to school with, store clerks, the parents of other students, teachers. All of these categories may add up to thousands of people. But if you have two or three very good friends, you are lucky.

In addition to treating the friends according to the modified Boy Scout oath listed above, true friends, as opposed to acquaintances, take lots of time and attention. You need to be available to do things with your friends and be available for assistance and sharing events of life. This is very important and is usually the problem when you do not have friends. Without friends, achieving goals can be lonely and perhaps pointless.

Doing a favor for a friend may be just the motivation you need to stay focused enough to have sufficient self-discipline to finish the project.

People need each other; people need friendships. But setting priorities to spend time to develop friendships is a difficult call. What is the balance between friendships and parenting and being a good husband, spouse, and son or daughter? There is a question in my mind whether there is enough time to devote to friends and family with just twenty-four hours per day. Time certainly is limited.

There is a bond between family members, but not one cast in stone.

A friend is a jewel that must be earned.
How to have friends is something you already have learned.
Deciding that you want to have a friend is not enough.
Earning the position of friend takes time and can be tough.

18F. WORK FROM *THE BOOK OF VIRTUES* BY WILLIAM J. BENNETT

"Work" is defined in *Webster's New World Dictionary*, third edition, as "physical or mental effort exerted to do or make something; purposeful activity; labor; toil."

Purposeful activity is a place to start. Work along the path of your life's vision is definitely a purposeful activity. On the other hand, work without any plan and just working, moving in one direction for a while and then in another direction for a while, will not be considered a purposeful activity and definitely will only be accidently successful. Working will be essential if you are ever to be successful at any chosen field. The "purposeful activity" phrase is particularly descriptive to what must take place.

If you are a student, your out-of-class assignment, or "homework," is a critical complement to the direction of the class and for your success in the class. Doing the homework, and more importantly *understanding the homework*, is critical to your success in the class. Without homework, and lots of it, it will not be clear to you whether you have worked hard enough to actually learn the material. You will not have established whether you have achieved purposeful activity or whether your efforts are just activity leading nowhere.

Work, as a virtue, is important because without work, virtually nothing will happen. Without your effort, you will achieve very little in either the short term or the long term.

If you are an athlete, work definitely is a critical virtue. And you must work with the intensity and quality necessary to refine the skills to a sufficiently high quality to produce skill improvements. Only this level of work will improve your competitive position. The work is to make you better at what you do as an athlete and for you to know what you will be able to do for the team in a predictable fashion.

Work—anything done can be work but generally desired work is associated with accomplishing tasks—but more. Accomplishing something—seeing what you have done is very satisfying and important to ones ego, confidence, and self-concept. Being given something without having to work for it does not accomplish the same gain in ego, confidence, and self-concept.

A gift alone is nonproductive. A gift of a resource to a person with self-discipline, responsibility, and who is willing to work may instill virtuous work into a person. It may not. They, more than likely, will use the resource to achieve some goal or produce a useful product.

Work makes thing happen; self-discipline keeps it going; a plan sets its direction.

Physical and mental effort were work to Noah.
He made something out of his work, you betcha?
Work is work, be it in Chicago or Arabia.
Purposeful activity and labor are work . . . comprehenda?

18F. COURAGE, FROM *THE BOOK OF VIRTUES* BY WILLIAM J. BENNETT

"Courage" is defined in *Webster's New World Dictionary*, third edition, as "the attitude of facing and dealing with anything recognized as dangerous, difficult or painful instead of withdrawing from it; quality of being fearless or brave; valor."

This is another important virtue, the virtue of courage. As *Webster* envisioned, courage is to face dangerous situations without withdrawing.

Courage is not necessarily placing one's life or basic integrity at risk. That is being stupid!

Fear of failure can stop any progress. Anyone taking an action takes a risk. Taking that risk takes courage—a virtue.

The lack of courage can paralyze any activity or undertaking.
Fear of failure can be totally stifling. All the great accomplishments throughout history required courage to be achieved, courage to overcome fear . . . such as fear of ridicule, fear of financial failure, fear of injury or death.

Courage, along with the other virtues, is an excellent predictor of success in life. Without overcoming an overwhelming fear of taking an action, nothing would occur. That fear must be overcome to achieve greatness or even to achieve a routine day on the job.

In many cases, it takes courage to face the day for many of us. It takes courage to drive the expressways. It takes courage to face the bully whether he or she is the thirty-five-year-old peer or supervisor or the kids on the bus or the brute in the lunch line at school. Meeting that fear and moving forward takes courage.

One person's courage is another's baby step.
The degree depends on where the shoes have been.
Miles traveled magnifies one's prep.
Courage is a virtue; being a coward is akin to sin.

18G. PERSEVERANCE, FROM *THE BOOK OF VIRTUES* BY WILLIAM J. BENNETT

"Perseverance" is defined in *Webster's New World Dictionary*, third edition, as "continued, patient effort; the quality of one who perseveres; to continue in some effort, course of action etc. in spite of difficulty, opposition etc; be steadfast in purpose, persist."

Never give up; know where you are going; develop your plan; and never give up until your goal is accomplished.

How many times did Abraham Lincoln have to overcome defeat in order to achieve the presidency? Think of what would have been the result if he had retired from political life after the election just before he ran for and won the presidency.

I am sure that every person who has accomplished anything has a significant level of perseverance.

Sure, some things come easy for some people—but not all things. Everyone who is successful must exhibit perseverance. They persevere through sports, developing the skills and exerting the energy to achieve excellence. They persevere through college. They persevere up the career path through the company hierarchy, and on and on. They work and strive to achieve.

A Hall of Fame baseball hitter fails two out of three tries. Lincoln only won two or three elections before he won the important election for the presidency of the United States. Persevere, have courage, remember your friends, work hard, and be compassionate.

Perseverance means to stick it out, stick it out.
Set your course and shout it out.
Focus on your course, your daily route.
Stick it out, be tough, it will make you want to shout.

18H. HONESTY, FROM *THE BOOK OF VIRTUES* BY WILLIAM J. BENNETT

"Honesty" is defined in *Webster's New World Dictionary*, third edition, as "the state or quality of being honest; refraining from lying, cheating or stealing; being truthful, trustworthy or upright; sincerity, fairness; straightforwardness."

They say honesty is the best policy. I say "it is the only policy."

The so-called need to lie or being dishonest occurs only when you are afraid or ashamed to say the truth. Why put yourself in the position in the first place where you feel that you are afraid or ashamed of the truth?

Think through what you are about to do and eliminate those actions or thoughts that you believe, in the future, you will be ashamed or afraid to tell your mom or dad. Call this the mom-and-pop test. Think through what you are about to do, and if you think you will be hesitant to tell your mom and pop, don't do it!

Life is extremely complex with its many decisions. Why add to the complexity by doing or saying something that you are afraid or ashamed to tell the truth about.

Anticipate the results and the perceived results from your actions to keep yourself in a position for which you can be honest and proud. It sure keeps your life simpler in a very complex world.

So many activities are pushed on TV as being the norm but are really deviant. Bounce potential actions off your value system—not the value system insinuated by the media as being normal. Give it the "mom and pop test."

Tell the truth . . . do what's right . . .
Saves you from a daily fright.
Fear of deeds being brought to light.
Honesty, frees you to keep your vision in sight.

181. LOYALTY, FROM *THE BOOK OF VIRTUES* BY WILLIAM J. BENNETT

Loyalty is defined in *Webster's New World Dictionary*, third edition, as "quality, state or instance of being loyal, faithfulness, or faithful adherence to a person, government cause, duty etc."

Childhood neighborhood and grade/high-school friends are to be counted on and are friends, which you should be appreciative of the rest of your life.

The same goes for the values of your youth.

All should be held in high esteem your entire life.

New friends and new understandings of early values will come into your life. But, the test of character comes when one observes how you are loyal to your old original friends and values.

The other virtues also must be brought forward also . . . Friends change too. Life's influences can change them and move them out of the game of acceptable behavior or thinking.

You can be loyal to certain people, products, areas of the state, or sports teams. We all have loyalties or favorites.

Loyalty has limits. Its strengths should not exceed your value system and the value system of your family.

Friends deserve the same to their face . . .
As you would say when they are nowhere near your place.
Portray them always at their best.
In difficult times, your friendship will pass the test.

18J. FAITH, FROM *THE BOOK OF VIRTUES* BY WILLIAM J. BENNETT

"Faith" is defined in *Webster's New World Dictionary*, third edition, as "unquestioning belief that does not require proof or evidence or unquestioning belief in God, religious tenants, etc."

Faith is a confidence that something exists without being able to actually see it, feel it, or hear it.

Mostly, faith is used in a religious sense for supporting our belief in God and Jesus.

We have never seen them, and only through faith do we believe that they exist.

Faith in God and Jesus is one of the two criteria for entering eternal life in heaven with them.

Faith is used in Alcoholics Anonymous. In a religious sense, faith means confidence in your abilities to handle a situation or task.

Faith in your friends will come through jointly dealing with stressful bonding situations; faith in yourself will come from accomplishing difficult, real life issues, which challenge your abilities as you set out to accomplish your vision.

But faith without the other virtues in place is not sufficient except for coupling with repentance of your sins for salvation. In every other situation, faith must be accomplished with the other virtues. Having faith that all "will work out" without putting the efforts implied by the virtues into it will be a shallow hope.

Self-discipline, compassion, responsibility, friendships, work, courage, perseverance, honesty, loyalty, and faith are important in life's journey.

Believe in what is without proof.
This is not an order to blindly accept what is not true.
No need for faith in an elaborate spoof.
Search, think, know ... what is true for you.

19

Are You Trying Real Hard? John H. Johnson And Lerone Bennett Jr.

"Son," she said, "are you trying hard? Real hard? Well," she said, closing the conversation, "whenever you're trying hard, you're never failing. The only failure is failing to try."

Effort: the importance of effort appears in every success-oriented or motivational book, essay, or writing.

Planning and hard work, both important, go hand in hand. One without the other is not nearly as effective.

One, you, me, really can't be given credit for trying without planning the effort first.

Overcoming the inertia of laziness, or misspent time, is the biggest obstacle to overcome to succeed in life. Just the satisfaction of knowing that you actually gave it your best is enough to look back to your life as being successful.

If the only thing in life that you are good at is working and trying very hard at whatever you are doing, you will be a success.

Then with some planning and luck along with your hard work, you may accumulate happiness and wealth.

But that cannot be the measure of a successful life . . . not at all.

Your happiness will lie on the doorstep of being good at something. And you certainly can be happy without being wealthy.

No matter what your talents and brain power are, if you try hard, real hard, you will be good at something. Excelling in even one category is worth being proud of and will be a source of pleasure and satisfaction. And I believe that you will be successful as measured by your happiness and even your material wealth as well.

On the other hand, failing to try hard will be deflating to your ego, downright depressing, and will make you feel like a loser. And you probably will be a loser if you really don't give your opportunities the effort they and you deserve!

You can't lose when you try hard.

Ending the battle before the pedal goes down . . .
Singing a song without uttering a sound . . .
Painting a picture with no paint on your brush . . .
All will lead you around and round.
Knowing you tried hard will bring you a victorious rush.

20

"I Will Permit No Man To Narrow And Degrade My Soul By Making Me Hate Him." Booker T. Washington.

The fact that hate consumes so much of our energy is reason enough to follow Booker T. Washington's advice and creed. You do not have to like everyone. No matter what, every person has value, and there is something to appreciate in every person. As long as you can keep yourself in a position of not being hurt or negatively impacted by the other person, there is no reason to dislike or hate.

I believe that is the key; unless you choose, don't be impacted over any significant period by the other person.

Even something as simple as a little drip of water, time after time, will evoke hatred in a person. You know, the ol' Chinese water torture: a person is tied down, and a cold drip of water falls on the tied-down person every once in a while. After a period of time, depending on the length of the time and the frequency and temperature of the drops, the tied-down person will eventually hate the captors.

Water has value; even the meanest people have value; however, a behavior that annoys or negatively impacts another will evoke strong dislikes or hatred. Avoid that situation; get out from under the drip, so to speak. Don't allow the drip to consume your reserve energy.

Stay away from people and situations that evoke strong dislikes and opinions.

There are too many pleasant and courteous people that are not a drip, drip to your soul. A drip, drip is still an irritant, avoid them. There are just too many nice and pleasant people to be with to waste much time on the irritants.

With the world full of those in need . . .
Why let one cause you to take heed.
The person that caused you strife . . .
Is reason to avoid them for life.

21

"Of Course, It's The Same Old Story. Truth Usually Is The Same Old Story," Margaret Thatcher.

Truth makes your life so simple. Live a life that allows you to always tell the truth. Lies, half truths, white lies complicate your life and take creative energy away from accomplishing your goals.

What did I say? What did I do? Can I say that to him? How often do these come up when you have lies/untruths out on the table and you fear being discovered?

Covering up time and fretting away time both waste the time you can use to achieve the accomplishment you have set forth as your goals.

There are people who lie when there is no reason to lie. There are people who lie, think they have a reason, and have absolutely no fear of being caught or guilt if they do get caught.

Don't trust these people; don't associate with them; don't depend on them.

Observe people in the daily routine of life. Select the truly honest people for your friends.

Success should never come at the expense of another person. And it does not have to if it is accomplished honestly and with your own effort.

Telling the truth makes it easier to repeat the same story to others. There is no need to keep track of what else you told someone. The truth is the same old story, but it certainly makes you more credible, and your life will ultimately be more pleasant and successful.

The truth is and always will be . . .
The story stays the same, you will see.
With a clear vision of what you know.
The truth will be in your tomorrows.

22

"We Are All Worms, But I Do Believe I Am A Glowworm." Winston Churchill.

Everyone needs to feel that they are special and have value. Being special should be earned, not just claimed.

To be credible in your specialness, you must earn that status by being good at least one thing.

Being truly good at one thing will give people confidence in their abilities. Achieving this skill requires practice and hard work to cause you to stand out when among your peers.

We are all people surviving in a world with some good and some bad happenings.

If there is just one thing in which each of us excel, that will build our confidence and allow us to feel like the glowworms among the other worms.

Hopefully each person will have his or her specialty where he/she feels that he/she excels.

What I Would Have Said . . .

Glow little glowworm, glimmer, glimmer.
Hard work and persistence will make them famous.
A glow worm is a slimy little critter . . .
But he makes the point without a jitter.
Winston's life was a primer.

23

"What Really Is Worthwhile?" Nardi Reader Campion, *Reader's Digest*, July 1994

If we don't want to "cumber" our lives, there are four things we can do:

- drop pretense;
- don't worry;
- let go of discontent; and
- let go of self-seeking

What is worthwhile, who gets to say?
Being able to make a choice—win or lose . . .
Puts you in the driver's seat and on your way.
Really worthwhile? It is yours to choose.
You set your standards for every day.

23A. DROP PRETENSE, FROM "WHAT REALLY IS WORTHWHILE?" BY NARDI REEDER CAMPION, *READER'S DIGEST*, JULY 1994

Don't try to convince someone that you are different from what you really are. Pretending or lying about your personal situation is unfortunate and does tend to continue a falsehood. Keeping track of "whom you told what" gets too complicated and complicates your life. Keep it simple; tell the truth.

Be honest with yourself and others. With character and personality traits described in these pages, your being will be prepared to be viewed and assessed by anyone. You will be free to be yourself.

If you are afraid to portray yourself as you really are, you need to change anyway.

Keep your life and your character in a position that you are proud of or at least satisfied with "who" and "what" you are. Then there will be no need to use pretense to project the image you wish to portray.

When trying to fool those you meet.
Pretense tricks you too and not so discreet.
The "fooler" is oft the one in retreat.
Straight up . . . be what you are.
Truth simply can't be beat!

23B. DROP WORRY, FROM "WHAT REALLY IS WORTHWHILE?" NARDI REEDER CAMPION, *READER'S DIGEST*, JULY 1994.

For sure, do not worry about what is not under your control. Health, for example . . . don't worry about your health. Keep a healthy diet and exercise as well as avoid the smoking and drinking beyond one-drink-per-day lifestyles.

The theme here is . . . don't set around worrying and fretting.

Do something about it. Setting around and worrying about something is totally nonproductive.

Whatever the issue, you should think through the situation and take action to prevent the problem from continuing, or minimize it as much as possible.

No matter what the situation is, it is easier to plan how to prevent a problem than to let the problem happen and then try to live with the event. Living with the problematic result on top of trying to think through and worry about why in the world you didn't take action to keep the problem from happening . . . gets you into the worry, woe-is-me cycle.

Worry not.
Plan a lot.
Wheels spinning are such a waste.
Worry too wastes . . . to my taste.

23C. LET GO OF DISCONTENT, FROM "WHAT REALLY IS WORTHWHILE?" BY NARDI REEDER CAMPION, *READER'S DIGEST*, JULY 1994.

Let go of being dissatisfied with your situation in life without committing to doing something about it.

I will have to say that if you do not care for your situation in life, do something about it. Discontent without action is a terrible waste.

Take action if you are dissatisfied; wasting energy sitting and being dissatisfied is unfortunate.

Assess and build on your positives: your health, your family, your job, your knowledge, your abilities, and so on.

There must be positives, and if you are not terminally ill, you have a future that you can build on. Focus on the positives and set short-term goals.

Achieving these goals will give you a sense of accomplishment and confidence for your future.

Let go, let go, be free.
Decide what you are and what you will be.
Complacency is not for you or me.
Discontent is too much to carry!
Turn to your vision for life quickly.

23D. LET GO OF SELF-SEEKING, FROM "WHAT REALLY IS WORTHWHILE?" BY NARDI REEDER CAMPION, *READER'S DIGEST*, JULY 1994.

Self-seeking at the expense of others must be avoided. The capitalistic economy runs based on self-seeking in our business lives. All achievement comes from those of us who work to achieve personal, group, and team excellence.

The capitalistic economic system does not necessarily bring success at the expense of others. It can but shouldn't. Self-seeking at the expense of others must be avoided.

For interpersonal relations, do not think of satisfying your needs first while climbing over the backs of others.

Think of your friends, your mate, and associates first. Being served first from the coffeepot, being first through the door, being first to see the world, being first to enter the house—all should be avoided. Think of your friends and associates first.

Achievement is not being discouraged through this writing! The theme is just the opposite, but taking away from others is being discouraged. The bounty of this country and our economic system is limited only by what we/you can achieve. Our bounty is not a limited pie to be cut up by the participants of our economy. The economic pie can expand and expand to the limits of our collective ability, creativity, and hard work.

With your life's vision setting your path . . .
Success as you define will suffer no wrath.
Nothing you do to achieve your goal . . .
Should be shunned when no one hath . . .
To lose . . . I here forth extol.

23E. WHAT ARE THE THINGS IN LIFE THAT WE SHOULD KEEP, GUARD, USE? AR BROWN. FROM "WHAT REALLY IS WORTHWHILE?" BY NARDI REEDER CAMPION, *READER'S DIGEST*, JULY 1994.

When evaluating the value produced by your life, what will you have to show?

When your final stone plunges through the surface of the still lake... how far out and how long will the ripples portraying your life continue to be seen?

Our ripples will not last forever... for sure. So leaving some real evidence that you actually lived and spent time here on earth should be factored in your decision. When answering the question, "What are the things in life that we should keep, guard, use?"—things like family and institutions come to mind.

Number one... what is in your heart... have you done your best? Being able to say *yes* to this question should be a life goal as something you "keep, guard, and use" throughout your life. This strikes me as something that is really worthwhile.

Number two would be the character and quality of your family. Has the younger generations of your family copied your desire to do their best? A *yes* here is another very important lifetime accomplishment and are things in life that we should definitely strive to keep, guard, and use.

Number three... but not third in importance, for my stressing the need of keeping, guarding, and using is the requirement for spending eternal life with God in heaven. Therefore keep, guard, and use your repentance of your sins and your faith in God and Jesus.

Always striving to do your best...
Would be among the rest.
A cross and a heart would show your zest.
I am seeing our new family crest.

23F. BE WISE IN THE USE OF TIME, FROM "WHAT IS WORTHWHILE?" BY ANNA ROBERTSON BROWN, *READER'S DIGEST*, JULY 1994.

Time is limited to twenty-four hours per day for everyone. How one uses that time is the variable that we have to make or break our health, our families, our jobs, and really all aspects of our life.

Proper rest and sleep are needed and must come off the top. The remainder of the twenty-four hours per day must be used to achieve a balance between health, your families, jobs, and the rest.

How we use the remaining time will dictate essentially everything about our life. With our life built around with the philosophies expressed in this book, our life should be healthy, happy, productive, sharing, and financially secure. And I suppose that goes a long way to living a successful life.

Time is one treasure we all share.
Equal portions—that's fair . . .
But some achieve so much more without flair.
Don't be wasteful, and after a while, you will not despair.

23G. VALUE WORK, FROM "WHAT IS WORTHWHILE?" BY ANNA ROBERTSON BROWN, *READER'S DIGEST*, JULY 1994.

Value work because work is the tool needed to accomplish all of our objectives. Work can be thought of as storing energy, which can be called upon later to produce results or enjoyment.

Appreciate that fact, the fact that nothing gets accomplished without someone or numerous someones expending work.

Value work and value the concept that you should pick a vocation you enjoy doing because you will be doing a lot of it through your lifetime and will need to do it well.

Appreciate both the concept of work and the actual activity so that you are doubly reminded that work has value.

Work as a value is often rare.
Nothing happens without work!
Relying on the work others work is not to care.
To endorse less than your best means you are a jerk!

23H. SEEK HAPPINESS EACH DAY, FROM "WHAT IS WORTHWHILE?" BY ANNA ROBERTSON BROWN, *READER'S DIGEST*, JULY 1994.

Seek happiness each day! Don't plan your life such that your happiness is always over the horizon. If you are not approaching life such that you are not enjoying yourself each day but hope that someday you will, you may never reach that happiness. With the uncertainties of life, that happiness may never come.

Happiness can come from helping others. And here, the possibilities are infinite. Help at the "soup kitchen," at political fund-raisers, needy cause fund-raisers, the neighbor down the street, or generically with volunteering at university events.

Happiness can come from a walk in the morning, wherever you want . . . in the woods, in the mall, or on the golf course. It can be a walk with your spouse, your dogs, your grandchildren . . . again these are endless possibilities.

Happiness can come from writings such as this or shopping or reading the paper, playing video games or playing basketball or studying for the test. Create in life a series of perhaps small events that you enjoy doing throughout each day. Small happiness events add up to a happy life!

Remember, if you value work, even doing your job or other necessary components of what it takes to provide your income can bring you happiness. It is your job to make yourself happy, and the more people you can bring with you, the better off the world will be.

Seek some every day.
Joy, happiness, hopefully is your goal.
Enjoy what you do—I say . . .
And do what you enjoy, it's your role.

231. CHERISH LOVE, FROM "WHAT IS WORTHWHILE?" BY ANNA ROBERTSON BROWN, *READER'S DIGEST*, JULY 1994.

Cherish the fact that there are people who love you. But what is love, you say?

Defining the love first is an important element of this conversation. Read 1 Corinthians 13:1-13. A biblical version of this definition comes in the New Testament: 1 Corinthians 13: "Love is patient. Love is kind. It does not envy. It does not boast. It is not proud. It is not rude. It is not self-seeking. It is not easily angered. It keeps no record of wrongs. Love does not delight in evil, but rejoices with the truth. It always protects, always trusts, always hopes, always perseveres. Love never fails . . ."

Love such as this is predicated on a firm and sound foundation of common courtesy and sensitivity to your mate, child, teammate, or friend or to others in the world around you.

Never ever expect this idealistic definition of love to exist when common courtesies are not offered in return. The flow of love will ebb and flow as the common courtesies and trust extend from one to another; ebb and flow; ebb and flow; ebb and flow.

Love, when it exists, should be cherished and when present, may never totally disappear. It will ebb and flow commensurate with the extent common courtesies and trust match expectations. Love varies: love for a mate; love for a child; love for a dear parent or grandparent; love for a friend or associate or pastor or coach. All are different; all should be cherished.

Love for a child or parent will never end and will always be cherished. Whether the child is a friend and someone you do things with is another story. This relationship will ebb and flow depending on the courtesies and trust that develop over the years.

The love for a mate is definitely conditional and will ebb and flow depending on the extent common courtesies and trust match expectations. And the love for a mate can be much more intimate and intense if the couple adequately pays attention to common courtesies and trust. The love for a mate and a child can be like the love that one feels for one's own arm or eyesight—a strong emotional attachment, which you share their joys and oppose their difficulties.

Love for nonfamily members is more conditional and more a statement of friendship than it is a statement of strong affection.

Galatians 5:14-15: "The entire Law of the Bible can be summed up in a single command, 'Love your neighbor as yourself; If you keep on biting and devouring each other, watch out or you will be destroyed by each other.'"

Love love.
"Cherish" is a French word for "love."
Love love.
Savor and respect love.

23J. KEEP AMBITION IN CHECK, FROM "WHAT IS WORTHWHILE?" BY ANNA ROBERTSON BROWN, *READER'S DIGEST*, JULY 1994.

Ambition, the desire to be successful and outstanding in whatever field of endeavor you choose, is extremely important to achieving your goals.

Goals must be achieved, however, without injuring others. The "pie" of "successful opportunities" is never ending. Other individuals do not have to be damaged for you to achieve your goals. You do not have to take away from others for you to enjoy and achieve success! Opportunities are endless in the United States of America!

Keep your ambitions in check. Control your ambition such that no one individually gets injured from your seeking your goals. It isn't necessary, so do not let it happen.

Worthwhile issues still must be resolved. What is worthwhile still must be resolved. The priority of other elements in your life must be assessed. The importance of your family and their needs must be determined. The importance of maintaining a diet and physical plan must be maintained. All aspects of your life must be assessed, and your direction must be chosen.

Goal-seeking ambition has to be kept in perspective with all other priorities so that your life will be balanced. The value of judgment of whether the activity is truly worthwhile, when balanced against the other aspects of your life, must be measured and found to be important.

Galatians 5:16-22: "Live by the Spirit and you will not gratify the desires of the sinful nature. Defining what is a worthwhile ambition is the key. The sinful nature desires what is contrary to the Spirit and the Spirit desires what is contrary to the sinful nature. They are in conflict so that you have a standard against which you can compare your actions."

If you are led by the Spirit, you are not under the law. The acts of sinful nature are obvious: sexual immorality, impurity and debauchery, idolatry and witchcraft, hatred, discord, jealousy, fits of rage, selfish ambition, dissensions, factions, and envy, drunkenness, orgies, and the like. I warn you, as I did before, that those who live like this will not inherit the kingdom of God.

Debauchery means excessive indulgence in sensual pleasures, such as eating and drinking.

But the fruit of the Spirit is love, joy, peace, patience, kindness, goodness, faithfulness, gentleness, and self-control. Ambition, which incorporates these values, is never to be discouraged. And when ambition does drift in opposition to these characteristics (joy, peace, patience, kindness, goodness, faithfulness, gentleness, and self-control) . . . you are heading in the wrong direction!

Ambition that grinds a friend into the ground.
Is not particularly sound.
Ambition that carries your friends along with you.
Is the kind of vision which I value.

23K. EMBRACE FRIENDSHIP, FROM "WHAT IS WORTHWHILE?" BY ANNA ROBERTSON BROWN, *READER'S DIGEST*, JULY 1994.

Proverbs 27:10: "Do not forsake your friend and the friend of your father and do not go to your brother's house when disaster strikes you—better a neighbor nearby than a brother far away."

To have a friend, you must be a friend. It takes time to be a friend. Friends outside your family take time away from your family . . . so there are definite life choices!

Life is a series of checks and balances. Balancing family and friends is difficult.

To be a friend, you must be a friend—involved with your friend's life; helping, doing things with; being there when assistance is needed. The same is true for families; to be supportive of your family, you must be involved and be there when you are needed and to enjoy one another's company.

Your family is your first priory. Practice random acts of kindness to people in your environment. Do favors and nice things for the people with whom you come in contact.

Value people. The extent to which you can stay with a friend and be helpful and loyal over time depends on the family and work commitments you have. Seek to support your friends and family.

Friends indeed take time.
And no doubt they have their own mind.
Yet helping others should be your goal.
A trail of good deeds should be your role.

23L. DO NOT FEAR SORROW, FROM "WHAT IS WORTHWHILE?" BY ANNA ROBERTSON BROWN, *READER'S DIGEST*, JULY 1994.

Isaiah 60:1-20: "Arise, shine for your light has come and the glory of the Lord rises upon you . . . I will make you the everlasting pride and the joy of all generations . . . for the Lord will be your everlasting light and your God will be your glory . . . and your days of sorrow will end . . . Then all your people will be righteous . . . and they will possess the land forever."—A Biblical picture after God establishes His kingdom on earth. Sorrow will end. To end . . . sorrow had to have occurred.

It is a certainty that sorrow will enter your life. Sooner or later, intense and mild . . . all forms of sorrow will enter your life.

Live your life without regard to the sorrow, which may come from the injury, sickness, or death of friends and loved ones and the sorrow, which may result from broken relationships. Do not avoid friendships because of a fear of receiving less in return commensurate with expectations. Focus on what you can do for others and not on potential disappointments and sorrow.

Enjoy your life; consider the wisdom of this task to the extent you deem it wisdom and move forward. Support and give to others and do not look back to second-guess yourself.

Sorrow will come, maybe not today, but certainly tomorrow.
Make your moves, based on your vision, not fear of sorrow.
Fear must not guide your ways!
Make the very best of all your days.

23M. CHERISH FAITH, FROM "WHAT REALLY IS WORTHWHILE?" BY ANNA ROBERTSON BROWN, *READER'S DIGEST*, JULY 1994.

2 Chronicles 20:20: "You have faith that the sun will come up each morning and that it will set each evening. You are certain that fall follows summer, and that winter follows fall and that spring follows winter. Faith is a belief that something will occur without absolute proof of that fact."

You are reasonably certain that when you turn on the faucet, water will flow. Likewise, if you turn on the light switch, the room will be flooded with light. Also, you are reasonably certain that your wife will be faithful and your child will not take drugs.

You also must have faith in God and Jesus and be repentant (sorry for your sins) in order to enter their Kingdom.

Almost any activity involves a certain amount of faith. Faith is critical to functioning. Cherish that fact. Appreciate the importance of faith in a world of many opportunities and dangers.

Expecting with little support . . .
Seems to be what they call faith, I report.
Faith in what the Bible says is true.
Faith that education and hard work will be the best for you.

24

"Raising A Can-Do Kid: Seven Traits That Encourage Self-Esteem In Your Children," John Rosemond, *Better Homes And Gardens*, March 1990

24A. RESOURCEFULNESS, FROM "RAISING A CAN-DO KID: SEVEN TRAITS THAT ENCOURAGE SELF-ESTEEM IN YOUR CHILDREN," JOHN ROSEMOND, *BETTER HOMES AND GARDENS*, MARCH 1990

Resourcefulness is the skill of being able to solve problems with or without formal tools. A creative problem solver is another way to describe a resourceful person. Obviously, this is a skill we wish for our children.

Resourcefulness is stifled when the child is showered with every toy, computer game, or convenience known to mankind.

Letting kids solve problems or have fun on their own is a challenge because of the dangers of youth. Opportunities are necessary if they are to end up exhibiting the resourcefulness necessary to excel in significant areas of their life.

Making the most of everyday situations, things, and items is resourcefulness. A resourceful person is a leader, a problem solver, and a winner.

Children with stifled creativity and resourcefulness follow and are not problem—or issue-solving people and do not see tasks that need to be accomplished to achieve a vision.

Encourage the skill of creating something from a maze.
Finding a way to win will mostly amaze.
Today, victims abound . . .
But not when the resourceful ones are around.

24B. IMAGINATION AND CREATIVITY, FROM "RAISING A CAN-DO KID: SEVEN TRAITS THAT ENCOURAGE SELF-ESTEEM IN YOUR CHILDREN," JOHN ROSEMOND, *BETTER HOMES AND GARDENS*, MARCH 1990

Sure, this is what we want, but how do you instill imagination and creativity? This is difficult because the things that support creativity are giving the kids opportunity to amuse themselves by giving them books to read, reading to them, or giving them unusual toys like articles for them to develop uses.

But kids today often have TV, video games, organized sports, and dumbing down in school. So are we creating/raising kids with imagination and creativity?

It is hard to say, and my biases come out. It is a mixed bag—video games do require a great deal of imagination and creativity to get through the maze of tunnels, waterfalls monsters, rock slides, etc . . . . to the treasure, so to speak! Nonviolent video games . . . maybe but no mindless TV Disney, teenager shows, and most cartoons.

It is important to interact with our children; spend time with them; know what they are doing; look at their schoolwork; set standards; enforce your standards; discuss issues and their schoolwork with them; discuss world and local issues; keep your life and your actions consistent with what you are telling them.

Creatively and imagination are taught and learned attributes rather than behaviors one can inherit.

I think you can be a possibility thinker by forcing yourself to identify a problem and then determine alternatives for solutions. Follow that by picking a game strategy and then develop pieces and rules for the game. There should be no house repair issue, tool or bicycle malfunction in which less than an hour of repair time is spent before seeking outside help! This is being a creative thinker and using your imagination.

Reorder the dust and what do you see?
The results of imagination and creativity.
That's what we need in our society.
Directed by the ten rules of the Nativity.

24C. DETERMINATION, FROM "RAISING A CAN-DO KID: SEVEN TRAITS THAT ENCOURAGE SELF-ESTEEM IN YOUR CHILDREN," JOHN ROSEMOND, *BETTER HOMES AND GARDENS*, MARCH 1990.

Help children grow into adults with determination. To assist your children with achieving that determination during their youth, you must start by giving them goals, objectives, tasks that are attainable and fair, but they have to work to achieve. They will be able to attain the goals with effort and that skill will grow if you continue to guide their progress.

Always saying no or setting impossible goals or standards or even being consistently negative is damaging to their determination and spirit. Eventually, the goal setting must be assumed by the child in order to achieve greatness.

You exhibit determination by setting out for what you want to accomplish and then not allowing yourself to be turned away from succeeding at reaching that goal. Think through what you want and need to achieve and then set about to achieve it.

Determination is an important attribute in any field of endeavor or any activity.

A determined student, a determined athlete, a determined business man/person is an asset to each of their organizations.

And your knowledge that you will stay in pursuit of a goal until you attain that goal will very strongly encourage your self-confidence and self-esteem.

Determination, grit your teeth, and set your path.
Know where you are going to be sure.
And never be turned by wrath.
Make your way and keep it pure.

24D. SELF-SUFFICIENCY, FROM "RAISING A CAN-DO KID: SEVEN TRAITS THAT ENCOURAGE SELF-ESTEEM IN YOUR CHILDREN," JOHN ROSEMOND, *BETTER HOMES AND GARDENS*, MARCH 1990.

Depending on oneself and being self-reliant are important attributes for people you want on your team.

The quality of the American people most representative of what it took to settle this country and make it successful is self-sufficiency.

Getting things done using your own energies and creativity is self-sufficiency.

No person is totally, totally self-sufficient. We depend on one another for our personal needs . . . think of this relationship as all being part of a team.

The self-sufficient left Europe either because they were not treated properly in the Europe of their day, or they believed the opportunities to succeed were better somewhere else. They arrived in North America and survived against all odds using their self-sufficiency.

The self-sufficient are independent and can act and think for themselves. This instills in a child the attribute of being confident enough to depend on him or herself and rely on personal abilities. Self-sufficiency is an advantage that the child will enjoy and use during an entire lifetime.

When the final plays out . . .
I don't have to shout.
You are going to be the one . . .
Who makes the hit and drives in the run.

24E. RESPONSIBILITY, FROM "RAISING A CAN-DO KID: SEVEN TRAITS THAT ENCOURAGE SELF-ESTEEM IN YOUR CHILDREN," JOHN ROSEMOND, *BETTER HOMES AND GARDENS*, MARCH 1990

People need to be convinced that they are responsible for their own actions. This is very important!

Naturally, people have rights; Americans have rights, the Bill of Rights come to mind as expressed in the U.S. Constitution and interpreted by the courts including the Supreme Court.

People have a responsibility to obey the laws; they have a responsibility to treat others with common courtesies before they have any right to base treatment they receive on inherent rights protected by the constitution . . . this is my opinion of course.

If everyone treated everyone else with common courtesies, there would be no need for courts because everyone would be following the laws that have been adopted or the moral laws of the Bible. Our responsibilities of following laws and the moral laws of the Bible have been replaced by those in our country, wishing to totally do away with any trace of a religious based moral code. Their secular and individually focused code of conduct concept—if it feels good to us personally, we should be able to do it regardless of how it overrides the rights of others.

If only people would carry out their responsibility, no one would have to worry about protecting their rights. They would not be threatened by the other people out there in our world.

The secular moral code, Civil Liberties Union types should not make judgments as to the morality or efficacy of what one does . . . They say . . . society has no right to make judgments on individual performance. The result has been a breakdown of society by thoughts that go with a do-what-feels-good philosophy.

Being responsible would end all this lawlessness, immorality, and the breakdown in values, which has devastated our families.

What I Would Have Said . . .

A key word for every day of our life . . .
Being responsible would stop most strife.
Our constitution assures what's right.
It is character that makes us responsible with all our might.

24F. RESPECTFULNESS, FROM "RAISING A CAN-DO KID: SEVEN TRAITS THAT ENCOURAGE SELF-ESTEEM IN YOUR CHILDREN," JOHN ROSEMOND, *BETTER HOMES AND GARDENS*, MARCH 1990

You are to be respectful of laws and show respectfulness to each other.

Oh, if everyone respected the laws of our country and respected the rights of others with whom we come into contact, we all would be much better off. There would be peace between countries, and the jails would be empty.

There would be peace between people, and the creative energies of people could be focused on accomplishing positive things—not trying to overcome others, getting even, or repairing the damage caused by angry or disrespectful actions.

Respectfulness is similar to the Golden Rule, "Do unto others as you would have them do unto you."

Treat others the way you want to be treated; respect others and their rights.

It is their unwritten right to be treated with respect. You are not doing them a favor. You are supposed to treat other respectfully.

The same concept apples to the way you treat animals, the environment, your possessions, and your own body. Treat them all like precious jewels—respectfully.

The kid can do it all it seems.
Skill abounds in reams.
Does he remember the courteousness and perks.
Because without such, his picture will hang in the hall of jerks.

24G. AUTONOMY, FROM "RAISING A CAN-DO KID: SEVEN TRAITS THAT ENCOURAGE SELF-ESTEEM IN YOUR CHILDREN," JOHN ROSEMOND, *BETTER HOMES AND GARDENS*, MARCH 1990

Seek to be independent and self-sufficient. Seek to be confident in your actions enough to not be led by the crowd.

Know what you need to do and do it without being redirected again and again by the crowd.

You will need to have relationships with people in many ways, but strive for an independent approach for dealing with right and wrong so that you won't be led down the wrong path by people who simply do not have the same high level set of values.

Autonomous for the sake of operating alone is not the point. The point is that you need a vision of where you are going and when you will be there. Armed with the vision or plan for your life, you will have a reason not just to follow the crowd. You will be able to follow your own path and be a leader to success as you define it.

An independent soul, there is a fine line.
Working well without direction is a skill.
A youth with talent to work alone is fine.
This portrays autonomy with an iron clad will.

25

A Millionaire's Notebook: How Ordinary People Can Achieve Extraordinary Success, Copyright 1996, By Steven K. Scott.

INSIGHTS

25A. INSIGHT 1: PAST ACHIEVEMENT IS NOT A TRUE PREDICTOR OF FUTURE SUCCESS.

Past achievement is not an absolute predictor of future success.

Past achievement is one of many predictors of future success.

If you wanted to pick a baseball team, a football team, a staff of sales people to begin operations in a new area, or a pilot to attack an enemy fighter jet approaching your position, you would absolutely pick the candidates based on past performance!

There is no chance you would do it any other way but to base your decision on past performance. However, there are some "no-brainer" add-ons, which may eliminate the importance of past performance.

The value of this statement, "Past achievement is not a true predictor of future success," is that if your performance in the past was not so good, you have the potential to turn yourself around and turn around your performance. There is hope; do not be discouraged. Intelligence, drive, "heart," motivation, speed, size are all additional indicators of success and performance but are not absolute or true indicators either.

For example, a person may have been the world's fastest human and won every race he or she was in . . . but was in a diving accident and now is paralyzed from the neck down. The past achievements really don't mean much. What the person does from now on out will determine the level of any residual quality of life.

What you did in the past,
If you were like the wind,
You probably still are fast.
A broken leg would cause the speed to end.
The predictor would not be the last . . .
To tell how you will contend.

25B. INSIGHT 2: IF YOU CAN DO ONE THING WELL, EVEN IF IT DOESN'T SEEM SIGNIFICANT, YOU HAVE THE POTENTIAL FOR PHENOMENAL SUCCESS, FROM *A MILLIONAIRE'S NOTEBOOK: HOW ORDINARY PEOPLE CAN ACHIEVE EXTRAORDINARY SUCCESS*, COPYRIGHT 1996, BY STEVEN K. SCOTT.

If you can do one thing well, you should be confident of your abilities, and you should feel good about yourself.

If you can do one thing well, you should be able to figure a way to ride that skill to financial success and happiness throughout your working career.

If you can do one thing well, you should be extremely encouraged and in no way act sad or depressed about your chances in life.

A focus on one's abilities and successes has been a continuing theme of this writing project. Once you identify the activity in which you have skills, you will begin to gain confidence. Being able to look around and know that there are very few people who can do something as well as you has to be ego building and satisfying. Building on that knowledge, the knowledge that you are very good at some skill, will give you the confidence and motivation to use the same practice to identify other skills and preparation schedules to achieve great things toward your visionary goals.

Success will come your way . . .
If there is at least one feat . . .
Everyone would agree and say . . .
On that one thing . . . you can't be beat!

25C. INSIGHT 3: TAKE A CLOSE LOOK AND DISCOVER WHAT "INSIGNIFICANT" SUCCESSES YOU HAVE HAD AND FOCUS ON THEM. THEY COULD WELL BECOME THE FOUNDATION OF YOUR FUTURE ACHIEVEMENT, *A MILLIONAIRE'S NOTEBOOK: HOW ORDINARY PEOPLE CAN ACHIEVE EXTRAORDINARY SUCCESS*, COPYRIGHT 1996, BY STEVEN K. SCOTT.

Successes and doing things well will all have the same theme; and remember, you don't have to do everything well.

If you can do one just thing well, practice that one skill until you are the very best at that, and your career will be one that brings you considerable enjoyment.

Every stage of life can be, and should be, a stage for future growth and achievement.

With a vision of what you are wanting out of life and what you want to accomplish, life can be a systematic path of accomplishments. Reassessing your direction, at the same time you are building and purposefully preparing yourself for the future, will bring you great success. You will be purposefully moving toward your goals.

Unfocused accomplishment off in one direction and then off in another direction will not serve any purpose and will not serve to build a proper foundation to what you might want to accomplish later in life.

Unfocused accomplishments will not likely become the foundation for your future achievements. If they do serve as any basic foundation, they will represent a thin and shaky foundation, which ultimately must be further expanded with focused accomplishments.

When you get to a nongoal end point by accident . . . it will not be satisfying. A long-term vision with successes, even small or insignificant successes along the way, will lead to a life of achievement.

Look to discover what you can do . . .
With "insignificant" successes . . . I'm telling you.
Focus on them and follow through.
There will be achievements . . . it's true.
They continue for more than a year or two

25D. INSIGHT 4: PAST FAILURES DON'T HAVE TO LIMIT YOUR FUTURE, FROM *A MILLIONAIRE'S NOTEBOOK: HOW ORDINARY PEOPLE CAN ACHIEVE EXTRAORDINARY SUCCESS*, COPYRIGHT 1996, BY STEVEN K. SCOTT.

It is an admirable attribute if you don't let past failures limit your future.

Learn from your failures, but know that they can be overcome by hard work and a vision of where you want to be one, five, and ten years down the road.

The reference to past failures implies that you have tried something or things, and at least some of your attempts have resulted in failures. No problem . . . as long as you learn from these failures; make adjustments and then try again.

Everyone who has ever secured accomplishments has had failures in the process of their efforts. Electing to seek accomplishments that will ensure automatic success will not be in the direction of expanding your abilities and expanding your experiences. A streak of successes can be beneficial, but eventually, you need to go back to the more difficult tasks so that overall your long term vision will be attained.

Everyone needs to know that they are good at something. Search for it and make corrections so that your future and achieving your vision can evolve along with your skills.

Your past should not be the sign!
Failures and you need not be entwined.
Take notes, make changes, if you will.
Your future can be a thrill.

25E. INSIGHT 5: "THREE STRIKES, YOU'RE OUT" APPLIES ONLY IN BASEBALL, FROM *A MILLIONAIRE'S NOTEBOOK: HOW ORDINARY PEOPLE CAN ACHIEVE EXTRAORDINARY SUCCESS*, COPYRIGHT 1996, BY STEVEN K. SCOTT.

Baseball has other examples of the importance of persistence. The best hitters in baseball only get a hit one-out-of-three opportunities.

Who said try and try and if you fail, try again?

Life does not guarantee you success at the end of every effort. The American promise is to guarantee you equal opportunity but not equal results!

Lincoln often comes to mind because of his many election defeats before he was elected president.

Don't be bothered by a strike if you learn from it. Just like a strike, if that helps your learn what to expect or what will happen next, the strike was used constructively. If nothing is learned and you focus on the failure rather than on what you learned and what to do next time, you have missed an opportunity.

Opportunities to learn are invaluable. Relish them, and your life can be a series of learning experiences and wins/hits. Go get them!

Three strikes in baseball means you're out.
Three strikes in bowling means you scored low.
Learn and you can turn it about.
Show the world you are in the know.

25F. INSIGHT 6: WORK TO MEET YOUR NEEDS BUT DREAM TO GET AHEAD. YOUR DREAM OR VISION OF YOUR FUTURE IS THE FOCUS OF YOUR WORK, FROM *A MILLIONAIRE'S NOTEBOOK: HOW ORDINARY PEOPLE CAN ACHIEVE EXTRAORDINARY SUCCESS*, COPYRIGHT 1996, BY STEVEN K. SCOTT.

It is safe to say that hard work, even at minimum wages, will meet your basic needs. Perhaps food and basic housing could be paid for with wages earned at minimum rates.

Admittedly, this is an extreme case, but to get ahead, really ahead with special results for a career of work, you must have a vision or dream of where you want to be in one year, five years, ten years, and so on down the road of life. Your efforts must fit into your dream or vision so that your efforts fit into the pathway of your life. Then your efforts will contribute toward moving you along the way toward your vision.

Ideally, most of the productive activities of your life need to be or should be directed at achieving your dream or vision.

If it is your dream to teach, your vision would lead you through developing a depth of knowledge and participating heavily in speech, acting, or musical activities, and preferably all three. Plus, you should study and begin investing in the stock market. Playing sports would be important because your vision may involve coaching a sports team or participating on other teams such as debate, math bowl or other scholastic team activities. If teaching is your dream, there are numerous areas of expertise, which are essential to being the best teacher you can be. Consider the following:

- Depth of knowledge in math, writing, grammar, history, science, and literature: depth of knowledge is important because you will need to be able to impart your knowledge to your students. Without depth to your knowledge, your students will be able to see through your shallow perception of the topic and lose confidence in you.
- Participate heavily in speech or acting or musical activities and preferably all three; you need to be very comfortable in front of

- an audience, and this variety of performing will be very helpful for teaching.
- Study and begin investing in the stock market. With a teaching career alone, you will never, just from your teaching, earn a great deal of money. If you learn and start early, over a lifetime, you will earn and can accumulate a great deal of resources. Also, if you develop a system for teachers to accumulate wealth, you may be able to write a book or give workshops or provide training in some other way to further expand your income and change your career altogether later in life.
- Playing sports are important because your vision may involve coaching a sports team or participating.
- If it is your dream is to practice medicine, your vision would lead you through developing a depth of knowledge especially in the math and science areas.
- Depth of knowledge math, writing, grammar, history, science, and literature: a depth of knowledge is important because you will need to be able to first be able to score high enough on college and medical school entrance exams. Later a very thorough knowledge base is important when dealing with real life-or-death situations. Knowledge and skill are extremely important.

The point of this is your dreams will be very important in determining how far you go in life and what you actually achieve. A dream or vision will be critical to the focus of your work and what you actually accomplish. And remember when you are young, it is much, much easier to have a dream and base many of your life's decision and efforts in the direction of your dream. When you are older or old and wonder why you didn't accomplish what you wanted, it must be attributed to your lack of a dream. Consequently, you did not follow your dream or vision as you made your life's decisions because you had none.

Life's work . . . looking ahead can be planned.
Your will to follow that map need not be perfection.
Years will stack on years as the beach's sand.
Follow that dream, your life's work will warrant no objection!

25G. INSIGHT 7: DON'T LET SMALL MINDS LIMIT YOUR THINKING, FROM *A MILLIONAIRE'S NOTEBOOK: HOW ORDINARY PEOPLE CAN ACHIEVE EXTRAORDINARY SUCCESS*, COPYRIGHT 1996, BY STEVEN K. SCOTT.

Most advice toward approaching the future involves the person preparing to set out on a journey of life and giving your options considerable thought. Without a plan or vision or dream, there will be unnecessary limits on the speed and, consequently, the distance you travel in your lifetime.

When you are young, now, there should be no artificial limit on what you choose to accomplish with your life and energies. As you get older, more of your decisions are made either by you or for you in the absence of your reasoned thought. Decisions on your options regarding what you want to do with your life diminish as you get older. When young, it is your "small mind" that limits your achievements when there is an absence of vision.

Absolutely no option for key events in your life needs to be rejected early in your life's travels. There is no reason to reject any option. Don't let anyone with a small, shallow, and limited mind restrict your thinking, your vision, or your dream!

If it will not damage your health, it is legal and doesn't infringe on the rights of others, consider the action in your dream. If they fit in your long-term vision, consider all aspects of your options.

Keep in view,
That the small mind may be in you.
The horizon is distant, it is safe to say,
Except when a tree is in your way.
Move, dodge, wiggle, and make your move.
Life will eventually set your groove.
Where it is? I dare not care.
Will it be here or there or high in the air?

25H. INSIGHT 8: "YOUNG AND INEXPERIENCED" IS NOT A VALID REASON TO IGNORE OR STIFLE CREATIVE IDEAS AND ACTIVITIES, FROM *A MILLIONAIRE'S NOTEBOOK: HOW ORDINARY PEOPLE CAN ACHIEVE EXTRAORDINARY SUCCESS*, COPYRIGHT 1996, BY STEVEN K. SCOTT.

No one's creativity, whether they are young and inexperienced or postcollege training, middle aged, or a senior citizen should be stifled. Creative ideas and activities are a treasure in any organization or family and never should be ignored. If each person's creativity is not being used to the fullest, the manager, coach, parent, teacher is not taking advantage of all the resources at their disposal.

The challenge is to recognize and utilize the creativity from any age. The role of the parent, the manager, the coach, or the leader is channeled directly into productive concepts. Their challenge is to recognize and utilize the creativity from any age.

Any new and creative idea can be channeled directly or indirectly into productive concepts. A sure way to guarantee the creativity of the young and inexperienced person, or any other person as far as that goes, is to allow the full focus and application of the creative person to be used by going into business for himself or herself.

Otherwise, unless you are coupled with a manager, supervisor, parent, or the like, who can take advantage of your creativity, your creativity will likely be stifled. And . . . if you feel that your creativity is being stifled, you have choices to make by either going into business for yourself or using you creativity to convince the manager, coach, supervisor, or parent that you are creative and that your ideas deserve to be implemented.

In any case, you must be able to produce results for the organization whether you are producing points or dollars in products made or sold. You must be able to convert creativity into results.

Dale Carnegie's "six points to win friends and influence people" are the following:

- Become genuinely interested in other people.
- Smile.
- Remember that a person's name is to that person the sweetest and most important sound in any language.
- Be a good listener. Encourage others to talk about themselves.
- Talk in terms of the other person's interests.
- Make the other person feel important and do it sincerely.

The operative phrase here is how to "influence" people. You use your creativity to take advantage of Carnegie's six points so that the people, manager, coach, supervisor, or parent you are dealing with will recognize you and your creativity to help the organization succeed.

If you are creative as you think,
You will not be stifled for a wink.
Age . . . too much or little . . . cannot be a link . . .
To your being stopped at the brink.

251. INSIGHT 9: YOU MAY BE A LOT SMARTER THAN YOUR BOSSES, FROM *A MILLIONAIRE'S NOTEBOOK: HOW ORDINARY PEOPLE CAN ACHIEVE EXTRAORDINARY SUCCESS*, COPYRIGHT 1996, BY STEVEN K. SCOTT.

If the bosses are smart at all, they will hire people who are smarter than they are.

A boss is not a boss necessarily because of his or her brilliant intellect. Theoretically, a boss is the boss because the boss has leadership ability and is expected to lead the team to accomplish the selected goals.

And if you are as smart as you think you are, you will work very hard to make the boss look good and will convince him or her that his or her success is at least partly as a result of your quality efforts and hard work.

The same goes for your relationship with your teachers, coaches, and even parents. You may be a lot smarter than your bosses and your teachers, coaches, and even parents; but if you don't work with them to make the overall organizations look better, your success will be limited. A sharing and cooperative relationship with bosses, teachers, and coaches will be highly advantageous. They will have a desire to see you succeed and will more likely continue to put you in positions where you can succeed and will promote you to others to the advantage of your career.

Who is to say . . .
Who is the smartest . . .
On any given day?
Math smart is one test.
But when digging, it's in the way!
I'm not going to say who's the best . . .
But to be prepared for today . . .
A breadth of knowledge should be your quest.

25J. INSIGHT 10: A PERSON WHO BELIEVES IN YOU IS A TREMENDOUS SOURCE OF POWER, FROM *A MILLIONAIRE'S NOTEBOOK: HOW ORDINARY PEOPLE CAN ACHIEVE EXTRAORDINARY SUCCESS*, COPYRIGHT 1996, BY STEVEN K. SCOTT.

Knowing that one person believes in you and can be counted on to support you in your endeavors within the organizations, often called a mentor, should be a big boost to your confidence. If there is just one person who has observed you in operation and has seen you perform and still appreciates your value to the organizations, this may be all that is necessary to motivate and support you to the top of the organization.

It can be, and usually is, a parent who also believes in you almost unconditionally. Often the support can be tainted when day-to-day living experiences get in the way; taking out the trash, cleaning up your room, getting your homework done, helping with the chores, and how late you can stay out causes irritations, which might appear to weaken that unconditional support in you.

In actuality, it doesn't weaken the support. Most young people either go through that kind of relationship with their parents or learn early that if they do the things they are supposed to do without being told, they are much more apt to be treated with the respect they feel they deserve. And most teenagers want to be "treated as an adult" but have not figured out yet that to be treated as an adult, they need to act like the adult. They also need to observe that the way their parents act and behave is close enough to the way the parents believe the teenager should act (as an adult).

It can be a teacher who sees the special talent you have and helps bring out the best of your scholastic talents. The special mentor teacher can suggest that you move into situations where you can try out for parts in the school play or urge you to seek elective office as a class officer. The mentor teacher may encourage you to join certain school clubs or get involved with certain service to the community activities. All of these suggestions from mentors will enrich your education and give you experience, which will be extremely valuable to you later in life

It can be a coach who recognizes your special talent and helps you refine you skills until you are one of the very best. The mentor coach will want to be able to identify when you are having a bad day or when you seem to be having difficulty with a performance. The coach who believes in you will be likely to spot what you are doing wrong and help you make adjustments rather than just blast you for your mistakes. The mentor coach will put you in situations where you can succeed and will trust you to be in the game when the outcome is on the line.

It can be a supervisor who appreciates your abilities and recognizes your importance to him or her to accomplish the objectives of the unit in the overall organization. This is the way it should be. Supervisors need help and the full cooperation of all the employees in their organizations. If they get the cooperation and dedicated effort from the employees, the group is much more likely to be successful. And if the group is successful, the supervisor is more likely to advance in his or her career. To advance in the organization, the employees must receive the sponsorship of the group's supervisor. The supervisor is obligated, at least more likely, to mentor or support the advancement of his or her employees if they have significantly contributed to the success of the organization.

One person may be all that it takes in your organization. One person who believes in you is a tremendous source of power. Earn that confidence.

By birth, a parent will be your mentor first of all.
Your teacher develops trust if you deliver, don't you recall?
The coach knows your heart, will and passion, and what you have on the ball.
A supervisor recognizes your commitment; your career receives the windfall!

25K. INSIGHT 11: DON'T BE GREEDY, SHARE THE WEALTH, DON'T HOARD IT, FROM *A MILLIONAIRE'S NOTEBOOK: HOW ORDINARY PEOPLE CAN ACHIEVE EXTRAORDINARY SUCCESS*, COPYRIGHT 1996, BY STEVEN K. SCOTT.

Never ever be greedy with what you have. It is appropriate to expect people to work for what they get, but always be fair, clearly fair, with everyone.

If you have one person walking around who has experienced you being stingy with them and trying to give them less than they were due, this is one person too many. You never ever want anyone to be able to say that you were greedy with them or tried to cheat them or were not fair with them in every way.

Working hard and accumulating wealth for your future prosperity is fine. You definitely should be rewarded for your extraordinary effort, and you should be encouraged and motivated to succeed to the pinnacle of your chosen vocation or occupation.

You should keep in mind that there is not a limited amount of wealth or earnings potential in the United States. This country offers equal opportunity . . . not equal outcome for our efforts! There is room for, for example, twenty millionaires living next door to one another in this country. Your success and wealth are wholly dependent on your hard work, skill, persistence, intelligence, and sense of opportunity. Your chance for success is not weakened by the fact that you live next to nineteen other millionaires on the same block of the same street.

Share the wealth, but do not feel responsible in any way to give away what you have earned. Share the wealth by mentoring others on the way up. Share the wealth by being fair with everyone you deal with and ensure that they receive from you an honest day's pay for an honest day's work. Share the wealth by doing business with those willing to work hard and can be trusted to always do a great job. Share the wealth by making an occasional gift to someone who has worked hard, tried, and still needs some help. Never help someone who doesn't try to help themselves, hasn't recently worked, and *expects* you to help them. Share the opportunity for wealth more than actually giving money away.

The admonition to "don't hoard it (wealth)" is not a warning to avoid initiating a savings program. You should always initiate a savings program to get you to the point of being able to survive without being able to work. I say that if you certainly are not greedy as discussed above and are willing to share the wealth, it is almost impossible to do what some might say is hoarding wealth.

Greed is a nasty word to bear;
To treat it, just be fair!
Wealth can be shared without gratuities.
Effort put forth will earn the amenities.
Don't hoard it, lord over it, or place it in a bin.
But to be without . . . as a senior . . . is a sin.

25L. INSIGHT 12: WHOM YOU WORK FOR IS AS IMPORTANT AS WHAT YOU DO, FROM *A MILLIONAIRE'S NOTEBOOK: HOW ORDINARY PEOPLE CAN ACHIEVE EXTRAORDINARY SUCCESS*, COPYRIGHT 1996, BY STEVEN K. SCOTT.

Whom you work for is important.

From the positive side pertaining to importance, whom you work for can be very important. Successfully working for a company that has a positive national reputation as being successful, demanding in its hiring practices, and has company traditions generally considered positive to traditional American values will be considered positive for inclusion on your resume.

From the negative side, if you work for the mafia/mob, or for a pornographic magazine, or for the government, or as a used-car salesman, or a Democrat politician, whom you work for will be a negative influence on your career choice.

What you do is important because what you do tells a lot of the story about you; but not the whole story. To know the whole story about you, one needs to know what you do to earn a salary; what you do with your family; what you do with your spare time; what charities you contribute to; what other causes you contribute to; what church you belong to; and how you treat your pet.

More important are the questions: do you work, and do you think?

For future employers, they want to know . . .
Where you work . . . you reap what you sow.
What you do is important too.
Also, character, experience, motivation, to name a few.

25M. INSIGHT 13: THERE IS NO GREATER MOTIVATION THAN LOVE, FROM *A MILLIONAIRE'S NOTEBOOK: HOW ORDINARY PEOPLE CAN ACHIEVE EXTRAORDINARY SUCCESS*, COPYRIGHT 1996, BY STEVEN K. SCOTT.

"There is no greater motivation than love" may be true, but there are numerous definitions of "love." Look at *Webster's* for a few:

- fond of or tender feeling;
- warm liking;
- strong or passionate affection;
- attachment;
- something charming and delightful; or
- strong liking.

Consequently, there are numerous varieties or bases of motivations. Love implies passion, and you must have passion to be a winner; you must be motivated to be a winner. OK?
Love is too often used, and you would be better off using and thinking of another word to describe your emotional status.

Love means fond or tender feeling.
Love means warm liking.
Love means charming and delightful.
Love means strong liking.
Love has too many meanings, it's frightful.

25N. INSIGHT 14: COMMITMENT AND MOTIVATION ARE MORE IMPORTANT THAN CREDENTIALS OR RESUMES, FROM *A MILLIONAIRE'S NOTEBOOK: HOW ORDINARY PEOPLE CAN ACHIEVE EXTRAORDINARY SUCCESS*, COPYRIGHT 1996, BY STEVEN K. SCOTT.

What are you going to do; What are you determined to do; What you will do is more important to the success of any initiative than what you have done in the past.

One possible basis for judging what you are capable of doing is to look at your resume. Sure, that is an indication of what you have done in the past and potentially what you will do in the future.

But the real indication of what you will do with your education, training, and experience is your level of commitment and motivation. The real indication of whether you will get the job accomplished is . . . no matter what the job is and what your education, training, and experience are . . . your motivation and commitment to make things happen are the best indicators.

Select the most committed and motivated of the equals in education, training, and experience when picking someone for accomplishing a task.

Assess your own commitment and motivation when deciding whether you are the one needed to accomplish the task. How hard are you willing to aggressively seek to accomplish the task at hand necessary to make the organization successful? You must be willing, motivated, and committed to do what is necessary to succeed. If not, you should do something else. This is for your own good because of the need for being successful and for accomplishing things to be happy mentally. Unless you are willing to meet and exceed what is expected of you on a given task or assignment, do something else because your customer will not be satisfied, and there will be opportunities for conflict and dissatisfaction. You do not want that!

Meet and exceed what is expected of you on a given task or assignment. There is joy in being the best!

Thomas R. Wallin

Resumes tell a story about the past.
The future is more important to what you will do.
Commitment will get you out of the blocks fast.
Motivation will make dream come true.

250. INSIGHT 15: IT IS IMPORTANT TO NEVER OVERESTIMATE THE INCREDIBLE WORTH OF THE RIGHT PARTNERS (FRIENDS, TEAMMATES, MATE), FROM *A MILLIONAIRE'S NOTEBOOK: HOW ORDINARY PEOPLE CAN ACHIEVE EXTRAORDINARY SUCCESS*, COPYRIGHT 1996, BY STEVEN K. SCOTT.

A partner, without going to *Webster*, is an individual who shares an activity with you and has the status of an equal and shares more or less equally with the responsibility, rights, work, and profit.

If the task requires a partner, it is extremely important to select the right partner.

Bridge, the card game; doubles on tennis; badminton; ping-pong; two-on-two basketball, to name a few, are activities that require a partner. In these and similar activities, never overestimate the incredible worth of the right partner. With the right partner, your team can be the absolute greatest; or with the wrong partner, your team will be mediocre or worse.

Likewise, marriage and raising children are extremely dependent on the right partner. Selecting a marriage partner occurs at a time when you are actually not looking for the characteristics that will make the best marriage partner and coparent. Notwithstanding your passions of the time, this is one of the biggest, if not the biggest, decision of your life. Make the final decision one or two years after you graduate from college. Other sections of this book will be helpful with making the right decision.

The worth of the right friends needs to be stressed as well. Unfortunately, for many critical years, the opinion and values of friends are more important, if not solely important, than the opinion and values of parents. Look for friends with a strong sense of right and wrong and families that at least appear to have acceptable values and live a life commensurate with biblical and the Golden Rule values.

A partner in business is never mandatory, and you certainly can do most any business activity without a partner given the right set of extenuating circumstances. A business partner usually evolves out of a business need, and an individual is accepted as a partner only after some, probably extended, working familiarity with the individual or individuals. By the time the partnership is contemplated, you will know—and this is very important—if the potential partner is trustworthy, motivated, has personality, passions, values, morals, sense of urgency, and attitude that meshes well with yours.

The incredible worth of Mr. or Miss Right . . .
Must be stressed with all my might.
Say hello to all, there is no reason for fright.
Investing time though is nothing to be taken light.
Your decision must be "out of sight."
From your heart is right!

25P. INSIGHT 16: DO EVERYTHING YOU CAN TO MAKE THOSE YOU WORK WITH SUCCESSFUL, FROM *A MILLIONAIRE'S NOTEBOOK: HOW ORDINARY PEOPLE CAN ACHIEVE EXTRAORDINARY SUCCESS*, COPYRIGHT 1996, BY STEVEN K. SCOTT.

Friends, business associates, peers, neighbors, old high-school friends, grade-school friends . . . all could be helped, and you would gain from their advancement. It is important to do everything you can to make those you work with successful.

Think about any athletic endeavor and consider your teammates. If they improve themselves and gain considerable skill, whatever position you play, your success will be enhanced by their improving their ability. If you play a backfield or running position and your linemen friends have a choice to work out with weight and improve themselves, certainly you will benefit from their improvement.

Or consider a situation in a business environment and you sell insurance for example. As each of your friends improve and expand their expertise and consequently expand their businesses, your opportunities will be increased.

The same if you sell computers or cars or offer legal services . . . all will be enhanced if the people in your circle of associates become successful or more successful.

Besides doing a good deed and helping your friends, your career opportunities will be improved if your friends are able to become successful.

Remember, do everything you can to make those you work with successful.

Friends, business associates, teammates, and family members all can use help and will be rewarded in direct and indirect ways by your helping them.

Thomas R. Wallin

A football guard who is all lard . . .
Won't make much of a hole.
Encourage him to do more than sit in the yard.
Your dash to the goal, they will extol!

A business man who can afford to pay . . .
Is a better one to offer a new line of paint.
Help him enjoy success in his day.
And you will be his saint!

25Q. INSIGHT 17: SHARE THE WEALTH, FROM *A MILLIONAIRE'S NOTEBOOK: HOW ORDINARY PEOPLE CAN ACHIEVE EXTRAORDINARY SUCCESS*, COPYRIGHT 1996, BY STEVEN K. SCOTT.

More appropriately, I say, share the opportunity to achieve wealth!

Never be greedy. Always be fair and always leave the perception that you treated people fairly both in fact and in perception. You must treat people fairly.

This insight should not be interpreted as meaning "to give what you worked for away."

Sharing the wealth is just a place marker for a much broader topic. Share your ideas, share your time, and share your knowledge.

People who suggest that you owe them a portion of what you worked hard to earn are mistaken. You should not only reject their request, you should avoid them totally. They are losers and will generally be uncreative and unmotivated and will try to soak up all that you can do for them and want more . . . showing resentment if you do not come through.

Share the wealth feels good to say;
What have you gained, at the end of the day?
When your wealth hasn't helped, come what may.
Do what is right but they don't get to say.

25R. INSIGHT 18: CONSUMERS (PEOPLE WHO YOU ARE TRYING TO CONVINCE TO NEED YOU AND WHAT YOU HAVE TO OFFER) ARE A LOT SMARTER THAN YOU THINK, FROM *A MILLIONAIRE'S NOTEBOOK: HOW ORDINARY PEOPLE CAN ACHIEVE EXTRAORDINARY SUCCESS*, COPYRIGHT 1996, BY STEVEN K. SCOTT.

Who was it . . . Lincoln who said . . . you can fool all of the people some of the time; and you can fool some of the people all of the time, but you can't fool all of the people all of the time?

Start every relationship with every new person you meet by dealing with them as if the person is an absolute genius and treat them with the utmost respect. In this way, you won't insult them if they are a genius; and when treating them with respect, you won't insult them if they only have a double-digit IQ.

This advice pertains to normal everyday interpersonal relationships with people you meet at church, the fast food restaurants, or other hangouts or on the street. Always start conversations with the assumption that you are dealing with a genius who expects to be treated courteously. Be perceptive . . . when you speak to a person, you can tell if their eyes begin to glaze over when you are speaking . . . if it looks like you are getting through, your assumption was correct, but if their eyes glaze over, and it doesn't look like their mind is processing what you are telling or saying to them, then make it simpler or try another approach to getting your point across.

Honesty too is critical to any relationship whether the person is a customer, friend, or just a casual acquaintance. Like Lincoln said . . . people can tell usually from what you are saying, the look on your face, your body language, or later when they have a chance to check out what you are saying . . . whether the relationship continues or not. They can or will be able to know whether you are telling the truth or not.

Your personal credibility is at stake, and you must be known as a truthful person.

You have less control over other aspects of your personality or the product you are selling, but you can certainly control whether you are telling the truth to the very best of your ability. If you don't know for sure, label the issue as something you believe, but tell the person you are dealing with that you will check further and get back to them. Even if you absolutely should have known the answer to the question or issue, but you don't . . . don't attempt to fake it . . . again, tell the person you'll check and get back to them with the correct answer. That way, you will know the answer to their question the next time the issue comes up, and they will never get the impression you are faking it or trying to deceive them.

Lincoln was certainly one of the brightest of the smart.
And he warns us from the start.
Everyone should do their part . . .
And show that telling the truth is not a lost art.

25S. **INSIGHT 19: ARTISTIC SWELLS. LOGIC SELLS, FROM *A MILLIONAIRE'S NOTEBOOK: HOW ORDINARY PEOPLE CAN ACHIEVE EXTRAORDINARY SUCCESS*, COPYRIGHT 1996, BY STEVEN K. SCOTT.**

If you want to get your message to the attention of the largest audience, your message should be flashy and if you will . . . artistic. Whereas once you get your audience's attention, you must be able to present a logical "argument" as to why your product or your position will be helpful or needed by your customer.

Dull and boring TV commercials just do not get produced. Just think back to the Super Bowl commercials. Coke, Budweiser, Progressive Insurance, Geico Insurance, Michelin Tires, Ford Motor Company, typically all have very "artistic" . . . flashy or eye-appealing or catchy commercials for a major events such as the Super Bowl. Super Bowl commercials have such a positive . . . entertaining . . . artsy reputation that often people watch the commercials and take their break during the play of the game.

The product must, however, meet a logical need for the customer. First, you catch the customer's eye with artistic beauty or a clever gimmick or beautiful scene . . . then convince the customer of his or her need for the product by winning them over with logic.

A bored customer will likely go to sleep . . .
Just when your main message starts to creep . . .
Across the screen without connecting even a peep.
Pizzazz and then facts will make your income grow in a heap!

25T. INSIGHT 20: YOU HAVE TO TAKE A LOT OF SWINGS TO HIT A LOT OF HOME RUNS, FROM *A MILLIONAIRE'S NOTEBOOK: HOW ORDINARY PEOPLE CAN ACHIEVE EXTRAORDINARY SUCCESS*, COPYRIGHT 1996, BY STEVEN K. SCOTT.

The most prolific home run hitters in major league baseball might hit a home run every ten to twelve times at bat. And if you assume that they take three swings each time at bat . . . that means that the best home run hitters will take thirty to thirty-six swings for every home run they hit.

Hank Aaron . . . lifetime at bats . . . 12,364 . . . lifetime home runs . . . 755
At three swings per at bat . . . 37,092 . . . about forty-nine swings per home run.
At bats per home run . . . sixteen.

Babe Ruth . . . lifetime at bats . . . 8,399 . . . lifetime home runs . . . 714
At three swings per at bat . . . 25,197 . . . about thirty-five swings per home run.
At bats per home run . . . twelve.

Mark McGuire . . . lifetime at bats . . . 6,187 . . . lifetime home runs . . . 583
At three swings per at bat . . . 18,561 . . . about thirty-two swings per home run.
At bats per home run . . . eleven.

Now, this was a literal discussion of the insight "you have to take a lot of swings to hit a lot of home runs." Baseball hitters know what they want or need to do . . . they want to hit and catch the ball. They must have a vision of what they want and need to accomplish. Even the best hitters get only four hits out of ten times at bat. They must keep swinging.

Similarly in life or in any situation, as long as you have a vision of what you want to achieve and are trying to reach your goal, you have a chance to be successful. Without trying, nothing will happen. Look at the election record of Pres. Abraham Lincoln for example. Check out the number of swings President Lincoln took before he became president . . .

1832 ... Ran for state legislature. He lost.
1834 ... Ran for state legislature again. He won.
1838 ... Sought to become speaker of the state legislature. He was defeated.
1840 ... Sought to become elector. He was defeated.
1843 ... Ran for Congress. He lost.
1846 ... Ran for Congress again; this time he won; went to Washington and did a good job.
1848 ... Ran for reelection to Congress. He lost.
1856 ... Sought the vice-presidential nomination; he got less than one hundred votes.
1858 ... Ran for U.S. Senate again. He lost again.
1860 ... Elected president of the United States.

As long as you're swinging you are "dangerous" I say.
Keeping the bat on your shoulder is no way to play.
As long as you are "swinging," you'll be OK ...
Whether it's a game or your workday.

25U. INSIGHT 21: NO RECRIMINATIONS FOR FAILURES, FROM *A MILLIONAIRE'S NOTEBOOK: HOW ORDINARY PEOPLE CAN ACHIEVE EXTRAORDINARY SUCCESS*, COPYRIGHT 1996, BY STEVEN K. SCOTT.

As long as you are swinging, you are in the game . . . you have a chance. Obviously, this is a necessary "insight" when one of your insights is the one above . . . "You have to take a lot of swings to hit a lot of home runs." The best of the three baseball players listed above . . . Mark McGuire had to take approximately thirty-two swings for every home run he hit. Can you imagine the grief recriminations would cause when a player was successful only one in thirty-two times? Admittedly, McGuire got a hit one time in four at bats and was on base four out of every ten times at bat.

Salesmen making cold calls can expect success is setting appointments with qualified customers once every ten calls. Again, no recriminations warranted here. One out of ten should be the expected result, and just making the calls is tough enough . . . much less having someone being critical of the results.

Lincoln lost seven elections before he was elected president. Hold off on the recriminations against the Lincoln performance.

Recriminations are like taxes . . . the more activities a person performs that he or she is taxed on, the lesser of that activity will be accomplished.

If a child tries something adventurous . . . beyond making sure they are reasonably safe from injury . . . let them be free to make their own mistakes and make their own corrections. Your allowing the children to experiment and try things without recrimination will greatly encourage an adventurous spirit, whereas recriminations will severely curtail such an adventurous spirit.

Just as taxes on creativity and production, recriminations on an activity will result in less production of such activity.

No recriminations on a maker of pizzas . . .
You certainly must deep six the nixes
Creativity, success, and other fixes,
Unlike the government adding a bunch of taxes.

25V. INSIGHT 22: SHOOT FOR THE MOON. IF YOU MISS, YOU'RE STILL HIGH! FROM *A MILLIONAIRE'S NOTEBOOK: HOW ORDINARY PEOPLE CAN ACHIEVE EXTRAORDINARY SUCCESS*, COPYRIGHT 1996, BY STEVEN K. SCOTT.

This insight relates more to setting a vision for what you want to accomplish and the desirability of setting that vision high. A high vision is one for which you believe it will be very difficult to attain but could be reached with a great deal of effort, creativity, and maybe even luck.

Setting the vision or target high is the key point here.

Girl Scouts selling their cookies is an example. The girls set a goal for the number of boxes they wish to sell based on their experience from the previous year, the sales volumes of other known girls, siblings, or goals necessary to achieve certain badges or awards they are seeking. They have a vision . . . a "shooting for the moon" . . . if you will vision or goal. Then they finalize their strategy for achieving the goal. They will never get anywhere close to a "moon landing" type of goal without a specific vision. And who knows, they may even achieve the goal, but if not . . . they certainly will have sold more cookies than if they had started without a high goal.

Have you ever seen the goals on sticker boards around the drive-up windows inside McDonald's restaurants? Sure enough, each store sets goals, I am sure they are stretched to reach high goals for the number of Big Macs or chicken sandwiches or mocha coffee drinks. The listing, I'm sure, includes most if not all of McDonald's products available either on the breakfast or rest of the day menus. Now I am not sure what the individual store clerk can do to influence the numbers of each product sold during each shift, but apparently, the McDonald Corp. believes that setting goals will contribute to higher sales. McDonald averaged $2.4 million in sales per store, while Wendy's averaged $1.4 million in sales, and Burger King averaged $1.2 million per store. I have never seen a similar daily shift goal in Wendy's or Burger King.

How about a twenty—or thirty-game win for a pitcher or a 300 or 400 batting average for baseball players? How many basketball players wish they could get a triple double once a week or once a year or even once a career for some basketball players? Many of the "greats" of baseball or basketball do set these lofty goals . . . in other words, they are shooting for the moon, and even if they miss, their careers will often add up to "Hall of Fame" performances.

Shoot for the moon!
Your coming close will not cause me to impugn.
Or to question you skill so as to lampoon.
Were I to question your skill . . . I would be a loon.

25W. INSIGHT 23: PREPARE. DO YOUR HOMEWORK, FROM *A MILLIONAIRE'S NOTEBOOK: HOW ORDINARY PEOPLE CAN ACHIEVE EXTRAORDINARY SUCCESS*, COPYRIGHT 1996, BY STEVEN K. SCOTT.

Like the Boy Scouts of America motto . . . Be prepared!

No one gets anywhere in life without preparing . . . Do your homework.

By preparing or doing your homework, you are not 100 percent guaranteed of being successful . . . but it can be said that any success or even any completed project will follow preparation.

Hard work does not guarantee success . . . Heard on the radio: "If you work hard, practice, etc., I can't guarantee that you will win a championship, but if you don't work hard, practice, etc., I can guarantee that you won't win a championship!"

What do you want to be when you grow up? . . . Start with the assumption that you can do it if you start early and prepare. The road to your final destination may be a little windy, and you may not end up where you originally thought you were headed. By building on your preparation work, you may want to adjust your goals, your vision.

Your career may be a series of steps . . . all of which requires preparation to secure, hold, and then move on from if your revised vision calls for you to move on.

Say, you want to do something in the health care field. To be a medical doctor, preparation might consist of . . . four years of college, three years of medical school, and then two to three years as a resident. That's a lot of preparation. But if your vision is to supply first aid kits to every home in Haiti, then the preparation might be to learn how to set up a foundation, then establish the foundation, the entity that organizes the fund-raising, do the fund-raising, establish the sources of the first aid kits, pricing the contents, collect funds, purchase the first aid kits, arrange for the shipping and the distribution funding, and the storage and distribution system in Haiti. Both medical-field goals but very different.

Refusal to prepare for anything may end you up as homeless, but even that requires some preparation if you want a grocery store cart to carry your sleeping gear from the homeless shelter to the food kitchen.

Anything you do ... I swear ...
Will always require you to prepare.
Why don't you compare ...
The homework for a French chef making an éclair ...
To a seasoned jockey on the world's fastest mare?

25X. INSIGHT 24: GO FOR IT.

The best preparation in the world . . . of all time won't lead to the accomplishment of a single goal if there is no implementation . . . in other words . . . if you don't "go for it," nothing will happen.

Another way of saying the previous thought is . . . nothing has ever been accomplished by man throughout history who was not preceded by someone saying or thinking, let's . . . *"go for it."*

On this day in history, December 27, 537, the Hagia Sophia Basilica cathedral . . . later a mosque and now a museum, in Istanbul, Turkey, was completed. Without a "go for it," nothing would have happened.

Again, this day in 1657, the Flushing Remonstrance was signed to give religious freedom to allow Quakers to worship in New Netherlands . . . New York City. Without a "go for it," nothing would have happened.

On this day in 1927, the Broadway musical *Show Boat*, the first true American musical opened in the Ziegfeld Theater in New York City. Without a "go for it," nothing would have happened.

On this day in 1968, Apollo 8 splashed down in the Pacific Ocean, ending the first orbital space mission to the moon. Without a "go for it," nothing would have happened.

And one last . . . one last day in 1978, Spain became a democracy after forty years of dictatorship. Without a "go for it," nothing would have happened.

Before now, I am sure you get the point of this insight that to accomplish anything, you must *go for it!*

In this little tidbit.
Everything is *it*.
From the beach which is sunlit . . .
To the pole that's totally frostbit.

25Y. INSIGHT 25: MINIMIZE THE LOSSES. SHARE THE WINNINGS, FROM *A MILLIONAIRE'S NOTEBOOK: HOW ORDINARY PEOPLE CAN ACHIEVE EXTRAORDINARY SUCCESS*, COPYRIGHT 1996, BY STEVEN K. SCOTT.

The phrase . . . minimize losses . . . can mean many things. How about considering these as my top-ten ways to minimize your losses . . . but not in any particular order.

Don't stay in the stock market when it is going down or about to go down to minimize your losses.

Don't waste money on buying new cars when buying a one-, two-, or three-year-old will minimize your losses.

Keep a vehicle until it is approximately ten years old as long as you are mindful of the mechanical condition of the vehicle.

Buy a smaller car . . . hopefully a car that meets your family or business needs but with economical gas consumption. A vehicle that attains 40 mpg should be possible for most family situations. This is another way to minimize your losses.

Secure or buy living space designed to fit your minimal space needs rather than choosing a large, showy home. The initial cost as well as property taxes and heating and air conditioning costs all will be much lower for a small, minimally adequate home. This is another way to minimize your losses.

If you own your home, be aware of the socioeconomic condition of your neighborhood. Sell before blight sets in. This is another way to minimize your losses.

Shop for groceries at lower-cost grocery stores, such as Aldi, Walmart, or Shop and Save. Or if you prefer, buy store-brand grocery items when shopping at nondiscount stores. All of these grocery shopping ideas will help you to minimize your losses.

Significant losses can be minimized by purchasing clothing on sale and from discount chains, such as Walmart, Target, or Meijer's. By watching sales, name brand stores such as Macy, Dillard's, Bergner's can also be very helpful in minimizing your losses.

Don't buy new electronic "gizmos" the day they come upon the market. Usually, two or three months after a new item comes out, a newer items come out, and you can purchase the earlier item at a much lower price.

If you sense the company that you work for is about to go out of business or is going downhill and you do not believe you personally can make enough changes to turn the company around, then begin to actively seek other sources of income to replace the income you believe you are about to lose. This is another way to minimize your losses.

Tell the truth always. Lies, half truths, deception, and backbiting comments behind someone's back will always cost you in the long run. As Lincoln said, "You are not smart enough to fool all the people all of the time," and if not, there will be losses. This is another way to minimize your losses.

To minimize your losses . . .
Steer clear of big spending mates and bosses.
Keep moving so your plans won't grow mosses
And remember to keep a steady hand when the financial seas are showing tosses.

25Z. INSIGHT 26: IF IT'S NOT FUN, YOU PROBABLY WON'T SUCCEED, FROM *A MILLIONAIRE'S NOTEBOOK: HOW ORDINARY PEOPLE CAN ACHIEVE EXTRAORDINARY SUCCESS*, COPYRIGHT 1996, BY STEVEN K. SCOTT.

A wise person once said . . . regarding selecting a career . . . "Pick out something you really enjoy doing and figure out a way to earn a living performing that activity." Someone just as wise said something similar by saying, "Try to find a way to make a living doing the activities of your hobby."

Personally, I approached the same result from another direction by selecting a career by picking an educational field . . . engineering . . . by getting a degree in a field in which I had natural skills—math. I was good at math in high school, and people suggested that I study engineering in college. This supports the current wise saying as well as a wise saying of someone else . . . maybe me . . . who said . . . "People enjoy doing things at which they are good."

This insight of Scott . . . "If it's not fun, you probably won't succeed," captures the meaning of the "wise saying," which I have previously heard and is equally true. Why do you think the insight is true?

If you enjoy doing something, hopefully you will do it well and often. "Well and often" suggests that you will have a quality product and plenty of it. Hopefully lots of people will want to buy quality products, and you will be able to make lots of money selling quality products to lots of people.

People also would rather buy quality products from a happy, smiling salesperson, engineer, accountant, or manufacturer. There just is something about dealing with a pleasant smiling, happy person, rather than an ol' grouch.

A happy businessperson is more apt to be concerned about your long-term satisfaction with his product and service after the sale. You should expect better long-term service after you deal with the happy person.

Then too, if you don't enjoy doing the activity, you won't be doing it long . . . you will be moving on from one thing to another and never becoming successful with anything . . . until you actually find something you enjoy. Potential for long-term service after the sale will be limited when someone is unhappy in their job.

If they think it's fun . . .
The battle is half won.
Success comes often . . .
When your smile reflects the sun.

25AA. INSIGHT 27: ANY OTHER WAY OF GETTING RICH IS A WASTE OF LIFE, FROM *A MILLIONAIRE'S NOTEBOOK: HOW ORDINARY PEOPLE CAN ACHIEVE EXTRAORDINARY SUCCESS*, COPYRIGHT 1996, BY STEVEN K. SCOTT.

Scott no doubt was speaking about personal habits pertaining to approaching life and success using these twenty-seven insights as guidance or a career map . . .

1: Past achievement is not a true predictor of future success.
2: If you can do one thing well, even if it doesn't seem significant, you have the potential for phenomenal success.
3: Take a close look and discover what "insignificant" successes you have had and focus on them. They could well become the foundation of your future achievement.
4: Past failures don't have to limit your future.
5: "Three strikes you're out" applies only in baseball.
6: Work to meet your needs, but dream to get ahead.
7: Don't let small minds limit your thinking.
8: "Young and inexperienced" is not a valid reason to ignore or stifle creative ideas and activities.
9: You may be a lot smarter than your bosses.
10: A person who believes in you is a tremendous source of power.
11: Don't be greedy; share the wealth; don't hoard it.
12: Whom you work for is as important as what you do.
13: There is no greater motivation than love.
14: Commitment and motivation are more important than credentials or resumes.
15 It is important to overestimate the incredible worth of the right partners (friends, teammates, mate).
16: Do everything you can to make those you work with successful.
17: Share the wealth.
18: Consumers (people who you are trying to convince to need you and what you have to offer) are a lot smarter than you think.
19: Artistic swells. Logic sells.
20: You have to take a lot of swings to hit a lot of home runs.
21: No recriminations for failures.
22: Shoot for the moon. If you miss, you're still high!

23: Prepare. Do your homework.
24: Go for it.
25: Minimize the losses. Share the winnings.
26: If it's not fun, you probably won't succeed.
27: Any other way of getting rich is a waste of life.

Succeeding in life by hook or crook . . .
Is not worth another look.
These tips offer a playbook . . .
And that, my friend, you can book!

26

"How To Be The Best," My Conversation With Jimmy Johnson, *Rush Limbaugh Newsletter*, June 1996.

26A. "TWO THINGS MAKE A CHAMPION. PRIDE AND WORK. I DON'T KNOW THAT I'VE EVER BEEN AROUND A CHAMPION, A TRUE CHAMPION YEAR IN AND YEAR OUT, UNLESS HE WAS WORKING, ALWAYS TRYING TO GET BETTER."

In simplistic terms, true pride and work make a champion.

Work, practice, passion (maybe this is pride too), dedication, commitment, among dozens of other similar words, reflect the energy that must go into being the best in any field of endeavor. And the work, or practice, must be targeted at being the best. It does absolutely no good to undergo a mediocre practice because that will prepare you to be good and mediocre and not among the best.

The champion also has pride and refuses to see himself or herself as a loser and just refuses to lose. Champions appreciate what it takes to win and repeat that performance time after time attaining the status of champion. The pride of a champion prevents the champion from losing to a person of equal ability and preparation. Hard work keeps the ability of the champion at a very high level.

With that combination of work and pride, the champion is a formidable competitor and is not likely to lose.

Jimmy has convinced me.
He knows how to be . . . above the rest.
With work and pride, you too can be . . .
The best, a champion . . . this is no jest!

26B. "THE ONLY WAY I KNOW HOW TO PLAY THE GAME IS TO GIVE IT MY ALL," MY CONVERSATION WITH JIMMY JOHNSON, *RUSH LIMBAUGH NEWSLETTER*, JUNE 1996.

As long as you keep score, or anyone keeps track of the score at all, you must give it your best, give it your all. Given a situation of equals or peers, if the score is kept, let the other side deal with the loss. A small child is different; let the child be competitive. Always let him or her feel like he or she believes they have a chance, and do let them win once in a while.

There is no reason whatsoever to do something, which outcome you or anyone else considers important enough to keep score, and you only put forth a half-speed effort, then lose.

If you are to be a champion, you must get in the habit of always putting forth the effort to be on top and be a winner. A sloppy effort here and a sloppy effort there, and before long, you will be good and sloppy, and no one will consider you the best at anything.

There will be times when the pitch might not go exactly where you want it to be. There will be times when the football doesn't have the zip. There will be times when you get blocked, and they score . . . but there should never ever be a time when your effort is anything less than 110 percent.

There is a fine line . . .
Between the great and ones on top, the top guns.
No matter how you spend your time,
Whether you are pitching or scoring hits and runs,
Your speed should be above a percent of ninety-nine!

26C. "AS HEAD COACH, I (JIMMY JOHNSON) DO THREE THINGS:

* One, bring in people committed to being the very best;
* Two, eliminate people not committed to being the very best; and
* Three, create an atmosphere so they can be the best,"

from "How To Be the Best," My Conversation with Jimmy Johnson, *Rush Limbaugh Newsletter*, June 1996.

Coaches, managers, and crew chiefs need to associate themselves with quality people who are committed to being the very best. As long as you can be selective with whom you associate, choose to be with people who are committed to excellence. Being around people committed to being the best spreads to everyone involved. Similarly, the attitude of one negative, pessimistic person who just doesn't care can and probably will spread.

* One, bring in people committed to being the very best.
  When you can choose and you are involved with an activity where the score is kept, choose people who can be counted on to do their best and really try to win. Given equal ability, always pick the person who always gives it his or her best; you can count on them. While others may be with you, trying . . . part of the time . . . because of one mood or another, they may not be totally there to help deal with the real issues at hand.
* Two, eliminate people not committed to being the very best.
  As indicated earlier, someone without a commitment to be the best can be a source of discontentment or negativism in your organization. Negative talk and discontentment flow from being around someone who is not giving their best. Allow them to move on as soon as possible.
* Three, create an atmosphere so they can be the best.
  People who are committed to being the best need less directing because they are actually thinking about how to be their best. They will not need to be told what to do to improve or will only need to be told once. They will be thinking ahead of you and will be focused on achieving the best. And with people all thinking how they can be the best with the team, perhaps the team can also be the best. That will be the challenge for the coach; how can the best people mesh together for the team to be the best?

The coach will need to establish opportunities for there to be win-win situations for all the teammates and the team. With a win-win situation for all the players, the team should be very successful. Similarly, with most activities in the business world involving teams, and most business situations involving a team concept, these comments accurately depict the manager's role in creating the most productive situation for the company/business and team settings.

People committed to being the very best;
Will be ready to exceed life's test.
Pick positive teammates above the rest . . .
And let them keep their zest.
Success after success will lead to a fest.

27

My American Journey, By Colin Powell, Copyright 1995. Colin Powell's Rules:

27A. IT AIN'T AS BAD AS YOU THINK. IT WILL LOOK BETTER IN THE MORNING.

No matter how good you are, no matter how hard you try to be the best, there will be times when the best results do not occur for you. It may be the project you attempt, it may be the test you prepare for and do poorly, it may be the key situation in the ballgame and you pop up, it may be the key business deal and you don't make the sale, or it may be the big case you can't solve.

Never be forced into making an assessment of the performance immediately after the event, later that afternoon, or even that evening. There is just too much passion immediately after the event, and there is no value in being forced into assessing the performance.

Jog, work out, play some unrelated sport: be active and don't vegetate in front of the TV and don't rehash the event with anyone.

Get a good night's sleep, and then when you are fresh, it will look much better the next morning.

Then talk to advisors, think through the event in which you did not perform up to your expectations and make one or two corrections, practice them a day or two, and then move on into the next exciting day filled with opportunities to be your best.

Problems faced at the end of the day . . .
Will always seem bigger by double or triple, or so.
A tired mind and body will get in the way.
A night's rest will help, I know.
Listen to what the general and I have to say!

27B. GET MAD, THEN GET OVER IT, FROM *MY AMERICAN JOURNEY*, BY COLIN POWELL.

Deal with issues or conflicts head on, and don't let them continue in a simmering manner. If you have to get mad, that is the way it is, but absolutely seek to engage in every conflict situation from the standpoint that you should resolve conflicts with each individual by getting something out of it. In each situation, negotiate to a win-win situation.

This discussion is not about the need to get mad. This discussion is about dealing with issues and not letting them fester or simmer without a conclusion.

Some people, try to get by with as much as they can without intending to allow the other party to win. People often approach the situations in life with the idea that situations will end with a "they win, the other party loses," and the winner will be happy and they don't care about the loser. Perhaps with their family history, that is their experience. They haven't learned yet that if someone disagrees with them, the other party might believe in what the party are saying very strongly and might not be willing to automatically agree to a friendly win-win conclusion. If you persist, the other part may get angry. Their passion may be difficult to overcome.

The same applies to you if you approach things with a win-win attitude, but the other party insists on a "you lose, and they win" approach. There is going to be a problem.

Part of the trouble here is that the other person doesn't really think the situation is a win-win situation or a win-you lose situation at all. They just do not think, period, and the things they do are done out of their not thinking more than intentionally doing something to make you lose. Examples might be someone in your organization or close to you spending more than their budget. Another situation is a political discussion with both sides being so polarized that it is impossible to achieve a win-win situation in any case; or another example might be someone using shared equipment and not putting it back or changing the place where something is stored and doesn't tell you. Another example might be the other person agrees to do something and then doesn't do it and fails because they did not try very hard.

After a few repetitions of that, perhaps you might get angry or mad. Going around sulking and pouting and grouchy for some unknown reason to them will not solve the issue. Meet the issue/problem head on, get angry if you have to, and then set a situation up where you both can win and move on. Often, once people realize that they won't get by without being fair, their behavior will change. Help them turn it around. If that is not possible, happily move on.

Get mad if you must!
It may take that to win their trust.
Do what you must, then move on.
A flame that simmers is not gone.
Help them but it will take crust.

27C. AVOID HAVING YOUR EGO SO CLOSE TO YOUR POSITION THAT WHEN YOUR POSITION FALLS, YOUR EGO GOES WITH IT, FROM *MY AMERICAN JOURNEY*, BY COLIN POWELL.

Your ego should be built around two primary areas of your intellect: first, your faith in God and Jesus and the knowledge that you have an opportunity to spend eternity in Heaven. And, second, the knowledge that you are very good at doing at least one thing and always will try to do your best under the current situation. Having the reputation as a person with at least a partial vision toward Jesus and God as well as always doing your best and that you are very good at something or a few things will be a great foundation for a very healthy ego.

Decision making in many of our activities today is a group decision and must be made through consensus building with peers or subordinates. The consensus-building process allows everyone to collect enough information to make a sound decision which can be supported and enjoyed by everyone. Making the decision too early or without sufficient information will cause ego and other problems too.

In sports, say, baseball for example, the athlete must make the final decision as to style of throwing and hitting. That is acceptable, but if the success is not there, you need to make adjustments; listen to the coaches. If you are extremely successful, you make the decisions, especially if you are not open to advice.

Develop a position or vision, which will be the long-term direction of your energies. Along the way, there will be opportunities for numerous situations, which are interactions with teammates, peers, office mates, co-workers, and the like. These interactions are opportunities for win-win situations that will not require anyone's ego to go down in flames. Instead, that can be building to everyone's ego if properly formulated.

There are few decisions in life relative to sports or business or most anything in which the decision is worth a fight. Your life, other people's life, your reputation, and your future are a few examples that are worth fighting over. More than your ego, your life, the life of others, and your long-term future are worth taking firm, long-term positions. In most other areas, you can avoid having your ego so close to your position that should your position falls, your ego will not go with it.

Your ego is a wonderful tool
Your ego can lead you to or away from being a fool.
Because of ego, you can be stubborn as a mule.
Take charge over ego . . . you make the rule!

27D. IT CAN BE DONE! FROM *MY AMERICAN JOURNEY*, BY COLIN POWELL.

It is great being around people, individuals, who always think, "It can be done." The great events of our time or any time are created by people who think just that way.

People whose immediate reaction to any pending task or objective is "it can be done" are wonderful to work with. And it really is true; just about anything can be done. The only issue is, is it worth the effort? First, decide if it can be done. Then undergo a complete analysis to determine exactly what it will take to accomplish the task. At that point, you all can decide whether accomplishing the task is worth making the effort. The question is, is it worth the effort because most everything can be done or achieved?

This is clearly contrasted with others whose first reaction to a situation is that it can't be done, and they are willing to provide a complete listing of all the problems, which will keep you or your group from accomplishing the task.

My advice is to be a "can do" type person. You will accomplish more; your associates will accomplish more; and you all will be enriched in many ways for your positive attitude.

Avoid the "can't do" people and especially do not be a can't-do person yourself!

It can be done.
There is always a way under the sun.
Any task from great, great, great . . .
To lifting a two-pound weight . . .
Can be done first and the best . . .
By one who has a positive quest.

27E. BE CAREFUL WHAT YOU CHOOSE; YOU MAY GET IT, FROM *MY AMERICAN JOURNEY*, BY COLIN POWELL.

Actually choosing what you want to do in life might result in your achieving that goal. Making a choice, having a vision, is a key tool in accomplishing something in life beyond just doing the things that come totally natural, such as an hourly job at the tire store, a house full of kids, and a six-pack of beer on Saturday night. The word "choose" is the key. Be careful what you choose. You may get it.

The caution about getting what you choose is legitimate. Often young people choose a life's vision based on what their parents have done with their lives or what in their limited experience makes an impression upon them. Young people often set their vision early or have no vision at all about what they want to accomplish. That allows them to wander without a purpose for what they are doing in grade school and high school—maybe even in college. Math is boring; why do I need math? Why is history important? Or why is literature or poetry important?

How can they know if math or literature or history is important if they don't know what they will be doing?

That is why it is important for parents to set high scholastic standards for the young person until the young person knows what he or she will need along life's path.

Be careful about what you choose or let happen. Without careful thought and planning, your limited vision will make the life decisions for you. You certainly will accomplish more with your life by setting your vision yourself after thoughtful and guided preparation!

Choose what you want to be.
Be what you carefully choose.
Life can be years of glee!
But without a plan, you are likely to lose.
Looking back, you will clearly see.
With a vision of life, you will see blessings by twos.

27F. DON'T LET ADVERSE FACTS STAND IN THE WAY OF A GOOD DECISION, FROM *MY AMERICAN JOURNEY*, BY COLIN POWELL.

Make decisions only after you have enough information to believe your decision has a reasonable chance for being successful.

Very seldom, though, are all the facts lined up on one side in support of the decision you are considering. More often than not, there are facts in support of both choices, and the skill is to make the right choice; the one that most of the facts support.

This admonition is to not move too quickly into the decision phase by going ahead and making the decision, and then later . . . after being asked . . . trying to explain why you did something. It is much easier to collect the information you need in advance, think in advance before you act. And then ask yourself is there enough information to convince me that I should do it . . . should I make the decision? I also could say . . . never let the decision be made by inaction or just insufficient action.

The point to all this is, think and prepare before you act; know what you are going to do something and why you did it. Life's decisions are seldom black and white. Make sure the preponderance of facts in your own mind support the decisions you are about to make. Adverse facts will always be there, but after considering the preponderance of information, don't let the adverse facts stand in the way of a good decision.

Know why you act.
Never move without the fact.
Before, it is easier to ask and know why.
Than after and they all think it is a lie.

27G. YOU CAN'T MAKE SOMEONE ELSE'S CHOICE. YOU SHOULDN'T LET SOMEONE ELSE MAKE YOURS, FROM *MY AMERICAN JOURNEY*, BY COLIN POWELL.

Ultimately, each person must make his or her own decisions and choices. Ultimately, your choices are yours to make, and someone else should not be making your choices and decisions.

Man to man, woman to woman, so to speak, as an adult, your choices are yours to make, and someone else should not be making your choices.

As a baby and a child, this is not the case. Also, for people whose health has failed, they may not be able to make their own decisions; most of their decisions have to be made for them.

A baby has nearly all of his or her decisions made for him or her. Gradually, as the baby grows into a young child, and into a preteen and to a teenager, the young person begins to make more and more of his or her decisions. The degree of independence and the percentage of one's decisions will be proportional to the wisdom exhibited by the young person in the decisions they do make. The extreme in making very few of one's own decisions is the case of the person in prison or otherwise incarcerated. People in prison make very few of their own decisions. This predicament follows from their very poor record of making the decisions when they had a chance.

Given a normal youth, ranging in age from, say, thirteen to twenty-two, the degree of freedom you have and the percentage of time you will be forced to let someone else make your decisions will be largely dependent on you. Make bad decisions, and you will not have many opportunities to continue making your own decisions. Make good decisions and win the respect of the people around you, and you quickly increase the percentage of your own decisions you make.

Freedom to choose?
What do you have to lose?
Much . . . and a lot to gain . . .
As long as you maintain . . .
Life's thoughtful strategy!
Your decisions may make you seem like a prodigy.

27H. CHECK SMALL THINGS, FROM *MY AMERICAN JOURNEY*, BY COLIN POWELL.

Check the small things! Often it's the small things that separate you from your peers. Again, it's the small things that make the difference between the near great and the great. Having a vision is one of those small things critical to your being above the crowd.

The things that separate the 500 hitter and the 250 hitter are the small things. More than "keeping your eye on the ball," hitting is getting good advice and doing what the advisor tells you what to do . . . and practice. The 500 hitter needs a vision and desire to be good and must have a vision of achieving success in hitting a baseball. And the 500 hitter practices hitting off-speed slow pitches and practices hitting outside curve balls or inside fast balls. A 500 hitter must work very hard at being good. The 500 hitter must work at building strength and must be quick and have outstanding hand-to-eye coordination perfected with lot and lots of practice. These are individually small things, but taken all together, they add up.

The things that separate the A student from the C+ student are the small things. An A student takes notes; an A student works at really knowing the material. The A student doesn't just read the pages in the book; the A student really learns and tries to understand what is being taught. The A student makes it a point to actually learn the material, while the C+ student considers it enough to read the material. The difference between reading and actually knowing is significant. This is a small thing but very significant.

The things that separate the company president from the parts manager in the far-off district office are the small things. The company president has had a vision guiding his or her actions for a long time. With a vision of where he or she is going, the company president has made the career moves and secured the right education along the way to be at the right place at the right time. Without a vision, it is hard to make the sacrifices along the way necessary to move to the top. Sacrifices such as the extra long hours and commensurate absences from the family often must be offered for the success. The company parts manager might be just as intelligent and just as hard working. But without the long-term vision and other planning necessary, he or she advanced in career status but stopped along way before reaching the top of the organization.

The things that separate the Washington politician and the precinct committeeman are the small things. The Washington politician saw the precinct committeeman position as a stepping stone to the next and to the next and to the next level of elective office, while the precinct committeeman saw the job as a way to get involved while maintaining the regular job. The Washington politician had the vision of what he or she wanted to do, long term, and made the sacrifices along the way to move up the step-by-step process.

It's the small things.
No matter if you wish to sing,
To hit a ball or maybe its pitching . . .
Success along the way is more than wishing.
Small things add up to your achieving.

271. SHARE CREDIT, FROM *MY AMERICAN JOURNEY*, BY COLIN POWELL.

Every person of achievement on earth has someone or several someones who have helped her or him along the way. Share the joy, share the excitement, share the credit with them.

A vision of what the young person wants to do and where the young person wants to go is important and necessary for absolute success ascending to the highest levels of business or other vocational activities. But setting a vision any time will be helpful in elevating the person's lifetime success. Along the way, there will be numerous co-workers, supervisors, managers, and others who are participants in the same tasks and objectives who are also instrumental in the success of the venture. Share the credit with them!

During the educational process, there will be motivators and mentors who are instrumental with establishing the lifetime vision. Consequently, they are extremely helpful in establishing the direction and in achieving the success of the student. Share the credit later when success comes, and it will—to the young person who sets a vision.

Early in life, it may only take one person or the young person's parents who provide the motivation and mentoring to help with establishing the vision. Whether it is a lifetime in competitive sports, a lifetime of involvement in sports activities or recreational sports participation, the parents or someone close will be the ones to help the young person establish the vision to be inspired to head toward sports activities. Share the credit for the focus of your particular activity and for the considerable support necessary from family and friends.

Early in life, it can be a close family members, friend or parents who mentor and motivate the young person to develop interests and setting a vision toward a life of computer programming or animals or medicine or historical research. When the interest is developed early, the young person is blessed with a lifelong vision, which can be enriched, expanded, and revised throughout life. Share the credit later when success comes, and it will—to the young person who sets a vision early.

Credit is more than reading a list at your award.
Credit can be the recognition of your mentors.
Credit can be more than the victory you move toward.
Credit is deserved by all the victors.

27J. REMAIN CALM. BE KIND, FROM *MY AMERICAN JOURNEY*, BY COLIN POWELL.

In all situations throughout life, it should be your personal style to remain calm and be kind to other people and things.

No matter how stressful the situation is, and there will be many of them... be calm and kind to others. And this will be increasingly more challenging as you get older and are involved in more and more activities.

Ideally, throughout life, your challenges increase as your ability to deal with them also increases. The role of a parent and mentor comes in here to allow the difficulties and challenges to increase as your maturity and ability grows with your age. In all cases, the parents and mentors should be calm and kind to you. Not all of them will be kind and calm, but they should be, and you should expect it.

You have an obligation to be calm and kind with your parent and mentors, your peers and your subordinates. Always treat them with respect and give them an opportunity to preserve their dignity. Always give others an opportunity for a win-win situation.

You can really tell what is in a person's heart by the way they treat others, the way they treat those who are less fortunate, and how they treat animals. Absolutely avoid people who are cruel to animals.

Excessive excitement versus controlled excitement and passion defocuses the brain and makes a reasoned approach more difficult.

Being calm in life's experiences comes from life experiences. As you experience situations the second, third, fourth time, your ability to remain calm will improve, and you will truly be calm in situations that excited you earlier. Largely, early life's experiences are practice for later experiences in life.

Calm: Oh sure, remain calm he says with a grin.
Knowing full well that as practice seeps in.
Calmness will prevail for one whose kin...
Has seen the need for preparation to begin.

Thomas R. Wallin

Kind: Always be kind, there has to be a way.
Give people a win, give them their day.
Show them kindness and respect come what may . . .
Your day will be a success . . . you can say.

27K. HAVE A VISION. BE DEMANDING, FROM *MY AMERICAN JOURNEY*, BY COLIN POWELL.

Set a vision or direction of where you want to be and when. And similar to past statements in this book, set the bar high enough because you will certainly easily achieve "low bars" and the "low hanging fruit" . . . early.

Starting out in life without a vision is like playing the game of baseball and running the base paths from third to first to home to second and wondering why you are not successful at the sport.

Or in football, playing life without a vision would be like starting on a march down the field and then heading off into the stands and later heading crossing off to the other side before going back in the direction from which you started rather than heading down the field.

Similarly, starting life without a vision would be like studying history by studying the events of 1997 and then studying the events around sixty million BC and then studying events around 1492 and then studying the events around the time of Jesus.

All of these make no sense, and it would similarly make no sense to start out in life without a vision of where you want to go and when you want to be there. I hope this point gets made here in these words, and I hope the topic was adequately covered. A vision for a young person is both a gold mine of possibilities for life and critical for achieving success near to one's true potential.

Identify things you like to do and then develop a vision for ways to incorporate favorite activities into lifestyles that you seek and you enjoy doing.

Always remember to set the bar high enough because you will certainly achieve "low bars" and will be able to pick the "low hanging fruit" very easily with the focus of a vision. With a vision, you can and will achieve much and will be very happy with your life . . . both during life's events and then later, much later, looking back to reflect on events during middle age. Set the bar high. Without a vision of high expectations, you are not likely to achieve anywhere near your potential and reflecting will be emotionally painful.

Thomas R. Wallin

A vision can be like a key . . .
Doors will open, you will surely see!
Choose the door carefully . . .
Make sure the door for thee . . .
Goes to where you know you want to be!

27L. DON'T TAKE COUNSEL OF YOUR FEARS OR NAYSAYERS, FROM *MY AMERICAN JOURNEY*, BY COLIN POWELL.

Take counsel, listen to advice, study the situation, and use whatever good information you can collect concerning topics about which you are preparing to make a decision. Always think of the results your decision will bring about before you make the decision to do something. If you still want to go ahead, when you can anticipate the results, take the action of your decision.

It would be a mistake to only, when preparing to make a decision, think about the negative results or to only "listen to" your own personal fears or to negative people or naysayers.

Take counsel, listen to advice, study the situation from as many perspectives as you have time, but do consider all possibilities including your fears, the opinions of the naysayers, and unintended consequence.

Use whatever good information you can collect about topics when you are preparing to make a decision. Always think of the results your decision will bring about before you do something. If you still want to go ahead, anticipating full well what the results are likely to be, take the action of your decision.

Remember it will be much more pleasant to answer questions why you are thinking through the anticipated results of your decision than it will be to try to explain why you did something without thinking.

Don't take from one but be sure to take . . .
Take advice from all, including naysayers.
Listening only to "yes men" would too be a mistake!
The "OK-ers" find it easy but it takes more than prayers.
Hear both sides, make your move . . . sift though the layers.
The decision is yours to make.

27M. PERPETUAL OPTIMISM IS A FORCE MULTIPLIER, FROM *MY AMERICAN JOURNEY*, BY COLIN POWELL.

Thinking that you can do something is half the battle. Always thinking that something can be done is a big advantage. It is always better to be around an optimist who always thinks on the positive side, such as the proverbial glass is always half full rather than half empty.

Absolutely, the positive approach is the best and will be a big advantage for you in life. The positive approach must be coupled with the study of what it also takes beyond just the will and expectation to succeed. You must prepare and be ready to do what is necessary to accomplish the task when the time comes.

Even the Little Engine that Could had to exert the supereffort beyond just thinking that he, the engine, could. The engine did all that was necessary to pull the train over the mountain. From past experiences, from which he learned, the little engine knew he would need extra coal and water for steam. And he brought the coal and water with him. If he hadn't brought the extra supplies, no matter how good his intentions were, he would not have been able to pull the train over the mountain. He had the experience to know what was necessary, and he learned from those experiences.

Being teamed with others who have the same values system and motivation can definitely be a force multiplier. When there are multiple people on the same team and in the same group who have the same values and abilities, your skills will all be enhanced. And the opposition will not be able to focus on just one aspect of your organization. You all will be the better for being part of a group with great ability and positive mental attitude.

An optimist is the way to be.
Friends who are positive are a victory.
With several thinking that there has to be a way.
You will win on most everyday!

28

Pres. James A. Garfield's Cherished Personal Principles:

Thanks to some factual information from a *World Book Encyclopedia*, the following background information about President Garfield is provided.

James A. Garfield was the twentieth president of the United States and was only in office a few months before he was assassinated by a disappointed job seeker. He lived from 1831 to 1881 and was the last president to be born in a log cabin; that was in Ohio. He was the fourth president to die in office and was the second president to be assassinated.

Before becoming president, President Garfield was successful as a professor, college president, Civil War general, U.S. congressman and senator. He studied at colleges in Ohio and Massachusetts and also studied law and religion. Garfield rose to the rank of major general during the Civil War and distinguished himself for bravery and as a successful leader.

Garfield spoke and wrote well, read widely, and even composed poetry. He married Lucretia Rudolph on November 11, 1858, and they had five children, ranging in age at his death from eight to seventeen. She lived to be eighty-eight.

He was elected to Congress in the House of Representatives nine times and was elected to the U.S. Senate once. Before he took office in the

Senate, he was selected by the Republicans as a compromise candidate for the office of president in 1880. He was elected over Winfield Scott Hancock, the Democrat, by the small margin of 0.4 percent of the national vote.

A rejected job seeker shot Garfield on July 2, 1881 when he was traveling to attend the twenty-fifth anniversary reunion of his class at Williams College in Williamstown, Massachusetts.

His Cherished Personal Principles certainly do not warrant the same attention as the Ten Commandments of God, but I think they are sound and deserve attention in this writing. Although he was a religious man and occasionally preached at his Disciples of Christ Church, the principles are not religious and do not mention God and mankind's relationship with God.

His principles do offer excellent lifestyle suggestions, which deserve our attention and could serve as a model for our own personal principles.

28A. "NEVER BE IDLE", ONE OF PRES. JAMES A. GARFIELD'S CHERISHED PERSONAL PRINCIPLES.

Never be idle! Never be idle? How can that be . . . in a society that seems to be pushing more and more leisure time?

Never be idle is not an admonition to never participate in recreational activities or entertaining activities. No, I do not believe the "never be idle" statement goes that far. All activities should be part of your life's plan, and certainly an amount of entertainment and recreation will be warranted.

You should never be idle watching television because you can do any number of things while you watch television. Activities from folding and ironing clothes to writing checks to pay bills to reading the paper during slow times or commercials or sorting pictures to putting pictures in photo albums. The time does not have to be idle time. You can be very productive while watching television.

Some of your best personal planning and creative thinking can be done while you are jogging or other forms of exercising or while you are driving down lonesome, desolate sections of highways. Otherwise, the driving times will be idle except for guiding the vehicle. Surely you have enough brain power to do both, drive the vehicle safely, and plan and think about your life's vision. Now, if there are other people in the car and you are trying to drive, talk with the person, and think and plan about your future career or life in general, that might be a little much.

Overall, keep as much of your time productive, and not idle, as you can. Your life will be fuller and more satisfying to you. Your ego will be more satisfied, and you certainly will accomplish much more during a given amount of time than the person who allows idle time to creep significantly into his or her schedule.

Idle time is a time waste.
Years may be retrieved from the reapers trash.
Use that time, make haste.
Captured time is better than cash!

28B. "MAKE FEW PROMISES", ONE OF PRES. JAMES A. GARFIELD'S CHERISHED PERSONAL PRINCIPLES.

Make few promises. A promise is a commitment that you make, and you are obligated to fulfill all of your promises or commitments. Never make a commitment to any more than you can produce.

Most of us, myself definitely included, want to please other people, and our inclination is to make promises of things we'll do or try to do for others. This often brings out an old saying of letting our alligator mouth overload our hummingbird digestive system. We want to please and as a result, get ourselves overcommitted.

Do your best. Do all you can do, but don't feel compelled to promise to do more than you can absolutely do . . . well.

Commitments/promises are good and essential, just don't make too many of them, and don't make promises that you can't keep.

Commitments/promises to yourself, such as always doing your best, are important and must be made and kept.

Commitments/promises to family are important and must be made and must be kept.

Commitments/promises to friends are important and can be made and must be kept.

Commitments/promises to a spouse are important and must be made and must be kept.

Commitments/promises to God's commandments, Jesus, and God must be made and must be kept.

When it is all said and done,
A promise can't be limited to just one.
There is one for everything under the sun.
That's already enough to make one run!

28C. "ALWAYS SPEAK THE TRUTH", ONE OF PRES. JAMES A. GARFIELD'S CHERISHED PERSONAL PRINCIPLES.

There is no requirement to speak, but if you do . . . speak the truth. Tell it accurately and truthfully.

You must have the reputation of always speaking the truth. People, including your parents, family, and friends, must know that if any word comes out of your mouth, it will be the truth or an accurate portrayal of what you absolutely believe to be true. People need to be able to trust one another. If you speak the truth, always, it will be a wonderful asset for life. When issues come up, they will always feel safe coming to you for the truth because that is the reputation you earned and deserved.

It may be difficult sometimes. What happens for instance if you make a mistake and break something or get into a fender bender with the car? The problem has already occurred, and the issue is, how do you tell parents or the people who own the car that their property has been damaged? Tell them the truth, and do it as soon as possible. You can assume, you can be assured, that they will eventually find out about what you did anyway.

Not telling the truth will only make the second error, which will compound the first when the physical damage is done. Both the property and your credibility are damaged.

The trick is to think through what you intend to do and avoid the mistake that causes the damage in the first place. Then, you will not have to think up excuses for why you did something and worry about not telling the truth when describing what happened.

The truth keeps your life in glory . . .
Is more than an allegory.
Burdens add up . . . on your mind . . .
When facts differ from your story.
With truth, life will be more kind.

28D. "LIVE WITHIN YOUR INCOME", ONE OF PRES. JAMES A. GARFIELD'S CHERISHED PERSONAL PRINCIPLES.

Live within your income. Spend less money than you bring home. Use credit cards only to the extent that you will be able to pay them off when you receive the statement at the end of the month.

Many of life's problems are caused by not living within one's income.

Single individuals, couples, retired people, businesses, partnerships, corporations, and . . . yes, it's hard to believe . . . even governments all need a budget, a plan for allocating their income and outflow. While this is not meant to be a detailed family-budgeting dissertation, I will offer some observations and tips for family budgeting.

First, list all available income for spending. Income already accumulating inside IRAs, 401Ks, insurance policies, and the like should not be included in the spending plan but obviously should be considered as a part of your overall savings plan.

Second, identify all the spending categories that will be in your budget: savings, emergency fund, investments, housing (rent/mortgage/real-estate taxes), insurance, utilities (gas, electricity, water, refuse hauling, cable, phone, and Internet provider), transportation, contributions to the Republican party, and entertainment.

Third, allocate your income among all the budgeting categories included above—starting with savings a minimum of 10 percent and an emergency fund of 5 percent until the emergency fund will cover three months' income. If your income stretches to adequately cover all categories, you have a budget. As your income rises, your budget can be adjusted accordingly. If your income doesn't stretch to cover all categories, make adjustments but not to savings and emergency fund contributions. You must continue savings, and you will not regret that decision several years down the road. Make cuts in other budget items until projected income equals projected expenses. If that won't work, become an entrepreneur or take a second or third job to supplement your income.

The fourth and next step is to put into practice the budget and actually live with the budget. If you are part of a couple, the most difficult aspect of budgeting is yet to come—that is, to implement and live with the budget. Living with the constraints of a budget is important and almost impossible for some to do. If you or your partner have a difficult time following the constraints of a budget, then life will be difficult when you try to jointly follow the budget document. Having the cooperation of a mate is extremely important.

Live within your means . . . you say?
Spend less than you make.
This seems like an easy way . . .
To have a plan . . . for your future's sake!

28F. "NEVER SPEAK EVIL OF ANYONE", ONE OF PRES. JAMES A. GARFIELD'S CHERISHED PERSONAL PRINCIPLES.

There is an old saying . . . if you don't have anything good to say, don't say anything at all.

Rather than speaking evil of any person, by far the best thing to do is just avoid them totally.

If you speak evil of another person, what are you accomplishing?

Getting something off your chest?

Making yourself look better by making them look bad?

If these describe what you think you are accomplishing.
None of these strategies will work or develop into anything for which you are proud to be associated.

Speaking evil of another person may allow you to verbalize your frustration, but it will not be "off your chest." In fact, there is a strong likelihood that the issue will just get worse, especially if what you say gets back to the person about whom you were speaking.

Saying something bad or evil about another person will cause the person to whom you are currently speaking to be leery of you because they will wonder if you will speak evil of them as soon as you are out of their presence. Their comfort level of being around you will diminish. You watch their face and actions after you speak to them. Notice how their relationship with you cools.

Trying to accomplish nothing but speaking evil about another person anyway does not make any sense. Stop that!

Speak evil of no one . . .
I wish could be our cue.
And for everyone under the sun . . .
I wish would follow this too.

28F. "KEEP GOOD COMPANY OR NONE", ONE OF PRES. JAMES A. GARFIELD'S CHERISHED PERSONAL PRINCIPLES.

Keep good company or none at all. Who your friends are is important.

People can, or think they can, tell a great deal about you by the friends you keep. If your friends are all national merit scholars, Eagle Scouts, and high honor roll members, you will be judged to be one kind of person. If your friends are all school dropouts, wear black clothes, wear extrabig sizes, have long greasy hair and earrings, nose rings and tattoos, they will come to another conclusion.

And I firmly believe that there is a high probability that a person will be directly influenced by the people with whom they associate. Your value system will be influenced or tempted by your associates.

The best defense against undue influence by others is to have a fixed set of principles and an acknowledged value system. With these as a base, even the most negative peer pressure will have a tough time having any influence on you.

Garfield's position was, if your friends are not the clean cut, lawful type, it would be better to have no friends at all.

Keep good company or none at all.
Pals are important to chat with and affirm.
Sharing thoughts and times is a ball.
Similar thoughts and values you will confirm.

28G. "LIVE UP TO YOUR ENGAGEMENTS", ONE OF PRES. JAMES A. GARFIELD'S CHERISHED PERSONAL PRINCIPLES.

Do what you say, say it, and do it.

An engagement is a promise of appearance; you must appear when and where you say, and when and where you have agreed to appear. Living up to your commitment to engagements can be stated and manifested in actions many ways.

What a compliment it would be for you to be known as someone who does what they say and someone who commits to something and then does what they say.

Make few promises of appearance or engagement as with promises in general.

Most of us, myself definitely included, want to please other people, and our inclination is to make commitments of engagements to be nice to others. We do not wish to confront friends or associates because we do not want to disappoint them.

Do your best. Do all you can do, but don't feel compelled to commit to an engagement schedule more so than you can reasonably fulfill.

An engagement is that you will be ...
Exactly where you say ... you agree?
Too many places or times you will see,
Are an outright impossibility!

28H. "NEVER PLAY GAMES OF CHANCE", ONE OF PRES. JAMES A. GARFIELD'S CHERISHED PERSONAL PRINCIPLES.

"Never play games of chance" means never to gamble or bet on horses or play the lotto or play cards for money or go to the river boat to play slot machines or cards.

Most of President Garfield's principles are positives, such as "live within your means" or "keep your own secrets," but this principle is a statement of the negative: "Never play games of chance."

Negative statements such as this and "never be idle" or "don't marry until you can support a wife" or "never borrow if you can possibly help it" need to be tested against more all-encompassing standards of behavior such as the Ten Commandments or the rights of others protected by the U.S. Constitution and the Bill of Rights.

Of course you can be idle once in a while—maybe not often, but surely once in a while would be OK. The same for "don't marry until you can support a wife"; when *can* the normal person support a wife? First, today, most women want to work and do not need to be supported; women need to work for their own good if there are no young children in the home. Some women are like the liberals in Congress; they want more than they or you can afford anyway, so the time would never come to be able to marry them.

Games of chance range all across the board and are not prohibited by the Ten Commandments nor are they prohibited by laws. Excessive gambling can and has many, many times wrecked lives and families. If you have experienced excessive gambling wherein you started and did not stop until you lost all the money you had with you and money you could generate with you with credit cards, I definitely say, "Never play games of chance!"

On the other hand, if you occasionally play poker "with the boys" or play lotto weekly for $1 to $5, I truly see no problem with that. It must be small potatoes and done for entertainment and not for needed winnings. You must not play games of chance at all with family funds except for entertainment dollars, not food or shelter dollars.

Games of chance you say?
So you have never heard, much less had to play . . .
A game called chance in any way?
But the game comes to you each day . . .
From lotto to hearts to horses, to golf to croquette
All are fun but not for pay!

281. "DRINK NO INTOXICATING DRINKS", ONE OF PRES. JAMES A. GARFIELD'S CHERISHED PERSONAL PRINCIPLES.

There is a great deal of pleasure in waking up every morning feeling good and knowing that you have been in charge of your life over the past day or two.

Never become intoxicated; never drink more than two drinks.

Unlike some things you can do or take into your body, there may be some health advantage to drinking one or two drinks per day of red wine. The same thing may be accomplished by drinking red grape juice. But in any case, limit your consumption to two drinks per day.

As long as your age will allow you to legally drink intoxicating, alcoholic beverages, this is not one that I would make into an absolute. There is a balance, and there may be some health advantage.

The absolutes would be reserved for tobacco; do not smoke or chew, period. Do not smoke marijuana, pot. Do not take any drugs like cocaine, heroin, PCPs, or LSD. There are no positives to balance any of these. Avoidance should be an absolute.

Wine, beer, whiskey, and ale . . .
Are not drinks that I would push.
Yet still I would not wail!
Two will not make you a lush.

28J. "GOOD CHARACTER IS ABOVE EVERYTHING ELSE", ONE OF PRES. JAMES A. GARFIELD'S CHERISHED PERSONAL PRINCIPLES.

If there is one word that tells the story about you as a person, it is the word . . . "character." Your good character is important above all else.

Your character is a statement of how well you are perceived as telling the truth and basically how well you adhere to all of President Garfield's principles and the ten commandments plus one. You especially must be honest and have a reputation of never telling a lie. You do what you say, and you treat others consistent with the Ten Commandments and the Golden Rule.

You have to remember that character is very difficult to build and improve upon; it often takes many years to gain the reputation of having a flawless character. And while it may take years to build, character may only take a short time, one lie or error in judgment, to destroy or hold to tear it down sufficiently to lose what advantage you took years to build.

Hold character above all else because all of your good traits, hard work, and other actions supportive to others come together in the term . . . character.

> Character is at the peak,
> Many slip on their way to the top.
> Character is not for the weak.
> Don't let it stop!
> You are what you are, hopefully unique.

28K. "KEEP YOUR OWN SECRETS," ONE OF PRES. JAMES A. GARFIELD'S CHERISHED PERSONAL PRINCIPLES.

Never tell someone else something that you would not want to be spread all over town or school or the office.

Once you start telling others your secrets, you lose control and are dependent on them to keep the secret.

At any time, if your innermost personal thoughts or secrets are out in the open through your telling others, you are at their mercy to keep your secrets to themselves. This is not the kind of position you want to be in, and it is so easy to avoid. Just don't tell others your own secrets.

Telling your secrets is a needless loss of control. There is no need for this to occur. There is no need to tell what you would rather not have just anyone know.

A secret is not a secret once told.
If I were to remind you, am I being too bold?
Why would you tell someone, I scold . . .
Don't tell something you need not unload.

28L. "NEVER BORROW IF YOU CAN POSSIBLY HELP IT," ONE OF PRES. JAMES A. GARFIELD'S CHERISHED PERSONAL PRINCIPLES.

Never borrow money from a friend.

Never borrow money from the local mafia bookmaker.

Never borrow money from a family member.

Don't borrow money unless you believe you can pay it back easily out of current income cash flow. Only have one loan ongoing at a time in addition . . . perhaps . . . to a home mortgage.

While it is best to pay cash or debit card for things that you wish to purchase, it may be necessary from time to time to make purchases with a credit card or a short-term loan. Repay the credit card bill totally in your next. Paying for things in cash or debit card makes it much easier to know where you stand financially.

If you pay for all things with cash and if you know how much cash you have before and after the purchase, your financial problems will be minimized.

And if you don't borrow from friends or family, they will always be your friend and never your banker; it is best not to mix the two. And you won't be tempted to delay the payment or pay later and risk the friendship or lose the friendship altogether . . .

The local mafia bookmaker, loan shark, or your friendly credit card charge very high interest rates and make it very painful if you are, for some reason, not able to pay.

Borrowing money . . . it's done every day.
So I am not saying usury is rare.
Avoid taking the borrowing way,
And you will surely avoid that snare.

28M. "DO NOT MARRY UNTIL YOU ARE ABLE TO SUPPORT A WIFE," ONE OF PRES. JAMES A. GARFIELD'S CHERISHED PERSONAL PRINCIPLES.

Oh, brother, you would never be able to always support some women. The test here for you to consider is to never marry unless you are absolutely certain that both you and your prospective mate have the same tendencies regarding financial affairs.

It is not as though today, "in the '90s . . . twenty-first century," that you will be supporting her. You will be creating a life and a family together, and you need to be like minded when it comes to key issues of the day. Family finances are only one of the critical issues families face.

Timing today would be more related to "Are you ready to spend the rest of your life with this person?" You may not need to support her, but marriage, especially when children are involved, is a minimum of a twenty-year commitment and should be thought of as a lifetime commitment.

Don't marry until you are able to come to a complete agreement on what your family's approach to resources will be and how you will resolve conflicting opinions surely to arise later in life.

Bringing children into the world demands such a thought coordinated process as well. Do not have children until you are married and able to support and care for them. This is a critical reminder for today with so many children being born into families with only one parent around to nurture them and provide financial support.

Do not marry until what . . . you say?
Support is a minor issue for some women today!
Wait till you've been a couple for many a day . . .
Before children are brought into the fray.

28N. "WHEN YOU SPEAK TO A PERSON, LOOK INTO HIS EYES, ONE OF PRES. JAMES A. GARFIELD'S CHERISHED PERSONAL PRINCIPLES.

Eye contact when you speak seems like such a little thing yet such a big deal is made of it, or the lack of it, when you speak to someone or they speak to you. If you speak to someone and do not look at them straight in the eye, they are likely to think of you as a weak person or you are hiding something without the courage to look them in the eye.

People can talk or text for hours over the phone lines and not come close to seeing the other person to "look them straight in the eye." People can communicate over the Internet without the eye contact, and the process seems to work just fine. Authors communicate with the world through the printed word, and they do just fine without the big eye contact.

The point is, communication can be completed just fine without the eye contact, but the protocol for today is definitely eye contact when you are speaking to someone, face-to-face. When speaking face-to-face, you must operate by the rule; the protocol calls for the eye contact.

Eye contact is such a big deal'
In Garfield's time as well as now.
Without it you are judged . . . its real.
Play the game as your courage will allow!

280. "SAVE WHEN YOU ARE YOUNG TO SPEND WHEN YOU ARE OLD," ONE OF PRES. JAMES A. GARFIELD'S CHERISHED PERSONAL PRINCIPLES.

Make hay when the sun shines. When you have the opportunity, that is the time to build up your cash reserves sufficient so that when the sun goes down on your ability to earn, you will have accumulated sufficient reserves to be able to survive and spend when your are older.

People's working career begins after high school or college and extends until they retire at, say, sixty-five. They have as high as fifty years to work, but maybe only thirty or forty years of sound productive work to earn sufficient income and reserves, which will sustain the person throughout life plus provide sufficient reserves to have to spend when older.

Social Security did not exist in President Garfield's time, and if everyone thought the way he did, Social Security would never have been enacted into law.

Social Security is helpful to those who did not prepare for their old age and did not accumulate sufficient funds to adequately take care of their needs when older. Social Security though is way oversold as an answer to supplying funds to spend when you are old. The quality of life under Social Security will not be anywhere close to what it could be if you saved when you were young and throughout life for spending when you are older.

The May of your life will become a December day.
I compared it to putting up the hay.
Work and prepare for your own needs when you are old.
Start now . . . don't wait and have to be told!

28P. "NEVER RUN INTO DEBT UNLESS THERE IS A WAY OUT AGAIN," ONE OF PRES. JAMES A. GARFIELD'S CHERISHED PERSONAL PRINCIPLES.

Never borrow money unless you are absolutely sure that you have a plan to pay back the loan.

Do not borrow money unless it is for a house or a car. The rest you can do without until you have accumulated the funds to purchase the article outright without the loan.

Never use a credit card unless you can repay any total upon receipt of the statement. You should always expect to repay the loan upon receipt of the statement.

Never borrow from anyone except an institution equipped to issue the loan and then to administer the transaction until it is repaid. Don't borrow from relatives or friends.

Conversely, never loan money to relatives or friends.

If you can afford it, consider money transactions between yourself and friends as gifts; and if they repay the gift, all the better.

Money will always be one of the biggest issues you must deal with throughout life. Always have a financial plan of what you want to accomplish with your money and when.

The financial plan should center on retirement and money for when you stop working. Include all the major purchases you might make throughout life. Prepare your financial plan around your income, your purchases, and your long-term savings needs. This approach to finances will save you, my dear one, from much grief and anguish during your life.

Thou shalt not borrow money unless you can repay.
Is not something that I, to you, would say!
Except for a home and maybe a car, thou shalt not borrow!
Impatience with "having" will cause you much sorrow.

28Q. "GOOD COMPANY AND GOOD CONVERSATION ARE THE SINEWS OF VIRTUE," ONE OF PRES. JAMES A. GARFIELD'S CHERISHED PERSONAL PRINCIPLES.

"Virtue" is defined in *World Book Dictionary* as "moral excellence; goodness."

Conversation with good company is the reinforcing bars to the concrete of virtue. The reinforcing bars and concrete are folksy ways of saying the same thing as President Garfield's sinews of virtue. Sinews are the muscles that hold the human body together, and reinforcing bars are the inner strength that hold the concrete together.

Associating with good company is extremely vital and is one of the very important personal decisions you will make. Associating with principled, moral, and good people who seek goodness is extremely important and is critical to keeping the virtuous person virtuous.

Consequently, do what you do with principled, moral, and good people who seek goodness. Their ideas will inspire and motivate you, and your ideas will inspire and motivate them.

Conversations on the issues of the day are important to strengthen and reinforce your virtue, your principles, morality, and your goodness. Dormant virtues or thoughts relevant to virtues, without being strengthened and reinforced, become weaker and weaker.

Good company means surrounding yourself with the virtuous!
Dialoging with those of virtue keeps your heart pure.
You must search them out, they are not ubiquitous!
Conversation with good company is a lifestyle; it is not a cure.

28R. "YOUR CHARACTER CANNOT BE ESSENTIALLY INJURED EXCEPT THROUGH YOUR OWN ACTS," ONE OF PRES. JAMES A. GARFIELD'S CHERISHED PERSONAL PRINCIPLES.

Your character cannot be truly injured except through your own acts. However, it is your act when your friends act inappropriately . . . and you are along. Often, you will be judged as exhibiting inappropriate behavior if your friends and associates do not act appropriately and follow the rules.

Maybe key words in President Garfield's principle are the "essentially injured" phrase. Your own personal behavior should be the absolute gauge as to your reputation and how you are regarded by absolutely wise and fair-minded people. Yes, that is the way it should happen, but unfortunately, that is not the way it always occurs. In fact, usually, you are judged by the company you keep, and your character may be injured through simply your association with a certain group of people.

This subject is covered many times and in many ways in this book but is very important. You are judged by the company you keep. If there are any drugs, alcohol, or illegal or immoral behavior in your presence, you will be judged along with your crowd. Your associates do not have to have the appearance of Harvard preppies. Not at all! But they had better not be involved with drugs, alcohol, or illegal or immoral behavior—whether you're one with them or not.

Your character can be injured in another's mind.
They see who you are with, they certainly are not blind.
Illegal behavior must be held afar.
It will be your character too, they will scar!

28S. "IF ANYBODY SPEAKS EVIL OF YOU, LET YOUR LIFE BE SO THAT NO ONE BELIEVES HIM," ONE OF PRES. JAMES A. GARFIELD'S CHERISHED PERSONAL PRINCIPLES.

Anyone can say anything they want to say about you.

Treat people fairly and honestly and basically treat them as you would wish to be treated; don't give them the motivation to say anything negative about you.

Live your life so that anything negative anyone would say about you would not match up with your character and with what people know and think about you.

Give them nothing negative to say and no reason to say it.

Someone in my family told me, "Live your life such that you never have to worry about something you did being a problem if it become known to others. This frees you up to focus on your accomplishments of life." Maybe I said it. I am sure that is a paraphrase, but the idea is important; if you live a clean and moral life, you never have to worry about someone finding out about what you are doing.

Your mind can be clear of guilt so that you can focus on your vision and can remain clearly on track for your accomplishments of life. This may seem like a small deal, but so much creative energy can be lost worrying about past behavior when you did not act as you should have acted.

Instead, let your continual behavior free your mind for accomplishment and creativity and give others no opportunity to cloud your vision of your future.

Claims of evil deeds will not stick;
Your life provides a Teflon coating, it's no trick!
Just like mud, lies about you will slide right down.
Guilt, fear, and worry can take its toll mighty quick.
With a clean conscience, your smile will replace any frown.

28T. "WHEN YOU RETIRE AT NIGHT, THINK OVER WHAT YOU HAVE DONE DURING THE DAY," ONE OF PRES. JAMES A. GARFIELD'S CHERISHED PERSONAL PRINCIPLES.

When near the end of the day, think over, and write down what you did. Keep this written in a leather-bound calendar from now on. This is much more satisfying and memorable than just thinking over what you have done during the past day.

This is the routine of keeping a journal. A month, year, decade, quarter century or longer of keeping a journal is maintaining the activities of life and maintaining the ability to keep track of lost time for future enjoyment. With activities, thoughts, and other events over the years kept in writing, you will not sense the loss of time. Not knowing where the time has gone will not be your problem. You know because you have kept a journal of the events of a lifetime.

Additionally, thinking over the events of the day is useful in assessing the activities of the day and planning the activities of the days to come. Being aware of your past activities and introspective about how your day went will help you make your future days successful.

Hopefully, you will be able to say at the end of every day . . . "That was a good day" or "That was a great day, but here are a few things I could do to improve the day" or "There are a few things left from today that I still need to do tomorrow."

Reflect on your day at its end.
Savor your wins; understand your losses.
Your next chance will come, my dear friend.
Be ready to show your bosses.

28U. "IF YOUR HANDS CANNOT BE EMPLOYED USEFULLY, ATTEND TO THE CULTURE OF YOUR MIND," ONE OF PRES. JAMES A GARFIELD'S CHERISHED PERSONAL PRINCIPLES.

If you cannot do something constructive with your hands, do something to improve your level of knowledge; read a book, learn a skill to improve yourself.

Totally idle time is a total waste. You can be productive by doing something!

Ironing, cleaning the car, cleaning the garage, taking your child to the store to get something that they need . . . all are productive activities, which are useful.

There may be times, however, when you cannot be productive with your hands. Consider the situation when you are traveling by car and you can do nothing with your hands. That would be an excellent opportunity to "attend to the culture of your mind." You can listen to educational tapes, learn a language, learn how to deal with difficult people, or learn how to repack your bags for the rest of your life.

Similarly, when you are traveling by air, and there is virtually nothing you can do physically while you are thirty thousand feet up in the air. Again, this would be a good time to have a tape of something you would like to learn. Or perhaps you would want to read a book about some topic, which has been escaping you for some time. Having the free time when flying would provide an excellent opportunity to read the book and learn about a topic or read about some particular part of the country or about some famous American.

Your hands may be still;
Your mind may be closed;
If both occur, you are ill . . .
And your ignorance will be exposed.

28V. "READ THE ABOVE CAREFULLY AND THOUGHTFULLY AT LEAST ONCE A WEEK," ONE OF PRES. JAMES A. GARFIELD'S CHERISHED PERSONAL PRINCIPLES.

These cherished personal principles of President Garfield are all valuable lessons of life and are valuable to guide us as we carry out our daily activities. Read the list daily or weekly and search out one to stress each time:

- Never be idle.
- Make few promises.
- Always speak the truth.
- Live within your income.
- Never speak evil of anyone.
- Keep good company or none.
- Live up to your engagements.
- Never play games of chance.
- Drink no intoxicating drinks.
- Good character is above everything else.
- Keep your own secrets.
- Never borrow if you can possibly help it.
- Do not marry until you are able to support a wife.
- When you speak to a person, look into his eyes.
- Save when you are young to spend when you are old.
- Never run into debt unless you see a way out again.
- Good company and good conversation are the sinews of virtue.
- Your character cannot be essentially injured except through your own acts.
- If anybody speaks evil of you, let your life be so that no one believes him.
- When you retire at night, think over what you have done during the day.
- If your hands cannot be employed usefully, attend to the culture of your mind.
- Read the above carefully and thoughtfully at least once a week.

While these are not as powerful as the Ten Commandments, they are very significant and would serve us well as a guide to our lives.

29

The Only Cure To An Identity Crisis Is Involvement In Life Outside Of Self; Sermon, December 15, 1996, Naperville, Illinois, St. Margaret Mary Parish, Pastor Rev. William O'shea.

An identity crisis is defined in the *World Book Dictionary* as a time of disturbance and anxiety when a person is in a self-conscience stage of personality development or adjustment, occurring especially during adolescence.

The thesis of Reverend O'Shea's sermon is that the only cure to an identity crisis is to get into the lives of others and help them. Often a person is "still trying to find him or herself" and can be said as having an identity crisis. The person is said to be having difficulty dealing with others because he or she doesn't know how he/she should act.

Should you handle the situation like a minister type or a bartender type? Your degree of comfort with how you handle a situation is often determined by how you perceive yourself and how you think you should act based on that perception. The identity crisis comes when you are not sure how to act around others and in the situation you find yourself.

A certainly safe action to take is one in which you help someone else. Helping another human being, even if it's only thirty minutes per day, may be the cure to your identity crisis. It can be as simple as reaching out and helping others. This is an assuredly safe approach to and clarification of the meaning of life—helping and doing favors for people. This is not to say that aggressive people should be allowed to take advantage of your generosity by taking your service. Your help given to others who can't demand something of you is a clear map through any identity crisis/fog.

The rewards of helping other people are so great that once focused on the situations of others and helping them deal with their issues, the problem of your identify crisis fades, and the focus becomes the assistance being given to others.

How can you focus on your problems and inadequacies when you are being recognized and appreciated for assisting others?

An identity crisis means . . . gee . . .
You wonder who you might be . . .
How will I be me . . .
And in the mirror . . . who will I see?
No problems remain . . .
When helping others is your domain . . .
Your life will no longer be the same.
So the sermon helped them through . . .
Who am I . . . I can't act blue!
The solution is easily in view.
Staying focused on others it's true . . .
Will certainly help you too!

30

Idleness, Selfishness, Recklessness, Envy, And Irresponsibility Are The Vices Upon Which Socialism In Any Form Flourishes And Which It, In Turn, Encourages," Margaret Thatcher, *Washington Times Weekly*, December 1996.

The following are vices upon which socialism in any form flourishes and which socialism, in turn, encourages. The following definitions are as the words are defined in the *World Book Encyclopedia Dictionary*:

- Envy: Discontent or ill will at another's good fortune because one wishes it had been his.
- Idleness: The state of doing nothing; not busy; not working; unoccupied.
- Irresponsibility: Lack of being responsible.
- Recklessness: The act of being rash, heedless, careless.
- Selfishness: Caring too much for one self and too little for others.

Socialism is a theory or system of social organization in which the major means of production and distribution are owned, managed, or controlled by the government, groups of workers, or by the community.

Socialism is a vice.
There is no reason to excel.
Someone else will ring the bell . . .
Or what must be done to deliver the ice.
Some will be idle . . . they think it's so nice!
Some will think life is just a continuing ball.
No need to work, no need to stand tall.
Others will carry the load for us all.

30A. ENVY

Envy is defined as "discontent and wishing something had been his." Socialism at first seems like a mismatched comparison with envy. But at second thought, envy probably was a major motivator for socialism. Wanting what someone else worked for and earned may have been the seed that grew into socialism.

With socialism, everyone can get what they need theoretically regardless of how hard they work. Socialism is the getting from each according to their ability and giving to each according to their needs.

The most minimal effort will get someone what they need under socialism without risking failure through their creative efforts. Using abilities to the maximum is where the big problem with socialism evolves. Socialists are not forced to use all of their abilities. Socialism truly is ill will or discontent. Socialism allows people to hold back on their effort and dedication and still receive enough food and lodging to exist. And in their society, there is no motivation to go further because the rewards of working harder are not there.

Socialists wish they had the products of the hard workers labor and creatively without the effort on their part. The envy of socialists has been compared with the greed of capitalist. This offers an interesting comparison. Envy is wanting what someone else has, while greed has been described as wanting more than your share and are not willing to work very hard to get the extralarge portion. I say, if you work extrahard for something, you deserve the larger share of the pie.

Envy is on the list of the ten . . .
And is closely associated with sin.
Wanting what you haven't been able to win.
Demanding without earning is envy's evil twin.

30B. IDLENESS

Idleness is the state of doing nothing. Not busy, not working fits totally with socialism when comparing the societies of socialist versus capitalism. The capitalist is working and highly motivated as a result of the potential rewards available to those who work hard with creatively.

Idleness and socialism seem to go hand in hand because it is possible to get by without having to commit completely to an enterprise. This gives the socialist lots of idle time. The socialist has the freedom from having to think of extra ways to excel and not having to put in the time either to excel. There are minimal rewards for excellence in the socialist system. Consequently, the idleness creeps in because people are not motivated to put the extra time in to excel.

The issue is not that a socialist doesn't work. The issue is, a socialist is not motivated and does not need to go that extra mile to excel when the rewards of excelling are certainly not rewarded.

Idleness is not the one for me or you too.
You won't see the idle giving it the ol' one, two . . .
The idle have time but not for you.
They see it all as what you should do.

30C. IRRESPONSIBILITY

Irresponsibility is the lack of being responsible. In a socialist environment, the state is the responsible entity. There is no need for the individual to be responsible when the people get what they need regardless of how hard they work and regardless of their commitment to the outcome of their work venture.

The socialists are not responsible for the care of their family. The state is responsible; consequently, not being responsible is routinely reinforced though the socialist economy.

Opportunities of people motivated by capitalism to desire to take charge of their destiny and accomplish great things through hard work and persistence is remarkable. With little sense of the relationship between hard work, results, and benefits, irresponsibility is encouraged.

I know you want to be responsible.
Me too, I am most capable.
Make effort is all it takes and you are in control . . .
Make responsible progress toward your goal!

30D. RECKLESSNESS

Recklessness is being rash, heedless, or careless. Capitalists can be equated with individuals being careless in that people must take risks to make the connection between their hard work and the resulting rewards. They can appear careless relative to the family income and family subsistence. I do not see the socialists as being rash or heedless. The socialist has minimal motivation to take chances or to be rash, heedless, or careless.

The socialist, versus a capitalist, can live comfortably without taking chances and without exhibiting the rash behavior of the capitalist who must take chances with significant risks because the rewards are perceived to be worth the risk.

Behavior that is rash . . .
Often is considered brash . . .
But so, who splits hairs.
The capitalist certainly cares.

30E. SELFISHNESS

Selfishness is the caring too much for one's self and too little for others. The term offers an interesting comparison of socialism and capitalism. Socialist do care about others, but that care is strong on the side of a verbal caring and less, usually much less, on the helping others or doing side. A socialist cares but likely will not generate the resources to actually do something about the caring. The socialist will take your money, decide who they will give it to and then feel good that they have been generous.

On the other hand, a capitalist will be motivated to work harder and bring home more fruits of his or her labors and might appear to care too much about his or herself. Yet the issue is that the capitalist really puts himself out and throws out personal care to achieve the overall goal. Then he has more to share with others. This goal achieving offers a capitalist the fruits to be helpful to the less fortunate. A rising sea of good fortune raises all boats—rich and poor. The issue here then is that socialist may care but does less, while a capitalist appears to care less, but they create the resources to do things for the less fortunate.

A stingy person must be understood.
Value must not be assessed just by what you see.
The capitalist will contribute more than anyone could.
The picture is not what they feel . . . but what they cause to be.

31

"Maturity Is A High Price To Pay For Growing Up," Tom Stoppard, The Plays For Radio 1964-91 (Faber And Faber), *Reader's Digest*, August 1996.

Maturity is equated here to acting responsibly.

A common phrase uttered today by many in our society is something to the effect of "I have a right to do this or that . . ." And they are probably correct. We have many rights in this country.

You have rights guaranteed by the Bill of Rights of the U.S. Constitution.

Something people often fail to state or even recognize is that people also have responsibilities that must be remembered as they consume their rights. All too often today, I see people gorging themselves on their rights while ignoring on their responsibilities.

Equate mature behavior with the behavior of the Ten Commandments and the love chapter of 1 Corinthians 13 in the New Testament.

Adult or mature behavior always does the right thing.

Kindness, thoughtfulness, generosity, patience, courteousness, etc, have always been examples of mature behavior. This was and still should be mature, adult behavior.

Constantly exhibiting these characteristics of maturity is difficult at times and reflects the high price for growing up. Acting maturely requires us to think through the circumstances of the situations we find ourselves in, including why the other person acts as he or she does, before reacting to the situation.

Maturity is the price you pay . . .
You can't grab, cheat, and steal;
You must behave in a responsible way . . .
So when you grow up, your values are real!

32

"When We Seek To Discover The Best In Others, We Somehow Bring Out The Best In Ourselves," William Arthur Ward, *Reader's Digest*, August 1996.

Seeking to discover the best in others is an admirable goal and one that offers a broad range of opportunities.

It offers us a challenge to be creative in looking for, developing, and refining the skills and attributes/values of others. In the process, we too are greatly benefitted.

First, seeking to discover the best in others involves an investigation ranging from the superficial notice that the glass is half full or that the sky is partly sunny, to the awareness that the person or situation is a jewel in the rough and begin working to improve upon the existing qualities.

Making the superficial observation that the glass is half full or that the sky is partly sunny in a casual conversation is a pleasant, polite way to be friendly and gives you an opportunity to initiate a conversation with a person and to show interest in the other person.

Compare the half full or partly sunny observation to the one in which the glass is half empty, woe-is-me, things-are-better-today-than-they-will-ever-be-again approach. As a half-empty person, your comments and presence to the other person or to the setting will cast a cloud on the mood of the scene rather than saying something positive and thereby not harming if not helping the atmosphere.

It is always best to leave "little packages of good will" or pleasant thoughts with people as you move through your day.

Second, but not second in relevance, is the effort of seeking to discover the best in a student, an athlete, a new engineer, or other worker. Each occurrence is another opportunity to seek the best in others and offer the potential to help the other person, especially if they are young, to achieve greatness.

Just the experience of helping another person will benefit you because you have a desire and a need to be helpful to others.

This also tends to bring out the best in us as we strive to help others. While helping a student learn the alphabet or learning the math tables or learning trigonometry or Plato or learning what it takes to be a world-class athlete, we will gain from the experience and will be better off for the experience.

If we all seek the best in others,
Even beyond that seen by their mothers,
We will bring out the best . . .
In ourselves and the rest!

33

"Hot Heads And Cold Hearts Never Solved Anything," Billy Graham, *Reader's Digest*, August 1996.

The Bible in Ecclesiastes 3:1-8 indicates that "there is a time for everything, and a season for every activity under heaven. A time to be born and time to die, a time to plant and time to uproot, a time to kill and a time to heal, a time to tear down and time to build . . . a time to love and a time to hate, a time for war and a time for peace.

Similarly, there is a time for having a hot head and a time for stealth and wisdom . . . and a time for a cold heart and a time for compassion.

People can say anything at any time, and I can only presume that Billy Graham's quote referred to a time when stealth wisdom and compassion were called for, and he was rebuking the application of a hot head and a cold heart.

The hottest head and the coldest heart in all history were and continue today to be exhibited by God. There is no more hotheaded and cold-blooded "person" in the written history of the world than the book entitled the Holy Bible.

I am sure Billy Graham would be astounded when I say that God's hotheadedness directly resulted in the death of millions and millions of people. Whole cities were destroyed; individual people were turned to stone. God acted as an extreme hothead at times throughout the Bible.

And what about the Passover when all the firstborn males of Egypt were killed and all the children of the Israelites lived because their parents spread lambs blood above their doorways? This had to have been one of the most cold-blooded acts in all history!

These situations in the Bible refute the blanket assertion that hot heads and cold hearts never solved anything. Also, as indicated in the Bible, there is a time for everything and a season for every activity under heaven. Billy Graham should have indicated that it is best to treat everyone consistent with the Ten Commandments and the Golden Rule of treating your neighbor as you would like to be treated and respect the rights of others. This kind of treatment will not create enemies for you to deal with and will then leave the situation open for you to use your creativity to accomplish great things.

There is a time for a hot head.
There is a time for a cold heart.
God was hot and cold the Bible has said.
Knowing when it's right is your part.

34

"A Great Many People Mistake Opinions For Thoughts," Herbert V. Prochnow, *Reader's Digest*, August 1996.

Webster defines "opinion" as "what one thinks; belief not so strong as knowledge; judgment."

Webster also defines "thought" as "what a person thinks; idea; notion."

The definitions are similar, but for both words, opinion and thought, we'll take the second definition as our operative phrase in both cases. (Opinion means belief not so strong as knowledge; and thought means idea.)

The words are very close in definition, and there are just subtle differences between opinion and thought, belief and idea.

Both can be based on long-term biases. In fact, everyone's opinions and thoughts are based on their biases.

This original quote would have been more meaningful if it had said, "A great many people mistake opinions for *facts*." Facts should be irrefutable and should not be based on opinion. Beliefs are not so strong as knowledge. Thoughts are what a person thinks . . . an idea or notion.

The absolute best example today is the large, but much smaller than it used to be, audience of the national television news reporters and programs on the major news networks: ABC, CBS, NBC, and CNN. Fortunately, people are learning that the major media sources are biased and are turning to other sources, including "talk radio" for their news. Don't waste time receiving information that is really someone else's biased or "factless" thought or opinion. Choose news sources and friends that base what they say on facts rather than bias. Fill your head with facts and use those facts to form your own opinions and thoughts.

Opinions are formed on a foundation of bias.
Thoughts are supported by bias as well.
Knowledge and facts are worth your focus.
All have biases . . . but facts . . . you can surely tell.

35

"Freedom, After All, Is Simply Being Able To Live With The Consequences Of Your Decisions," James X. Mullen, *The Simple Art Of Greatness* (Viking Penguin), *Reader's Digest*, August 1996.

Do you have any choice? You must live with the consequences of your decisions! You must live with the consequences of decisions you make with your freedom either as a free person or as a person without freedom.

Again, checking with *Webster* for a definition to form a discussion around, *Webster* defines "freedom" as "exemption or liberation from the control of some other person or some arbitrary power."

Freedom is discussed at two basic levels: the level of the family and the level of the country.

First, freedom from the standpoint of living in a "free" country like the United States is "having" to live with the consequences of your actions. In the United States, you can do anything that is not prohibited by law and doesn't violate the rights of another person. If you cannot handle your freedom and you make unlawful decisions or violate the rights of another person, your freedom will be taken from you, and you may be imprisoned or otherwise limited in movement or choices.

From the standpoint of the country, obeying the laws and not violating the rights of others are critical responsibilities to maintaining that freedom. Also, voting for candidates to occupy the various elective offices from local to state to national levels who will not further restrict our freedom or will not unnecessarily take our resources via taxation are critical to maintaining one's freedom.

Second, freedom from the standpoint of living within a family is different. More and more freedom will be given to a young person growing up in a family setting, as they show they can handle the freedom. If they make wise choices under close and strict parental supervision, more and more freedom will be given to them. With this newly bestowed freedom, they can make choices. If they act responsibly, the freedom will likely be expanded. If poor choices are made, the freedom is likely to be reduced.

Do you have any choice, you say?
Each must live with the choices we make.
Freedom from the start in the USA.
Break laws and from you they will take.
Families grant freedom in a different way.
Win their trust and it's a piece of cake!

36

"Slow Down, Simplify, And Be Kind," Naomi Judd, *Reader's Digest*, August 1996.

Most of life's problems for the achievers, the people accomplishing things with their life, can be helped by taking the advice offered here: slow down, simplify, and be kind!

Did you ever notice that many, many people who reach the very top of their field sooner or later begin to have problems with drugs, drinking alcohol, adultery, or some difficulty with their family and friends. I don't know whether it is safe to say as an absolute truth—but it is close—difficulties such as this happen to every superachiever, from sports, to business, to politics, to the arts, acting, and so on.

Beyond the superachiever, the middle class evolves into an operational mode that accomplishes some degree of success and they focus on activities, to the average person, seems that they are successful and very busy. This generates the same results as with the superachiever: too busy, too focused on things and activities, and prone to have problems with drugs, drinking alcohol, adultery, or some other difficulty with their family and friends.

I contend here that many problems of people who are achieving great things in their life and are successful in every material sense will be solved or dealt with successfully by "slowing down, simplifying, and being kind."

So you have done well!
You have attacked life and hit the bell.
Then, why does life seem like hell?
Slow down is the first thing I would tell.
Simplify it all, I would yell;
And be kind . . . it will help . . . I can foretell!

37

"We May Pass Violets Looking For Roses. We May Pass Contentment Looking For Victory," Bern Williams; *Reader's Digest*, August 1996.

What is a rose: a rose, according to *Webster*, is any of a genus *Rosa* of shrubs of the rose family, characteristically with prickly stems, alternate, compound leaves and five parted, usually fragrant, flowers of red, pink, white, yellow etc. having many stamens.

Also according to *Webster*, a violet is any plant of a genus *Viola* of plants of the violet family, having white, blue, purple or yellow irregular flowers with short spurs.

When you are out looking for roses, it is very important to know what a rose looks like or what a rose is! When you are looking for a violet, obviously, you must know what a violet is and how it looks.

Similarly, you need to know what victory is before you set out to conquer the world. A vision of what you are seeking is necessary before setting out!

Your definition of victory should include opinions on love, security, religious beliefs, status, educational level, relationships with others, general direction (such as technical, law, business, entrepreneur, or medicine or others). Your definition of victory would also need to include a balance of work, rest, and play.

As you seek your victory, the vision you set forth for your life, contentment will follow as you see your plan click into place. Simply shooting out from the starting blocks of life and going full speed ahead will not bring contentment. Contentment comes from the satisfaction of establishing a vision or a plan and then seeing that plan click into place and your vision come into view.

Roses are red . . .
Violets may be blue!
Contentment will be fed . . .
When your story comes into view.
Your vision will be the right med . . .
For a life seeking to be true.
Once you get out the lead . . .
And achieve your vision . . . I am telling you!

38

"Words Are Plentiful, But Deeds Are Precious," Lech Walesa, *Reader's Digest*, August 1996.

We all have known people who can talk and talk and talk and but don't deliver. They have all kinds of advice; I would do this, and I would do that . . . they say . . . but their advice is not consistent with their own life.

Others will tell you that they will do this and that for you or for the business but just don't get it accomplished.

Words are plentiful and often come from those without commitment and passion for your cause. Passion, action, and commitment are critical ingredients to securing quality assistance and partnering. When selecting the right partner for most any activity for life, look for the person who places importance on deeds before someone who just talks big. As indicated, passion, action, and commitment are important too. Without these ingredients, look further.

Deeds are precious, but deeds off in the wrong direction or deeds that are full of errors or deeds that don't reflect your standards of quality are useless.

Words of advice or direction . . . find someone who is committed and passionate toward the issues of life and liberty. Find someone who is skilled to your standards of quality.

Knowledge of when to give advice and when to offer deeds are equally valuable and represent qualities in a person to be treasured.

Words are plentiful, a point proven by TV.
Talk can be purposeful to see your way through . . .
Deeds are more precious, precious as can be.
Both wise words and effective deeds stand out in Lech's view.

39

"The Harder I Work, The Luckier I Get," Unknown Speaker, Talk Radio, December 26, 1996.

The harder I work, the luckier I get, of course, is a tongue-in-cheek statement, knowing that everyone would recognize the fact that the hard work generated the desired result.

You cannot count on luck. You cannot count on prayer. When God's will is involved, prayer won't deliver achievement and success.

The only thing you can count on is that hard work, especially targeted hard work, will serve you much better toward your life's goals than either luck or prayer.

To be outstanding in sports . . . practice, practice, practice. To be outstanding in school . . . study, study, and study. To be able to play the piano very well . . . practice, practice, practice. In anything, if you want to be the best or a leader in your field, you must practice and work and practice and work toward excellence. A half-speed effort will never get you more than halfway there.

What I Would Have Said . . .

Some may think that . . .
Hard work produces luck.
So please it keep under your hat . . .
Your work generates the buck!

40

"If You Are Going To Get Anywhere In Life, You Are Going To Have To Go Into Business For Yourself!" Unknown Speaker, Talk Radio, December 26, 1996.

Going into business for yourself will offer you an opportunity to achieve considerable success. Actually achieving success is dependent on considerably more than just going into business for yourself.

Most new businesses fail, leaving the owner of the business getting somewhere . . . but that somewhere maybe the poor house.

Even the businesses that succeed do not succeed to the point that the business owner could say that he or she really "got somewhere" with the business.

Some businesses do very well, allowing the owner to consider that he or she may feel that success was attained.

Salaried people can achieve a fair to outstanding salary. This may generate for the worker a reasonable lifestyle. Most salaried people earn modest incomes, which don't offer the worker an opportunity to boast that they have arrived. They can be happy though, if not wealthy.

Self-employment is risky, and many are not successful. But obviously enough are successful to keep people's excitement up about their chances and encouraging some to go into self-employment.

If you are going to get anywhere . . .
Financially speaking that is . . .
Your own business, you must bear.
But in business, success may be a fizz!

41

"Be Fair; Only Agreed-To Need Comes Before Fairness," The Author . . . Unless Someone Else Claims It.

A major, major rule in dealing with people is to be fair in your exchanges with them. When you are doing the giving . . . you get to define what is fair.

When politicians use the term "fair," they are using their sense of what is fair, and that usually means that you get to share your hard-earned wages with people who expect you to share, and they basically hate you for having so much. Hardworking people will never be able to satisfy the "takers" that the givers are being fair. The Constitution guarantees equal opportunity in the USA . . . not equal outcome.

Always try to exceed what people expect from you in each interaction with them. People should always understand that you will be fair with them. There should be no question that you were fair with them in these interactions. There should be no question about this point in anyone's mind.

This goes from your relationship with parents, peers, teachers, coaches, parents of your friends, baby-sitting customers, waitresses, supervisors, and bosses when your start working at jobs outside your home.

You must treat them all fairly and should expect them to treat you the same.

The lone exception to meeting and exceeding fairness is the situation when you are dealing with two or more individuals, and one clearly needs the item of issue much more than the other. The issue of the greater need of one person versus the other must be addressed. There can not be of any doubt of fairness in your mind and hopefully not any question in the mind of the others involved as well. The people involved should be told what you are doing and why you are doing it. Remember if you are a giver, you get to decide what is fair.

For fairness, you all must clearly understand what is expected and deliver that and more. Always understand what is expected of you and exceed that by a noticeable amount.

Fairness, you all must clearly understand.
Parents, friends, and teachers and all should know . . .
Where you are coming from to give them a hand . . .
"To be fair and then some" is for you to show.

42

"The Most Important Trip You May Take In Life Is Meeting People Halfway," Henry Boye In *National Enquirer, Reader's Digest,* January 1997.

Compromising is often thought of as meeting people halfway, and that is often a very good and healthy approach to dealing with friends, family, and just acquaintances alike. Taken literally, when deciding where to do lunch, pick a site halfway; that is a great way to decide where you will meet a friend. Likewise, meeting people halfway is a reasonable approach in deciding how you two split up the chores: each should do approximately one half of the chores. That is fair and right, and that is the way it should be.

On some really important issues, compromising is not acceptable at all for coming to conclusions.

When deciding how to live your life and are discussing issues with a non-Christians, nonbelievers, nonnice people, which half of the Ten Commandments do you follow and which ones do you ignore? You can't do it; you can't meet them halfway on your core values!

When deciding whether your country balances the budget each year or spends more than what it takes in, do you compromise and just spend half as much over the budget as the other person wanted but still spend more than the country takes in as income? You must spend equal to or less than you take in as income or your children and grandchildren will end up paying for your compromise.

You must have a set of core beliefs or values, and those may not be compromised!

The most important trip you may take in life may be in meeting people halfway; but the most important decision is knowing when to meet them halfway and when to insist either they come all the way to your side or skip the "travel" plans.

The most important trip . . .
May be the "meet in the middle" one you take;
But equally important I quip,
Are the firm core value decisions you make.

43

"In Politics, There's A Fine Line Between Too Much Conviction And Too Little," Robert J. Samuelson In *Newsweek, Reader's Digest,* January 1997

The word "politic" in *Webster* means "looking out for one's own interests or showing wisdom or shrewdness or scheming, or crafty or political." *Webster* also defines politics as "the science and art of government."

This discussion of politics is as it relates to elected officials governing public bodies, such as cities, counties, states, and countries.

We basically want our politicians, our elected officials, to have convictions in the same directions and in the same things that we do. Convictions and passions are nearly the same thing to me, and passions have been written about at other locations in this text. Too little conviction on a topic, especially those topics affecting governments with all the pressures of the media and interests groups, is dangerous these days.

A person with too few convictions will flap in the breeze because they really don't believe deeply in anything. They will go one way for a while, and then, when the wind changes, because they have no real convictions in anything, they change directions and head toward a new target.

There are a few convictions that we must look for to be strong before we would want them to be over our government.

First, they should have strong convictions in a value system based on a belief of the Ten Commandments. They would not have to be Christian but believe in what the ten "thou shall not's" say.

Second, they should believe in the U.S. Constitution and all amendments as written and not with revisionist's interpretations or unstated, newly discovered rights. Any interpretation of the constitution needs to be officially added to the constitution rather than interpreted to mean something different from the actual words say.

So you see . . .
Convictions are important to me,
As long as we vote . . .
On the right bloke.

44

"High Station In Life Is Earned By The Gallantry With Which Appalling Experiences Are Survived With Grace," Tennessee Williams, Memoirs (Doubleday), *Reader's Digest*, January 1997.

Tennessee Williams is not someone I know and respect. Perhaps if I knew more about him, I could at least respect him. I do believe the quote attributed to him in this essay is very valuable.

It would be hypocritical to say that no one can achieve high station in life as a gift, without their personal effort. Rewards and success without effort certainly happen. Since it is impossible to pick your parents, achieving high station in life via receiving gifts is beyond your control and will not be suggested as a way to achieving the revered high station in life. Personal wealth is just part of the high station.

Highly ethical character is another concept or element of high station in life. Highly ethical character is desirable and achievable for everyone.

Earned is another important concept. Earned as opposed to awarded, or given, is the issue. The *Thorndike-Barnhart Dictionary* defines "earned" as getting in return for work or service; being paid; doing enough work for; bringing or getting as deserved; gaining as a profit or return.

Most people who accomplish things in life get there through considerable effort. You might get the impression that success has come easy to people who have accomplished a great deal in life. And for the most part, self-made people and their success stories are about people who have worked and worked and made many sacrifices to get where they are. They make it look easy because of the poised gallantry with which they accomplish their success.

Happiness and joy are another matter. Being gallant while dealing with appalling experiences does not guarantee happiness. Theoretically, it should guarantee confidence that you can deal with most events in this life. That, coupled with an expectation in eternal life to those who have faith in God and Jesus, and are repentant of their sins, are likely to experience joy—but there are no guarantees. Joy is to find things, events, situations, or anticipations that you enjoy. The little things are what I am writing about—not necessarily the biggies. Enjoyment/joy of the flower garden, the child's first step, the first words, the special moments together. These are all potential sources for joy. People must find their own joy and happiness.

High station is another word for success.
Gallantry means great bravery to us all.
Appalling experiences, the hard work that causes us to assess . . .
Whether we proceed with grace . . . or fall.

Through appalling experiences charge those who . . .
Seek to achieve High station . . . let's review:
Life provides a process whereby this is earned.
Their gallantry is judged to have been learned.
They must survive with grace no matter where they turned.
High station success will come, in time . . . it's true!

45

"The Attempt To Silence A Man Is The Greatest Honor You Can Bestow On Him. It Means That You Recognize The Other Person As Superior To Yourself," Joseph Sobran, Universal Press Syndicate, *Reader's Digest*, January 1997.

Throughout history, attempts to silence the wise and the wicked, has come from both sides; those in and out of power and those with good and evil in their hearts all have attempted to silence a vocal enemy. It is not possible to totally generalize that just the bad people or just the good people try to silence a person speaking an opposing viewpoint.

To silence an opposing viewpoint may be because you recognize that the opposing person is superior intellectually to you. Or it may be because the opposing person is espousing a viewpoint that is destructive to your family or destructive to the entire country and is not factually correct.

You definitely can silence a person falsely yelling "Fire, fire," in a crowded movie theater. The potential risk to the other members of the audience is to too great to allow the person to speak. In this case, the person may be silenced, and the question of superiority of thought is not raised.

This platitude parallels the virtue of free speech. The best examples of this quote that I can think of today involves two conservative Americans. The attempt to silence Justice Clarence Thomas, judge of the U.S. Supreme Court, by various members of the National Association for the Advancement of (Liberal) Colored People. The National Association for the Advancement of (Liberal) Colored People protests whenever Judge Thomas is scheduled to speak to any group. The second is the attempt by various women's groups, such as the National Organization for Women, to get the Florida Orange Juice growers to stop using Rush Limbaugh as a national spokesman for orange juice sales. In both cases, these are examples of having a great honor bestowed on these outstanding Americans. This means that the National Association for the Advancement of (Liberal) Colored People and the National Organization for Women recognize that Justice Thomas's and Rush's views are superior to theirs. They no longer feel capable of debating in the arena of ideas and must resort to some other action such as boycott or protests to stop the flow of wisdom from these two American leaders. Liberals and Progressives seem to believe that the U.S. Constitution protects only liberal speech and does not protect conservative thought and speech.

Silence a man . . .
If you can.
Letting him speak . . .
May make him meek!
Don't fear his right to say;
Truth will save the day.

46

"Never Let A Problem To Be Solved Become More Important Than A Person To Be Loved," Barbara Johnson, The Joy Journal (Word); *Reader's Digest*, January 1997.

For this quote to have any relevance at all, it must be applied in an extreme, fluffy, innocent, and fairy tale-like environment. In other words, this quote is not to be considered a "real world" situation involving real "white knuckle" problem solving.

Problems involving cruel people, killers, enemy countries, and even competitive sporting events beyond T-Ball and "Bumblebee" soccer all put the problem to be solved ahead of the person to be loved.

Never let a problem to be solved become more important than a person to be loved to decide who in the three-year-old preschool gets to stand in line first today. Solving the problems must take into account the fact that you must be loving and gentle with the children when you make your decision.

My convictions on letting the problem to be solved become more important than a person to be loved certainly weaken if, for example, the same person and you reach the same point at one end of the parking lot and the beginning of a parking row every day. If the other person, every time, assumes that you are going to let him or her go first to find the empty space, you are not dealing with a person who needs to be treated with love. If the person is always pushy about the certainty of getting his or her way, do not feel compelled to putting love of the person ahead of the problem. Selfish and stubborn people deserve little or no slack when it comes to dealing with issues.

Almost any activity, when you are not dealing with an outright cruel person or in a situation in which you are not keeping score as in a competitive game, you should never let the problem to be solved become more important than the person to be loved or the person to be treated with an act of kindness.

A problem to be solved . . .
Should never be,
To the people involved,
More than the love of thee.

47

"Love Is What's Left In A Relationship After All The Selfishness Has Been Removed," Cullen Hightower, *Reader's Digest*, January 1997.

What is love?
According to *The Living Bible*: "Love is very patient and kind, never jealous or envious, never boastful or proud, never haughty or selfish or rude. Love does not demand its own way. It is not irritable or touchy. It does not hold grudges and will hardly even notice when others do it wrong. It is never glad about injustice, but rejoices whenever truth wins out. If you love someone, you will be loyal to him (or her) no matter what the cost. You will always believe in him, always expect the best of him and always stand your ground in defending him (or her)."

Webster's New World Dictionary defines "selfishness" as "the act of being too much concerned with one's own welfare or interests and having little or no concern for others; self-centered."

With the above definitions as starting points, and some basic knowledge of what people bring into a relationship from their former status as individuals, this discussion supports the premise that love is what is left after the selfishness is removed.

This premise is, of course, a very perfect, but unusual situation. All the selfishness is never removed. You never ever reach a perfect or complete removal of selfishness.

Love is very patient and kind.
True! Love is patient and kind to the mate who is exemplary of the Boy or Girl Scout motto most of the time. In its broadest sense, it is easy to be patient and kind to a mate who is an absolutely giving person.

Can you always be patient or kind to a mate who is in your face to get his or her way? I think not!

Being treated with patience and kindness is a right. However, it is a right that comes with responsibilities. Like many areas of our society, it is wrong to expect rights without accepting certain responsibilities!

Love is never jealous or envious.
Expecting a mate to never exhibit jealousy or envy requires a responsible mate in return. It is totally unreasonable to expect a mate to never exhibit jealousy or envy when his or her mate flirts with, gives special attention, or even more, to others.

Always be sensitive to the feelings of your mate and how she/he will interpret your actions. Act in the presence of others of the opposite sex as you would want your spouse to act.

Love is never boastful or proud.
Love is never boastful or proud at the expense of the other person of the couple. There is absolutely never anything to boast or be proud of when it causes your loved one any discomfort. Really, there is no need to boast at all unless you are of the opinion that you need to try to make yourself look better than you think you look. Insecurity usually will be the reason for trying to make yourself look better by boasting. Often it is easier to talk about yourself when you are speaking to others because you know more about yourself than you know about anything else. In that case, use the "Carnegie" suggestions for topics; especially ask lots of questions and give the other person lots of opportunities to talk about themselves. That will ease the burden on you, and that will reduce the potential to talk about yourself, which is often considered boastful with excessive pride. Sometimes, that is a fine line. It has to be acceptable to talk about yourself, but never ever boast or exhibit pride to the detriment of anyone especially your spouse and partner.

Love is never haughty or selfish or rude.
Webster's New World Dictionary defines "haughty" as "having or showing great pride in oneself and disdain, contempt or scorn for others; proud; arrogant." A love relationship between a man and a woman, a husband and a wife, is not usually complicated by pride. Personalities are so complex; it is a wonder anyone stays married!

Being selfish or rude more often than pride or boasting is the cause of marital difficulties.

A selfish mate spends more than his or her fair share of the family budget. The income and expenses need to be discussed and agreed to by both members of the couple. After agreement, then they both need to adhere to the spending and income factors in the budget.

A selfish mate leaves messes around the house or apartment and expects the other to clean up for him or her. The selfish or rude mate doesn't clean them up and is indignant when asked to do so by the spouse. A selfish mate uses things of the other and does not put them back.

Someone who grows up in an environment where he or she can get by with being fiscally selfish, unthoughtful, messy, or rude is likely to be selfish and rude to a spouse after they are married. A person, when confronted with this selfish or rude behavior, is likely to evoke a rebuke and denial from the rude and selfish spouse.

Again, avoid being excessively proud, selfish, or rude to your spouse, the person you love.

Love does not demand its own way.
True, love does not demand its own way except when the "demands" are really just an expectation of being treated with common courtesies. Without common courtesies, there will be a continuing conflict in the marriage. The demanded common courtesies really should not have to be demanded. But in the absence of such common courtesies, one should feel free to demand them.

An overbearing and demanding relationship with your spouse is not acceptable. Your spouse is your partner, not your servant. You should be exceptionally fair with your spouse as to your perception of the division of labor around the house.

Love is not irritable or touchy.
Starting with a clean slate without the debris situations of living a life together, it is very easy to not be irritable or touchy with your spouse. As time passes, the likelihood of irritations or incidents of touchiness becomes greater. Now, if you are irritable or touchy, it still isn't good, but at least it could be understandable.

Love does not hold grudges and will hardly even notice when others do it wrong.
Ideally, the slate should be erased the next day after any misdeed, error in judgment, or verbal sparring between mates. After a few years, the memory is similar to a used recording, magnetic tape, or a slate that is wiped and not washed. There is some buildup that is not erased for the next use. When this occurs year after year and not totally erased, the recording tape or the chalk slate must be discarded because they are not usable.

Love is never glad about injustice; love rejoices whenever truth wins.
Never ever be glad about injustice, and always rejoice whenever truth wins out. This does not only apply to love, spouse, children, or parents. Fight injustice no matter who the affected party is. Justice and fair treatment should be everyone's right. Stand up to oppose injustice, and do your very best to ensure that they do enjoy freedom from injustice. Do your part to ensure that truth wins out.

Always believe in him (or her)
Always believe in him (or her), always expect the best of him (or her) and always stand your ground in defending him (or her).

Again, while I believe in the wisdom of Paul's writings in Corinthians, there are limits to the believing in the spouse, and there are limits in how long the mate can stand firm in defending the spouse. There are limits to these rights of thought and expectations. Rights without responsibilities are essentially worthless because you will never know for sure when you have reached the breaking point by exceeding your demand of rights without exhibiting sufficient responsible actions.

Many, many times has Paul's letter . . .
Been used to describe how you can do better.
Love is patient and kind . . .
The spouse is anxious to remind.

Yes, I know the Corinthian letter of love . . .
A one-sided picture from above.
A picture of rights, the right of quality treatment by a mate . . .
Isn't love great?

48

"Treat A Person As He Is, And He Will Remain As He Is. Treat Him As He Could Be, And He Will Become What He Should Be," Jimmy Johnson, Quoted By Jarret Bell In *Usa Today*, *Reader's Digest*, January 1997.

In a perfect and idealistic world, you might wish that human motivation was so simple as the premise of this section implies: "Treat a person as he is, and he will remain as he is. Treat him as he could be, and he will become what he should be."

Unfortunately, that premise just is not true as a universal truth. At least it is a major simplification, and for all intent and purposes, it just is not true.

There is no question that you should treat people as they could be. That is great, and the results, for the right person, at the right time in their life will be wonderful. You can truly have an apparent visible impact on their life.

This may be somewhat of a generalization, but most people that you come across in your daily activities will positively react to the Dale Carnegie philosophy in *How to Win Friends and Influence People*:

1. Become genuinely interested in other people.
2. Smile.
3. Remember, a person's name is to that person the sweetest and most important sound in any language.
4. Be a good listener. Encourage others to talk about themselves.
5. Talk in terms of the other person's interests.
6. Make the other person feel important and do it sincerely.

This level of treatment, coupled with treating people as they could be and with respect and dignity, will have the most impact.

Even with this though, without the close contact for example of a child in your home or an athlete on a team, there will be limited behavior modification because changing a person's behavior and approach to life is slow turning and a long time coming even when the person is very young.

There must be limits to treating someone with respect and dignity when they are not responding. Eventually, if they do not respond to treating them as they could be and their behavior is not satisfactory for the situation they are in, then they must be treated as they are until their behavior improves. This is sometimes a tough call for parents and teachers.

Treat a person as he could be, and that may motivate him to become what he should be to achieve in the higher ranges of his potential. Treat a person as he is though if his behavior is below normal or acceptable behavior for the family or classroom.

Says Jimmy Johnson the pro . . .
Treat a gifted athlete, I suppose, as he could be
And he will develop as an athlete and grow.
Treat him as he is and you will see . . .
The athlete will either remain slow . . .
Or the athlete will excel if he's savvy.

A child is another tale.
Life is a much longer but simpler test . . .
You don't dump them if they fail.
But show them the door if they lack zest.

49

"Suggestions For Making Life More Vivid, More Enjoyable, More Rewarding: Try To Be Surprised By Something Every Day; Wake Up In The Morning With Specific Goals To Look Forward To; Make Time For Reflection And Relaxation," Mihaly Csikszentmihalyl, *Creativity: Flow And The Psychology Of Discovery And Invention.*

What I Would Have Said . . .

Try to be surprised by something every day.

Daily, put yourself in positions that allow you to discover new things. Reach out and learn and discover.

A mind sunken in the mire of television watching is a mind not prone to reaching out and is not a mind being programmed with continued learning.

New experiences make the mind quicker, and the quality of life, overall, will be more exciting with the daily new experiences.

Wake up in the morning with specific goals to look forward to.
When you start each day, focus on the activities that you have ahead of you that you will positively anticipate. There may be some things you know you will need to do during the day that you will not particularly enjoy. Accept that fact, but focus on the things that you will enjoy.

Make time for reflection and relaxation.
This is a "stop and smell the roses" type suggestion for your lifestyle. One's life can and will get so busy that this admonition is actually essential to a more vivid, more enjoyable, more rewarding life. A young person in high school, and later college, most certainly will think that their age group is

the busiest of all groups, and all they have to do is to get out of college, and they will then begin to enjoy life.

Later, after graduation, they are busy with their first job and buying a car and buying a house and perhaps going back to graduate school, they are busy; but as soon as they finish that phase, they will not be so busy, and they, then finally, will have time for reflection and relaxation.

The planning for a wedding, getting married, honeymoon, and beginning a new life together, at some point, all will restrict time for reflection and relaxation. This cycle could continue throughout a lifetime.

At some point, you must take control and plan the use of your time so that there will be time for reflection and relaxation to enjoy what you have and who you are with so that your life will be more enjoyable and rewarding.

Try to be surprised by something every day;
Wake up in the morning with something nice to say.
But make time for reflection and relaxation too . . . come what may . . .
Your life will be above the fray.

50

"Honesty, Hope, Faith, Courage, Integrity, Willingness, Humility, Brotherly Love, Justice, Perseverance, Spiritual, And Service," Alcoholics Anonymous, Bill Wilson And Robert Smith, 1935.

The following are the elements of Alcoholics Anonymous's twelve-step self-improvement process: honesty, hope, faith, courage, integrity, willingness, humility, brotherly love, justice, perseverance, spiritual, and service. It is assumed here that these steps are helpful in dealing with an excessive consumption of alcohol because that problem/habit is the result of a lack of personal pride and confidence. Further, it is assumed that excessive alcohol is consumed in the mistaken intent to feel better. And the alcohol is being consumed by the alcoholic to overcome the lack of pride and confidence and to try to feel better about oneself.

Honesty will do;
Hope can do it too.
Faith? Expect it to come true!
Courage is a must for you.

Integrity is telling no lie.
Willingness . . . at least you try.
Humility, you cannot buy.
Brotherly love is more than a sigh;
Justice develops trust.
Perseverance is a sign of a thick crust.
Spiritual concerns controlling lust.
Service to others for confidence is a must.

50A. HONESTY

"Honesty, hope, faith, courage, integrity, willingness, humility, brotherly love, justice, perseverance, spiritual, and service," Alcoholics Anonymous, Bill Wilson and Robert Smith, 1935.

Honesty is a basic component of personal pride and confidence. Even if only you alone know you are honest, it will be a source of pride and confidence. Further, it is completely impossible to fool all the people, all the time resulting in, if you are not honest, other people knowing that you are a dishonest cheat. Pride and confidence for most people just will not be sustained when other people consider you dishonest, and you know that they are right.

Be honest with yourself, and put forth an honest and sufficient effort to exceed what people expect of you. Knowing this and knowing that they know will be a tremendous source of pride and confidence builder to you.

Honesty gives you time for creativity . . .
Once the burden of being caught . . .
Has been taken away by your honesty.
There will be time for being taught . . .
So expand your capacity . . .
By keeping honesty in your daily thought.

50B. HOPE

"Honesty, hope, faith, courage, integrity, willingness, humility, brotherly love, justice, perseverance, spiritual, and service," Alcoholics Anonymous, Bill Wilson and Robert Smith, 1935.

Hope is the anticipation that the future has reasonable prospects of being acceptable based on what you want. You want what you hope for to happen. And when you can have hope that something you desire might actually happen, your confidence and pride will be strengthened. Hope needs to be based on your experiences. If you grew up without hope that some, or even one, of your dreams will come true, hope would not be there, and pride and confidence would not be there either.

Assist children to grow up and mature with a sense of hope such that they believe at least one of their dreams will come true is an important component of raising a child. A child who has a reasonable chance of being successful will not be prone to binge drinking or depend on alcohol.

Hope keeps you looking up the hill . . .
As if the slope tilts downward still.
With hope we are encouraged to take the challenge on.
A child's personality built on hope lasts when you are gone.

50C. FAITH

"Honesty, hope, faith, courage, integrity, willingness, humility, brotherly love, justice, perseverance, spiritual, and service," Alcoholics Anonymous, Bill Wilson and Robert Smith, 1935.

Faith is the anticipation that the event in the future that you want to happen will happen. This is a stronger statement than hope although they both positively anticipate future events. The Christian religion is largely based on faith, not hope. Faith that Jesus died so that our sins would be forgiven if we are repentant, sorry for our sins, and that we have faith in God and Jesus. Faith goes further than just faith in God, though. While this is the faith that is the backbone of Christianity and includes the belief that our sins will be forgiven and at some point there will be eternal life in God's Kingdom, faith is necessary in almost anything we do and use. For example, you have faith that the car will start even though you have no understanding how the starting and ignition systems of cars work.

This kind of faith allows us to look beyond just the day-to-day life of going forth, living life, taking risks, and doing what has to be done. There is a bigger picture than just us and our understandings. This is very important . . . being able to accept certain realities on faith will be a basis of both pride and confidence. With generic faith, your mind will not be cluttered with doubt until you have time and choose to learn more about the topic.

This faith-based confidence and pride in yourself will discourage any dependence on alcohol or drugs beyond yourself and your faith.

What is there to see around the curve?
Even if there's a truck in my lane, I'll swerve.
Faith gives you confidence you can handle what comes your way.
Faith's light lets you have your day.

50D. COURAGE

"Honesty, hope, faith, courage, integrity, willingness, humility, brotherly love, justice, perseverance, spiritual, and service," Alcoholics Anonymous, Bill Wilson and Robert Smith, 1935.

Courage is extremely important for both pride and confidence.
It is extremely important to have the courage to say no in the face of pressure from your peers to say yes. Similarly, it is just as important to have the courage to say yes when there is pressure from your friends to say no. Courage to go against the flow when your judgment leads you to do so is a must for pride and confidence. Someone without this courage will suffer from a loss of pride and confidence when there is no courage to resist a popular but wrong direction.

I am thinking too that courage to face some of the rugged moments of life by being the gifted student, the linebacker, the quarterback, the wrestler, the baseball batter or hitter will push you along the path of pride and confidence. All require courage to face tests of skill as an individual before the public and peers. It should be a total boost to one's confidence and pride to be able to meet these challenges and know that you are equal to the test.

Life takes much to overcome its peril.
Dealing with the issues with no wail . . .
And being wide-eyed without fail . . .
Will keep the wind in your sail!

50E. INTEGRITY

"Honesty, hope, faith, courage, integrity, willingness, humility, brotherly love, justice, perseverance, spiritual, and service," Alcoholics Anonymous, Bill Wilson and Robert Smith, 1935.

Integrity means that you do what you say and say what you do, and you can be trusted to do and say the right thing. Knowing that people recognize this trait in you will be a source of confidence and pride.

Having the reputation of being honest and truthful means that you have integrity, and as a result, you should have confidence and pride in your approach to people and life.

On the other hand, if people decide that they cannot depend on you, this will reflect the absence of integrity and will bring scorn and rejection on you. That will no doubt result in the loss of your confidence and pride. The sad thing is, it is totally predictable and can be avoided. Live your life to achieve integrity, and pride and confidence will follow.

Mean what you say.
Hold a view and keep it.
Know what you stand for every day.
Make your actions count every little bit.

50F. WILLINGNESS

"Honesty, hope, faith, courage, integrity, willingness, humility, brotherly love, justice, perseverance, spiritual, and service," Alcoholics Anonymous, Bill Wilson and Robert Smith, 1935.

Willingness to do what's right and a willingness to avoid what's wrong is what we are looking for here. Willingness to support your fellow human beings' will put you into a position to achieve confidence and pride. Willingness must be coupled with some generally accepted positive personal characteristics to cause people's reaction toward you to reflect back to you and produce confidence and pride. The lack of positive feedback will generate negative reactions internally to you. Then people's reaction to you will be negative and will produce a negative impact to your confidence and pride. This is to say that your detection of their negative reaction will reduce your confidence and pride.

It is important for you to have willingness to:

- help with duties;
- say the right thing to support a friend;
- be with and get to know and enjoy family beyond parents and siblings;
- work for what you want and need;
- treat others with the same respect as you wish to be treated; and
- forgo instant gratification for the sake of long-term achievement.

Willingness is important to pride and confidence from a positive standpoint only if you are willing to do the right thing.

Skill pent up has little value.
Offer and follow through.
Agreeing to help is a virtue.
When it comes to help, let them think of you.
This is a willingness point of view.

50G. HUMILITY

"Honesty, hope, faith, courage, integrity, willingness, humility, brotherly love, justice, perseverance, spiritual, and service," Alcoholics Anonymous, Bill Wilson and Robert Smith, 1935.

To be humble is to have humility with your situation. No matter how good things are today, they can be reversed as soon as tomorrow. Therefore, appreciate what you have with humility. Success comes to those who work for success. Success is not mandatory, and failure can come also.

It is not always possible to anticipate all the variables. Without accounting for all the variables, success might not result or might not result as anticipated. Humbly appreciate what your current status provides for you, and realize that reversals are possible at almost any time.

The more "things" you have, the more things you have to protect and maintain. So be thankful and share your successes and good fortune with others!

A basic and clean past . . .
Gives a confidence that will last.
Be true to your principles . . . be steadfast . . .
And appreciate what you have . . . life will be a blast!

50H. BROTHERLY LOVE

"Honesty, hope, faith, courage, integrity, willingness, humility, brotherly love, justice, perseverance, spiritual, and service," Alcoholics Anonymous, Bill Wilson and Robert Smith, 1935.

Realize that most people want the very same for themselves and their families as you do. Therefore, they merit your respect and affection, brotherly love—if you will.

Brothers in interests and motives warrant your affection: brotherly love.

Look at the people with whom you deal as a friend and as a person with similar interests and needs. This is brotherly love.

The fact that you silently acknowledge through your actions, the fact that other people have similar wants and needs for themselves and their families will be important to your pride and confidence.

Knowing that you treat people as they should be treated, and how you want to be treated, will be a source of pride and confidence.

Be a friend of one and all.
Let no one short or tall . . .
Or of any color of winter, spring, summer, or fall . . .
Receive less of a handshake when you are on the ball.

Love them all, a friend you should be.
Most people are nice, you will see.
There are many ways love leads to glee.
Love's many faces will be for you appropriately.

50I. JUSTICE

"Honesty, hope, faith, courage, integrity, willingness, humility, brotherly love, justice, perseverance, spiritual, and service," Alcoholics Anonymous, Bill Wilson and Robert Smith, 1935.

"With liberty and justice for all." That is what we demand as citizens of the United States! More than receiving justice, our being just with those with whom we deal, based on shared values, can be a basis for our confidence and pride.

Most people would experience some guilt if they cheat someone. Maybe there will be just a tiny amount of guilt for some, but there will be guilt or even a lot of guilt in some particular situations.

Most people will feel guilt when cheating or treating others unfairly or blaming something on them or telling a half truth, which makes them look worse than they deserve.

This will result in a reduction in the instigator's pride and confidence. And if it doesn't, it certainly should. Assuming people have a conscience, their telling lies or half truths about another will result in loss of pride and confidence.

Everything, every act that you undertake, should build or support your fellow human being and add to your pride and confidence as well. If your actions cannot do both, rethink your approach to dealing with people.

Justice for all has a lot of quirks and bends.
Justice for the slayer—when does his life end?
Justice must at one time be defined.
Justice must be clear as to what it take to be confined.
Justice in the nineties ... who to blame?
Justice must be the same.
Justice must be the same for the fame and the infame.
Justice: what to give and who to retain.

50J. PERSEVERANCE

"Honesty, hope, faith, courage, integrity, willingness, humility, brotherly love, justice, perseverance, spiritual, and service," Alcoholics Anonymous, Bill Wilson and Robert Smith, 1935.

"Be determined," "persistence," "tenacious," and "never give up" are a few synonyms of perseverance.

First, know where you are going and what your vision is!

What do you want to accomplish?

Perseverance when you don't have a vision is close to worthless. This makes the point of going hard in the wrong direction. Once you know what you want to do or what you want to accomplish with your life or even the next period of time of your life, then perseverance is an attribute that will give you confidence and pride.

A determined "never give up no matter what your target" attitude is a valuable resource and advantage over others with whom you compete. Perseverance in this situation will give you confidence and pride and can be a building block for the future. Most, if not all, of our country's most accomplished leaders, either from business or government, must have exhibited perseverance in order to overcome the obstacles before achieving success.

Abraham Lincoln lost many more elections than he won, yet he is still regarded as one of the top-five presidents in our country's history. The most gifted athlete must persevere to stay at the top. Without perseverance, the athlete, the musician, or any performer will drop back into the pack.

Unless the performer is willing to "be determined," "be persistent," "be tenacious," and "never give up," the field soon catches up, and there is no recognition for excellence and thus . . . no building block for pride and confidence.

History is full of those who used this tool.
Success comes to those who end on top.
Quitting is stopping before you win, don't be a fool!
Be tough, persevere . . . don't stop!

50K. SPIRITUAL

"Honesty, hope, faith, courage, integrity, willingness, humility, brotherly love, justice, perseverance, spiritual, and service," Alcoholics Anonymous, Bill Wilson and Robert Smith, 1935.

Spiritual values surrounding the main beliefs of Christianity are important to pride and confidence. Christians believe that there is an opportunity to spend eternity with God and Jesus in Heaven if one has faith in Jesus and God and if the person is repentant for his or her sins. One would expect that Christians with faith who are repentant would have confidence in the future and they would be proud of their stand on such an important issue.

Believing Christians have it both ways because they have eternity with God to look forward to. And it is possible to have a very happy and successful life here on earth resulting from their practicing Christian virtues. Christians avoid many of life's perils and thereby are not plagued by many of life's difficulties. This is not because of prayer but because of the nature of their lifestyle. That will leave time to find success in a career, or in school, or in sport, or various combinations of these and other endeavors.

Pride and confidence will result from a happy anticipation about the future and even the smooth, relatively trouble-free present.

Christians believe that the path to heaven . . .
Is based on a faith in God and His Son . . .
And a repentant heart to keep the balance even.
Without these truths your life and eternity will be on the run.

50L. SERVICE

"Honesty, hope, faith, courage, integrity, willingness, humility, brotherly love, justice, perseverance, spiritual, and service," Alcoholics Anonymous, Bill Wilson and Robert Smith, 1935.

Little can match the satisfaction of providing a useful service to other human beings. As has been indicated at other locations in this book, so much good comes to the provider of positive service that it is easy to see how service can be a source of pride and confidence.

Being able to help others gives you a great feeling. Whether the help is in providing a free service, just in a gratuitous act of kindness or service or whether it is a service provided for a fee such as in an accountant, engineer, police, or airplane pilot.

Providing service to your fellowman, or woman, is an opportunity to go forth and do good. It will provide an opportunity to achieve happiness, and that will also be a source of confidence and pride to you.

Service is a task for you!
Daily perform at least one good deed . . .
That will help another . . . even when not in full view.
Add service to your creed.

51

Salada Tea Taglines:

Where or when these sayings were first published is not clear. A friend of mine, Ed Dolby, had collected them. Later, Ed made them available to me. Since most of them made sense as a useful saying or piece of wisdom, I wanted to include them in this writing.

51A. SALADA TEA TAGLINES: A PAT ON THE BACK IS MORE POWERFUL THAN A KICK IN THE PANTS.

If you believe, and I do, that everyone needs to be appreciated, then you believe that for most situations, a pat on the back is more powerful than a kick in the pants. The skill comes in designing situations in which the people you are dealing with achieve something that is recognizable as deserving a pat on the back.

If your child is charged with watering the plants but forgets and all the plants die, how can the child deserve a pat on the back? Obviously, they don't. They deserve a kick in the pants.

Well, if a pat is more powerful than a kick, why wouldn't you give them a pat? The pat must be credible; the receiving person must accept the pat as a credible reaction to their efforts or the pat on the back is wasted.

The trick is to put your children, your subordinates, and others in our life with whom you deal into situations in which they can succeed sufficiently often to truly warrant a pat on the back. Sometimes, that requires much management or parental skill, but it is a necessary prerequisite to a successful leader.

Encouragement is right to pass the test.
A pat or congrats is best . . .
When the deeds warrant such a bequest.
Don't reward less than best . . .
That too must be stressed.

51B. SALADA TEA TAGLINES: YOU CAN'T IMPROVE YOUR PHYSICAL FITNESS BY RUNNING DOWN YOUR FRIENDS.

This is a tongue-in-cheek statement with a play on words.

Don't run down your family or friends at all. There is no need to run down anyone. And certainly, if you do, there is absolutely no fitness benefit. Generally, if you don't have anything good to say about someone, don't say it; don't run them down.

And if doesn't improve you fitness, and it doesn't, why do it?

Family and friends expect and deserve loyalty and support, not behind-the-back derogatory statements.

You should feel sorry for those who believe they must run other people down. I think they do it because they feel inadequate themselves and hope to gain some psychological advantage to build themselves up . . . by running someone else down. It is like eating sweets or potato chips. You think chips or candy will make you feel better because they taste good. But they truly don't make you feel better either in the short or longer range. The same goes for running another person down. You may think it will make you feel better, but both in the short and longer range, such behavior generates a hollow victory because most people see through what you are doing.

If you don't have something positive to say . . .
Save it for another day.
Don't let those little zips pass your way.
Build up, not tear down, should be the self you portray.

51C. SALADA TEA TAGLINES: NO MAN CAN DO MORE THAN HIS BEST NOR SHOULD HE DO LESS

Always do your best. If you agree to do something for someone, exceed what they expect of you.

Everyone has a certain tolerance for being on the spot where their absolute best performance is required. Where your performance is being assessed, and your performance is being assessed most of the time you are in public, you must do your best. People see your effort and judge you. Never give people an opportunity to see in you anything but the best.

There are some who never know when to quit because they do not know what their best is and really are left continually with indecision . . . not knowing when enough is enough.

Through your best efforts, can you greatly exceed the expectations of some, just barely exceed the expectations of others, meet the expectations of others, or just not matching the expectation, of certain people with whom you are dealing. Different people have different expectations.

Negotiate the task, and make sure you meet and exceed what people truly expect of you. A combination of your efforts and clarifying what people expect of you will enable you to achieve the challenge of always exceeding people's expectations of you.

Do your best or lay down the bat . . .
There is little value to aiming low.
Those without desire to wear the champ's hat . . .
Drift downward and watch challengers grow.

51D. SALADA TEA TAGLINES: BE SURE OF YOUR FACTS OR BE PREPARED FOR DISAPPOINTMENT.

Everything that occurs is based on facts . . . and you can't have your own facts . . . everyone must share the same facts. What time is it? A fact that can make or break your life. How much does it cost? Where can I get it?

Where am I going? What do I want to be? What do I want my life's work to be? What happened? What will happen? All facts, which, if not known, will set the scene for your happiness or disappointment.

Pointing out everything that we do that requires facts would soon become so nitpicky that a presentation of even the simplest activities would seem so complicated and so obvious that the reader would be turned away or "turned off."

Suffice it to say that reading any document including this one, performing any business operation, discussing any issue all require facts.

Without these and similar facts, your life's experiences will certainly bring disappointment. You will find out that knowledge is power. Facts trump opinions and feeling. The *Wall Street Journal*, the *USA Today*, and *Reader's Digest* are all great sources of facts to rebut opinion and feelings. I recommend reading and digesting all three to receive a balanced education of current events. Because of limited memory, most people must keep the discussion targeted to have sufficient knowledge to defeat opinions and feelings with facts.

Get it right.
Facts aren't so trite.
Without them, you drop out of sight.
There is no reason for fright . . .
Know your facts with all your might.

51E. SALADA TEA TAGLINES: DRIVE DEFENSIVELY. AN ACCIDENT THAT DOESN'T HAPPEN HELPS BOTH YOU AND THE OTHER DRIVER.

Be careful and make sure you anticipate accidents before they occur.

It is easier to explain what you did to avoid an accident than to explain why you didn't do something and an accident occurred.

It is easier to think first than to explain later.

It is easier to take heat for the delay than it is to take heat for not thinking.

Make sure you know the rules of the road distributed by the Illinois Secretary of State.

Think about everything that you do when you are driving before you do them. This will give you an opportunity to make changes in what you are going to do and avoid accidents.

Driving a car is an expensive and potentially deadly activity. There is no margin for error; when you do something while driving a car, it must be correct the first time.

It is so much easier to think before you act . . .
Than to have to scrape up a thought, looking back.
Reasons for making a move, looking ahead . . .
Are so much better than explaining the past instead.

51F. SALADA TEA TAGLINES: A JOB WELL DONE REQUIRES AN ENTHUSIASTIC BEGINNING FOLLOWED BY INTELLIGENT DETERMINATION.

This is another way of describing passion for succeeding in an undertaking along with a vision for what the person wants to accomplish.

First, you must care whether you will achieve a job well done. If you don't care about the outcome, spare potential partners and teammates from your participation.

If you truly don't care, do all your potential partners and teammates a favor and tell them you really don't care about the outcome and give them an opportunity to select another teammate, if that is the case.

An enthusiastic beginning is another way of describing passion for successfully starting out toward completing the task.

A strong passionate beginning followed by a vision of where you want to head or what you want to accomplish is important to the mission's success.

To do a job well . . .
Know about yourself, feel swell.
Start with vigor . . .
Stay with it with rigor.

51G. SALADA TEA TAGLINES: THINK HOW HAPPY YOU WOULD BE IF YOU LOST EVERYTHING—THEN FOUND IT AGAIN.

Losing everything and then finding it again is not a recommended process to find happiness. There is absolutely no reason to put yourself through the process of losing everything and then finding it or earning it back again.

You would be happy later, but immediately before finding "your lost treasure," whatever it is, again you would be very unhappy. Besides being very hard on your immune system, too much of your energies focused in a catch-up mode will be counterproductive. It will be much better to be focused on a positive direction and your successes. Avoid the losses and plan only to move forward with hard-earned successes. This will be much better for you in the long term.

Getting back what you lost . . .
No doubt would be a happy thought.
But a loss comes with a cost.
Best to keep it all and not get caught . . .
A loss of value for you will belike the coldest frost.

51H. SALADA TEA TAGLINES: PEOPLE WHO GET DISCOVERED AND THOSE WHO GET FOUND OUT ARE VERY DIFFERENT.

This is a play on words. "People who get discovered" in the common language meaning describes the process of discovering someone who has real value. "People who get found out" means something else and generally describes finding out about someone who does evil or has the reputation of not doing things well.

It follows, then, that you should make sure your actions are sufficient quality that you are one of those who needs to or deserves to be discovered.

Don't be in the group that people are trying to find out about you because of the bad things you have done. Conduct yourself in a way that you are pleased and proud of what you have done and want to be discovered. Avoid being in a position where you have to walk around with a fear that someone will find you out.

Huh, splitting hairs is the gist of this case.
A cutie with a smile upon her face . . .
Works hard and gets discovered.
The other sweats to avoid being uncovered.
Why such a difference in the first place?

51I. SALADA TEA TAGLINES: ALMOST ALWAYS THE LAST KEY YOU TRY OPENS THE DOOR.

Everything that occurs is based on facts. What key opens the lock? The right key may be a fact that can make or break your life. Life-altering facts are facts that, if not known, will set the scene for your disappointment. As indicated, be sure of your facts or be prepared for disappointment. Why carry a key that you don't know what it is for?

This saying may be a form of a Murphy's Law: everything that can go wrong will go wrong at the most inopportune time. Murphy's Law is a great reminder to plan to deal with emergencies and contingencies. Always have a plan and alternatives to deal with contingencies. The plan, your plan, is the most direct route to get from where you are to where you want to be. Then the contingency plans to deal with unforeseen situations that might end up being barriers to your success can be developed and used.

The last key has but one trait.
Such is the deal when you are late . . .
Guessing is not something you would equate . . .
To knowing what the key will facilitate.

51J. SALADA TEA TAGLINES: THE GREATER THE PROBLEM, THE MORE GLORY IN SOLVING IT.

The greater the problem, the more the glory possible from solving it.

This is a partial statement in the realities of life when fairness is a part of issuing credit. The bigger the job accomplished, the more credit should be given to the one responsible.

You should be concerned with solving the problem and put all your energies into solving the problem. You must not be concerned with the credit. Keep up the good work and effort long enough and successful enough and you will receive all the credit and glory you can handle. This is true whether it is being done from the perspective of the school student, educational perspective, the sports world, or the world of business. Solving big and significant problems will eventually bring credit and perhaps glory to you.

The other portion of the broad statement is, the bigger the problem. The more difficult it is, the more risks are involved with stepping forth to solve the problem.

The dream of a confident baseball player is to be up at bat, bases loaded, down by two, and needing a hit to win. The potential for glory is great.

On the other hand, the potential for failure is great and with that kind of exposure. The potential for being a scapegoat or the subject of ridicule is great too.

Difficult problems do bring risks to the leaders trying to solve the situation. Of course there are risks—but with sufficient training and practice, the person taking up the challenge should be confident of success. And after taking up the challenge, the endeavor should be successful with planning and a vision of exactly where you want to be at the completion of the project.

Demand to handle the tough story.
Anything less could be a little gory.
Take charge, you deserve the glory.
If you leave it to others, you will be sorry.

51K. SALADA TEA TAGLINES: THE TRUE WORTH OF WATER IS SELDOM REALIZED UNTIL THE WELL RUNS DRY.

Items that are routinely used are not fully appreciated until they are scarce. In most places we are personally familiar, water is plentiful and not fully appreciated. If the source of the water becomes dry, then water becomes a scarce, valuable commodity and the topic of every conversation in the city.

Similarly, for most things that we routinely use, their full worth is not appreciated until they are difficult to acquire in an adequate supply.

Gold is a good example. Since gold is limited in supply and money is printed to subsidize out of control government spending, gold's value in dollars is quite elevated.

The economic system that governs our society is one of supply and demand. The supply governs the demand and the price. Or does the demand govern the supply and price? The entire commodities market depends on the principle of value increasing as the supply dwindles. When the supply of corn is perceived to be abundant, the price drops. When the supply is perceived to be scarce, the price goes up. The relationship is not direct, but price is greatly influenced by supply.

Similarly, your value as perceived by your loved ones is sometimes increased if your presence becomes scarce or at least less abundant. This could be the subject of a PhD thesis but important. The bottom line truth is though . . . you will be appreciated more if you are occasionally scarce. Perhaps your value is enhanced by the life and your support given during your presence.

To the nonthinker who waits . . .
The dry well may be the first trait . . .
Of lost value beyond the gate.
Gone but not forgotten, we hope to retake . . .
That which we lost, if we get a remake.

51L. SALADA TEA TAGLINES: BE FRIENDLY AND YOU WILL NEVER WANT FOR FRIENDS.

This is the basic theme of Dale Carnegie's book *How to Win Friends and Influence People*. Be friendly and you will never want for friends . . . but not necessarily a true-blue, always-loyal friend.

Dedicating a life to doing nice things for people is sincerely a good way to ensure having lots of friends. And it isn't an artificial ploy to acquire friends. People enjoy and want to be with friendly and pleasant people. If you are friendly and pleasant, people will want to be with you, and you will never want for friends.

Some may say that you are artificial if you are always friendly, pleasant, or happy. But that isn't necessarily artificial; that is just seeing the glass half full rather than half empty. Being friendly is an attitude and approach to dealing with people. Why not be friendly? There is absolutely no reason not to be friendly.

The six Carnegie principles of winning friends are all very important for being "friendly. Genuine friendliness requires genuineness or honesty in your approach to applying these principles to your acquaintances.

It takes a great deal of time to be a friend. Being friendly is one thing—it is more superficial. Being a friend requires lots of time to be available in the good times and bad times to do things with and for the other person. Usually true friends bond through some difficult or challenging experiences in which they get to know and appreciate the other person.

You must recognize that there will always be people who develop an attitude about you in spite of your friendliness and good intentions. Being friendly just will not be enough with those people! They will never be your friend, but you should be friendly and respectful with them . . . who knows, maybe they will flip and become friendly if not a friend.

True, be friendly to win a friend.
A smile, a short conversation will transcend . . .
The space between travelers I contend.
Ask about them and start a trend.

51M. SALADA TEA TAGLINES: FIGURES CAN BE MISLEADING—BUT THOSE ON THE COST OF LIVING ARE ON THE UP AND UP.

This is a play on words, which rightfully implies that statistics can be misleading. This is true; depending on how some things are interpreted, statistics can be misleading. While figures can be misleading, you won't need figures to know that the cost of living will steadily increase.

Liars figure, but figures don't lie . . . but figures can be arranged in a way to mislead but perhaps not lie.

Annual increases in the cost of living will vary from 2.5 percent, as it was during the last ten years, to 19 percent, as it was during the administration of President Carter. Small increases in the costs of living are not necessarily bad.

Trust an analysis on data or reporting of analyses only if you totally understand what questions were asked regarding how the data was interpreted, and how the figures were arranged.

The cost of living may be going up . . .
But the cost of living you can interrupt.
Spend less than you make or it will be abrupt!
Overcome the desire to partake . . .
Never spend more than you make.

51N. SALADA TEA TAGLINES: YOUR MIND IS SOMEWHAT LIKE A PARACHUTE—NEITHER WORK UNLESS OPEN.

We all have seen the videos or movies of the parachutist screaming toward earth four thousand feet below with the unopened parachute trailing behind, rippling in the wind. What a horrifying sight? Can you imagine how that person might feel? What must he or she be thinking? I have heard in situations such as that, one's whole life flies past them as they scream toward the rock-solid landing. What if they had checked the packing of the parachute so that it would have opened? What if they had just packed the emergency chute? What if they had just not played around with that other skydiver and got the parachutes mixed up and tangled?

What a waste? A life goes screaming out of sight and will be doomed in a few seconds. That is what I think of when I am reminded of a young person who has a closed mind. How can a young person have a closed mind? What I am talking about? How can I speak of someone having a closed mind?

A young person with no willingness to dance is a closed mind. This was my single biggest mistake when I was a teenager. It doesn't sound serious, but when you consider countless social settings where I was unwilling to relax, dance, and have a fun time just being with my friends, this resulted in my feeling left out and uncomfortable with myself in situations where dancing was part of the agenda.

A young person unwilling to eat anything but certain foods and unwilling listen to the importance of nutrition is a closed mind. A young person without passion toward much of anything except video games, hanging out with buds, and staying away from parents during free time is a closed mind.

A young person unwilling to study and take advantage of the educational and other opportunities of youth is like the parachutists screaming toward earth although they may not have started screaming yet. They do not yet know that their life is being wasted by their closed mind keeping them away from fully taking advantage of their educational and training opportunities.

A young person unwilling to discuss their life and life's events with their family, parents has a closed mind. And the reason why they don't want to talk their actions over with their parents is because they have their mind made up and do not want input at all from their parents . . . and to some extent . . . peer pressure and not wanting to go against the "flow" with their friends. That is a closed mind as tight as the parachutist screaming down out of the sky.

A young person with a closed mind is and will be very much like the parachutist screaming down toward earth with a closed parachute streaming down behind that person. And if the mind doesn't open before hitting bottom, I fear the results will be sad for all concerned.

Keep an open mind.
Learn all the facts and you will find . . .
Knowledge is power; with it life will be kind.
And if closed the landing won't be sublime.

510. SALADA TEA TAGLINES: TIME SPENT GETTING EVEN WOULD BE BETTER SPENT IN GETTING AHEAD.

Getting even with someone for something that they did to you will not necessarily move you toward your goals. Moving toward your goals, or getting ahead, should be the emphasis of most, if not all, of your energies.

Usually, if someone does you a wrong, rather than retaliating and getting even, it is best to let them know in no uncertain terms that type of behavior must stop. And if it does, that can be the end of it for you, and you will be able to go ahead living your life and strive for your goals.

If they insist on continuing the unsatisfactory behavior and the behavior is harmful to your life's direction and vision, then your action must be focused on either stopping the unsatisfactory behavior or taking a few extra skips down the road rather than trying to get even with the person.

There are times when your action may appear to be getting even, and it really isn't. If you ask the person to terminate the unsatisfactory behavior and they refuse, they must believe that their behavior is appropriate for the situation and are rejecting your opinion that their performance is unsatisfactory. In this case, first give them a minor dose of their "own medicine," and that, maybe, is all it takes for them to get the message and terminate the unsatisfactory behavior. In my mind, it just does not sit well to plead with someone to "be nice to me." Like I said . . . give them a small dose of their own behavior. Not all will get the message quickly, and you may need to elevate the dose of their own medicine higher and higher until they finally do get the message. Remember, this is only if their behavior is harmful to your cause and you choose not to move on.

As soon as possible, divert your actions toward getting ahead "of the everyday" routine. Pack and strive toward your goals.

Getting even is often a waste.
Reaction should not be made in haste . . .
The best approach is to get ahead.
But once in a while, be them instead.

51P. SALADA TEA TAGLINES: YOU'RE A DIPLOMAT IF YOU CAN CUT A CAKE SO EVERYBODY THINKS HE HAS THE BIGGEST SLICE.

Looking at *Webster's New World Dictionary* and picking the definition of "diplomat," which seems most appropriate . . . "Diplomat" means "a person skilled in dealing with other people; a tactful person."

One simple rule is, the person who cuts the cake picks last.
You really don't need to fool people into believing that they are getting the largest piece of cake.

A diplomat, in normal circumstances, will have little trouble convincing the people that they all are getting an equal size piece of cake and everyone's piece of cake is pretty big. If this is done, they should be happy and you will be also.

This is a reasonable goal whether you are dividing the cake, marbles, company profits, or positions on the county board. If people are confident of your intent to be fair, they will consider you a diplomat and will trust your decisions.

A diplomat represents us—there.
A diplomat can be a member and be anywhere.
A diplomat must be able to split a hair.
And above all . . . a diplomat must be able to do it . . . fair.

51Q. SALADA TEA TAGLINES: YOU HAVE POISE IF YOU CAN BE ILL AT EASE INCONSPICUOUSLY.

Since it is good to know the base word, which represents the point of initiation of the discussion, again, *Webster* is consulted for the definition of the word "poise." In *Webster*, "poise" means "balance; stability; ease and dignity of manner; self-assurance; composure; the condition of being calm or serene."

Here, poise is the appearance of "balance; stability; ease and dignity of manner; self-assurance; composure; the condition of being calm or serene" while actually being ill at ease.

Most of the successful contributors to their particular fields of endeavor, be it sports, or politics, or entertainment, or you name it, must have poise. And in most highly visible competitive or combative situations involving their particular field, the individual will poses just the appearance of poise. This is true because the competitor's thoughts will be racing toward succeeding in the situation, without significant visible turmoil.

Poise comes with experiencing the fray . . .
Don't let anyone lead you astray.
Keep it light as if to play . . .
And you will soon be able to conquer all that comes your way.

51R. SALADA TEA TAGLINES: POLITICIANS ARE VERY ADEPT AT ANSWERING QUESTIONS NOBODY ASKS.

There are many generalizations that could be made regarding politicians; this is not necessarily the first one I would make.

Yes, some do and some do not answer questions.

Democratic politicians tend to bias their answers and their activities on the side of more and more government activities. They generally believe that a more and more powerful government is needed to provide for people who largely cannot take care of themselves. Did I say Nanny State? More and more people employed by and earning their income from the government will be the result. They make an error by letting the government make more and more of their decisions.

Republican politicians tend to bias their answers and their activities by assuming that people need to solve their own problems and government needs to do less and less to help its constituency. More and more people employed by and earning their income in the private sector will be the result. They will establish a government, which makes less and less of your decisions and expects you to be more responsible for more of your destiny.

There is a potential for illegal activity on either side of this issue, but this is a side problem and must be dealt with sternly as it occurs.

Do not tolerate any illegal activity from either side and always support the Republican's ... smaller government ... point of view.

When an answer is posed to you ...
Beware when the politician's actions come into view ...
There will be a difference between what they do ...
And what they say ... I am telling you.

51S. SALADA TEA TAGLINES: ALL TOO OFTEN, WHEN NOTHING REMAINS TO BE SAID, SOMEBODY SAYS IT.

The issue here is "who" decides when nothing remains to be said? If there are twenty people in the room, for example, there will be twenty different opinions as to when enough has been said on the topic. So if you are operating under the assumption that nothing else needs to be stated, there, very likely, will be nineteen other people in the room who disagree with you.

Actually, this is a very arrogant statement. Peering down and presuming, in a contested issue, at some point, there is nothing else to be said. That is pure arrogance.

Operate under the rules; use good common sense and your very best judgment and kindness. If you have something else to say, say it and to heck with the jerk in the room saying that everything has already been stated.

There is another side of course . . . every meeting needs to have a set time limit so that there will be a sense of urgency. Hold the meeting, set a definite time limit, and start with a defined agenda. Stick with the agenda and time limit and cover the topics fairly and finish on time.

What a touch?
When there is nothing left to be stated . . .
Some will dig deep but not say much.
And adjournment will be belated.

51T. SALADA TEA TAGLINES: TO AVOID MAKING MISTAKES, YOU MUST GAIN EXPERIENCE—BUT TO DO THAT, YOU OFTEN MAKE MISTAKES.

True . . . but a tangled web you say? A leader will spend all his or her life stretching abilities and capabilities. This means leaders will spend a lifetime of stretching and gaining additional experience; and of course, mistakes will be made.

In order to be the very best you can be, you must gain experience. You must not fear mistakes. Training and gaining experience will be the path you need to follow to be your best. The vision of where you ultimately want to be must be in your mind's eye. This will allow you to look beyond all the practice and mistakes as you gain experience. Keep in mind that the best baseball players only get a hit four out of ten times; the best basketball players hit the basket only one out of two times; President Lincoln lost many more elections than he won.

Work hard and smart, practice and train, do your best, and move through your mistakes with your head held high.

Practice is another form . . .
For gaining experience and skill.
Mistakes are forgotten as a norm.
Provided there is growth heading uphill.

51U. SALADA TEA TAGLINES: FRIENDSHIPS EARNED BEFORE YOU NEED THEM ARE ALMOST CERTAIN TO BE MORE LASTING.

There is a saying much earlier in this book something to the effect that "to have a friend, you must be a friend." That saying certainly applies in this case. Be a friend, and there will be hope, later when and if you need the help and support of a friend, the person, the friend, will be there for you.

Express friendship through smiling and being cordial and friendly with the people that you are around in school, teams, neighbors, and fellow workers. Friends are usually people with whom you share interests and goals. If they need help, offer the assistance willingly and with a smile on your face. Be there when they need you, and always do it with a smile on your face.

And do more than just the superficial offer of help. Try your best to help them almost to the point of being pushy.

These are one-on-one situations in which you must give of yourself, your time, your energy, and your effort. These situations make you, the person, and your peers evaluate you on what you contribute to the relationship, not just because of who you are and what you say. If you pass their test of a friend before you start asking or needing them for friendly favors, the friendship is much more likely to be long lasting.

A friendship because you are friends . . .
Is much more than a means to ends.
Too often it is not clear . . .
Are you a friend or are you there just to cover your rear?

51V. SALADA TEA TAGLINES: FLY INTO A RAGE ONLY AT THE RISK OF MAKING A BAD LANDING.

Flying into a rage implies going out of control. When you are out of control, your situation moves from one in which your actions are ruled by reasoned thought to one in which your situation is governed by wild reactions to static in your brain, a formula for trouble.

Obviously, the "fly into a rage" along with "the bad landing" are a play on words. If you fly off into a rage, you must land, and the result of a rage on you will not be pleasant.

This saying becomes a warning that you can expect a "double dose of bad" if you fly into a rage—the first dose being the problem that irritated you in the first place, the second dose being the negative impact of your rage.

My advice is to assess the initial situation that provided the irritation to you. If you are angry, walk away and think through what your measured and controlled response will be as opposed to a mindless burst of rage—as in flying off in a rage.

Do I always do this? No, but I should and I should have—but I have not always done this. Of course, this was my approach some of the time; maybe most of the time but not always. Looking back, I certainly believe a controlled response would have been best. This is my advice . . . assess the initial situation that provided the irritation to you. If you are angry, walk away and think through what your measured and controlled response will be.

A rage is not what to fly into . . .
Too often a cage is where they put you.
Space between you and your target . . .
Will save you from being the one they won't forget.

51W. SALADA TEA TAGLINES: A SPOILED CHILD IS A PERFECT EXAMPLE OF MINORITY RULE IN THE HOUSE.

First, what is a spoiled child? Looking to *Webster* for a definition of "spoiled child," I found the following as modified to fit this format: "a child who has been overindulged so as to demand or expect too much."

Determining whether a child is spoiled or supported very well is a fine line and usually difficult for parents to clearly ascertain. For parents who have progressed through their own childhood, their education both in high school and college and then marry before they begin to have children, supporting their children becomes a very important purpose to their life.

One of the greatest things you can do for your child is to raise them to expect a great deal out of life and to have the child believe that they certainly have a say in their own destiny.

Raising your child to do this and, at the same time, always being respectful of peers and adults is a wishful goal and is sometimes achieved.

No one person, including the parents, should always have absolute and always the final say about what happens in a family. Everyone should have a say, and everyone should at least occasionally get their way . . . with the understanding that the parents will have to OK the final decision.

This is not minority rule; this is an appropriate environment to prepare children for being an adult who will have an impact on the world.

Children must realize that while they are moving through the single-digit years and through the early teen years, they will have to take a secondary role to their parents. Later, they will assume more and more responsibility and authority in their actions.

Re . . . a spoiled child, the words are true.
But a clear picture as I think of another or two.
A parent with love in his (her) heart . . .
Must scramble to play his part.
Thus, the minority rule comes into view.

51X. SALADA TEA TAGLINES: EVEN THOUGH YOU MAY FAIL TO ATTAIN—YOU MUST NEVER FAIL TO ASPIRE.

Aspire is to have a vision of where you want to be with a focused effort. With aspirations, you set off in life with your plan for what you want to do with your time, the critical variable of life, as the groundwork toward your vision or aspiration.

Without a vision toward which you are working through your life's activities, it becomes impossible to measure success as well as failure. Without a vision, any definition of success or failure becomes arbitrary.

Never fear failure if you are certain the failure was along the path of achieving your vision. A failure truly is not a failure if you learned something and it was along the path of achieving your vision.

Pick the greatest political figure, the greatest business leader, the greatest athlete, or any other example of a person who has achieved greatness in their particular field. I am sure you will find a life with a vision and many failures along that route. Nevertheless, they may have achieved a great deal because they were relentless in the pursuit of their vision.

The people who were at the top, such as presidents Lincoln, Reagan, or Bush, or baseball players such as Ted Williams, Stan Musials, and Ozzie Smith must have visions and must have striven for their vision. Without a vision for just the regular person, life could sink into a purposeless swamp of hours and hours of TV programs and mindless other activities. Year after year such a life will become the basis for a sense of failure.

If you have a vision of where you want to be at various points in your future, that is extremely important. Expect a few failures and remember: the higher your vision, the greater the likelihood of more failures, but don't fear them. Expect them, learn from them, and move on toward your vision.

What I Would Have Said . . .

Aspire, dear one . . .
See clearly your vision . . .
having not won . . .
At each division.

Failure to attain . . .
Still is a gain.
Failure to aspire . . .
Is a loss; don't conspire.

51Y. SALADA TEA TAGLINES: EVEN NATURE IS NOT PERFECT. SHE LETS SPRING FEVER AND HOUSE CLEANING COME AT THE SAME TIME.

This is a cutesy little phrase about spring cleaning and spring fever coming at the same time.

Nature is totally not predictable.

But spring comes every year, and spring cleaning must be done whether you do it in spring or once a month or once a week.

The relevant point to make here is the fact that there will always be choices you have to make. There will be choices in the things that you would rather do for entertainment. For example, do you go on a picnic with these friends or go to a ball game with others? There will be many choices of entertainment rather than work or study. There will be choices to make among employment opportunities. Do you work for this company or that company? Do you choose to take a job in your hometown rather than let the first best job offer decide where to live when you get out of college?

The issue is not Mother Nature's perfection; the issue here is, what do you do with the choices you have or get to make? The fact of the matter is for most people, a decision comes along several times a day equivalent to the decision between spring cleaning and spring fever.

What do you do? Hopefully, you don't always choose spring fever, and you don't always choose spring cleaning. The key is to maintain a balance in your decisions consistent with your vision of what you want to accomplish in life rather than doing what the current fun thing. Balance fun and work consistent with your life's vision.

Though spring comes but once a year,
Decisions you make every day,
It soon becomes clear,
Will greatly guide what you have to do and say.

51Z. SALADA TEA TAGLINES: ALWAYS PUT OFF UNTIL THE DAY AFTER TOMORROW THE THINGS YOU SHOULDN'T DO AT ALL.

This is an opposite direction version of the anti-procrastination saying, "Never put off until tomorrow things that you are supposed to do today."

This saying is basically one which tells you to think before you act. Give yourself some time to think before you act if there is any question at all whether you should be doing something.

So why agree to do it at all if you're not sure? Day after tomorrow never comes because as long as you are not sure, the time you should be doing that item is day after tomorrow.

This is not an excuse to avoid doing something that needs to be done and that you are expected to do. This saying merely gives you an opportunity to set a time, get the proponent off your back, and then determine yourself if it should be done at all.

When and if you decide that the item should not be done at all, you indicate that you will not be doing that and stop scheduling it totally. If you decide the item should be done and you will do it, set a more-thoughtful date and time and then do the task well and promptly.

Tomorrow has an excellent sound . . .
To not do what you construe . . .
Will certainly get around town,
And make you parents blue.

51AA. SALADA TEA TAGLINES: ALIMONY IS SOMETIMES KNOWN AS BOUNTY ON THE MUTINY.

Mutiny on the Bounty is the name of a book by Charles Nordhoff. So this saying is a ploy on that title.

A dictionary definition of "mutiny" is "an open rebellion against lawful authority."

A definition of "alimony" is a fixed sum of money paid regularly to a former spouse under orders from a court.

The mutiny involved here is the ending of a marriage by one or both of the marriage partners filing for divorce. A judge from the court system would need to be involved as would lawyers and lots of expenses to say nothing of the damage to the two people's lives. If there are children involved, the damage is much worse.

The decision to get married and the decision to have children is not to be taken lightly. Notice the marrying comes first before the practicing to have children.

Prior to marriage, there needs to be true love, even passion between the partners, but there also needs to be an official, well-thought-out financial plan and an official well-thought-out plan to resolve conflict not resolvable between the partners.

A marriage ending in mutiny . . .
Does alimony get paid?
This deserves more scrutiny.
When tomorrow she's no maid!

51BB. SALADA TEA TAGLINES: TO END A WAR IS FINE, BUT TO KEEP ONE FROM STARTING IS BETTER.

The end of every disagreement should to be a win for each side, an application of the well-known phrase, win-win. At the end of the disagreement between people, or nations, both parties actually feel like they were a winner coming out of the disagreement . . . that is a win-win. This is the point of win-win.

It is not acceptable for the war, say, interpersonal disagreements, to be avoided by one party being the loser and the other party being the big winner. That is not an acceptable way to keep the war or conflicts from starting. However, if one party clearly started the belligerence, that party should be the loser. Somewhere in that point, fairness must be factored in too.

It will be difficult to avoid wars among individuals as well as countries with both parties ending as a winner: often there is a history to the issue that makes it difficult to have both come out as a winner.

If one party to a dispute is sitting on a considerable amount of territory once held by the other party or if the one party in the past did terrible things to the ancestors of the other party, coming to a win-win ending will be difficult. In a family argument between children and the argument is over something like one has the other's shirt, it is easy to go back to the conditions before the argument started and avoid the war. With adult family members, it gets more difficult because it gets harder to go back to conditions before the argument started.

An arbitrator needs to be involved at some point to assist in resolving the disagreement to aid in starting where they are now and coming to an agreeable end of the hostilities. Letting time pass plus accepting the fact that the other party exists and needs to be there . . . both are useful tools to end hostilities. They must end the hostilities and allow both parties to have some partial win allowing the win-win to occur.

Disputes grow into wars.
Alas it's true.
Men are from Mars . . .
Where does that leave you?

51CC. SALADA TEA TAGLINES: LIKE TEA, GETTING INTO HOT WATER TENDS TO BRING OUT THE BEST IN YOU.

Like the old saying, "When the going gets tough, the tough get going," this phrase implies that during tough times, certain people rise to the occasion to deal with the issues at hand. The saying "heroes are made, not born" implies the same thing . . . certain people rise to the occasion to deal with the issues at hand.

Adversity or difficult times give some of us an opportunity to use a greater percentage of our abilities.

Children, who are gifted scholastically, need to experience difficult situations to bring out their best and to stretch their abilities. Star athletes need difficult games and situations to bring out and expand their best. Lawyers need experience handling tough cases to sharpen their skills to prepare for specialized and advanced skills later in their careers. The same for surgeons; they need experience handling difficult surgeries to be able to confidently walk in and perform the more-complex operations on a patient.

All this describes the hot water, which is necessary to bring out the best of any of us.

Turn up the heat real slow . . .
And we will ride it out.
Let the heat quickly flow
And true leaders will turn on the clout.

51DD. SALADA TEA TAGLINES: AN OVERSIMPLIFICATION CAN GET MIGHTY COMPLICATED BEFORE BECOMING PRACTICAL.

Most accomplishments in life require considerable energy and thought to achieve. Cutting corners by skimping on either the energy or thought surely is an oversimplification of the solution to the problem.

When the oversimplification results in coming in lower than the targeted goal, complications can set in, and ultimately more effort will be required to undo the complications caused by the initial under achieving effort.

Doing something right by providing more than the targeted customer's expectations will save considerable effort in the long run by not having to redo the project. Exceeding expectations will assure that you will achieve a reputation with people by causing them to know that if something was done by you, it will be done well because you always do a job well and exceed expectations.

Easy becomes hard . . .
When the effort is not there.
If you rest in the yard . . .
Your results are nowhere.
Your basket will be bare.
And, you will have nothing to share.

51EE. SALADA TEA TAGLINES: A PERSON IS HAPPY ONLY WHEN HE BELIEVES HE IS!

Happiness is a state of mind. Is that what you have heard as well? Thinking that you are happy and knowing that your life is productive will be very satisfying.

What level of health or success, motivation, accomplishments or companionships are necessary to make a person think that he or she is happy?

There is no scale. That which makes a person happy is a totally arbitrary scale and will vary, even greatly, from person to person.

You have to convince yourself that you are happy. No one can make you happy, and no one can tell you to be happy when certain things happen. The elements . . . certain things and they vary . . . must happen, and those elements vary from person to person.

It is hardest to remain happy if you are depending on things and objects to keep you happy. Cars, houses, radio, and TV news, at best, should be a neutral in your life; neither making you happy or sad. They should not be the focus of your general feeling of happiness.

Focus on at least one thing in your life that you feel good about. There can be more, but at least focus on one thing or something that you enjoy and you feel good about. Let that be your guide to happiness.

To be happy here on earth, Christians should above all else think about where they will spend eternity. They expect to spend eternity in heaven with God, if they have faith in God and Jesus and are repentant/sorry for their sins.

Doing favors for people always brings a lift in overall well being or happiness. From letting the other person have the parking place when at all possible, to opening the door for someone, to letting the person with one or two items pass you in the grocery line, even the smallest favor or acts of kindness, freely given to others, can be uplifting and will give you a sense of well being and happiness.

Happiness is a satisfying thought;
Happiness is being kind;
Happiness can't be bought.
Happiness is a state of mind.

51FF. SALADA TEA TAGLINES: IF YOU MUST KILL TIME, TRY WORKING IT TO DEATH.

Time is the one thing in your life that, once it gets used, you cannot get back. Once gone, time is gone forever.

Killing time is equivalent to wasting a percentage of your life. Wasted time is wasted forever.

Everyone is entitled to entertainment, which should be scheduled as part of your life's activities and weighed against other activities of life. Sitting around in front of the TV is just killing time and should be avoided. If you wish to watch TV, watch it while you do some activity which is truly productive. Examples would be: folding clothes, ironing, sorting family pictures, or knitting. Use the time watching TV to do some work that must be done anyway.

Some television is worthwhile in itself; the History Channel or the Discovery Channel both are worthwhile. News that reports facts of occurrences around the world are relevant and worthwhile. Watching informative programs, reading the paper, and the like though are somewhat wasteful timewise if the knowledge gained is wasted by taking no action based on what you learn. Voting wisely by being informed is a very useful outcome . . . and I say then that a vote for the Tea Party, smaller government, lower taxes, candidate will logically follow.

It will, to a large extent, be possible to do something additionally productive while you watch these TV programs.

Doing something productive while you watch TV, for example, will give you a satisfying feeling of accomplishment after spending the time because something that you truly needed to have done would be accomplished as well.

There are too many opportunities in an involved life to just let time pass, kill time, without staying productive.

A productive life is a source of pride.
Start each day with a purposeful slate.
With your chin up, there is no reason to hide.
At day's end you will feel great.

51GG. SALADA TEA TAGLINES: IF YOU COULD REMEMBER ALL SALADA TAGLINES, YOU'D BE A BETTER CONVERSATIONALIST.

First, if your memory was great enough to memorize all the tag lines, even the ones listed here, you would be very bright. People with good and bright minds are the best conversationalists. They know more, and as a result, they have more to say.

The kind of knowledge represented by the taglines is basic common sense and colorful enough that people might be especially interested in the knowledge represented by them.

Some, if not most, have multiple meanings, which require a deeper concentration and reason beyond just a cursory nod of the head to understand the thought.

Salada Tea?
How far back in history . . .
Do you have to go . . .
To be in the know?

51HH. SALADA TEA TAGLINES: IT'S BETTER TO FACE UP TO TROUBLE SQUARELY THAN TO LIVE IN FEAR OF IT FOREVER.

I would say that it is better in most instances to go straight into the source of the fear as opposed to living in fear of that source. It was President Franklin D. Roosevelt who said during World War II that the people of the US "had nothing to fear but fear itself."

Well, there were a lot of German bombs falling everywhere, and that would have certainly created a tremendous amount of fear. But America's greatest generation went straight into the heart of the German nation and with the Allies help, and defeated them. America certainly did not live in fear forever.

Most athletes exemplify this point very well. Competition involves facing the trouble squarely and dealing with it rather than allowing the athlete to live in fear.

A life spent focused on fear loses the freedom to seek one's vision of what you want the future to be. A major quality of life is lost when you are controlled by your fears.

I say . . . go straight into your issues and you will be more likely to overcome all traces of fear.

Deal with your fears.
Set them straight.
Minutes become years.
Act before it's too late.

51II. SALADA TEA TAGLINES: IT'S A RECESSION WHEN OTHERS MEET FINANCIAL ADVERSITY; A DEPRESSION WHEN YOU DO.

In the cyclic nature of the financial security of our country, there are very precise definitions for "recessions" and "depressions." A recession occurs when there is zero or negative growth in our economy for two calendar quarters. A depression occurs when there is zero or very low growth in our economy for many more calendar quarters than a recession.

The conditions for a depression are longer and worse than for the conditions of a recession based on the formal definition.

And it follows for this tagline, when the financial problems relate directly to me, I would say the financial problem is a depression; and if the problem just impacted others, I would call the financial condition a recession.

The point here is that problems seem much worse if they apply close to home as with a personal situation. If the problem applies to others, they may appear less serious. A noncompassionate way of looking at it, but that is the way it is.

To paraphrase this a tad
There is still time to learn . . .
Your problems are not so bad!
Why do you toss and turn?
There is no reason for me to be sad . . .
While you do a slow burn.

51JJ. SALADA TEA TAGLINES: EVERYBODY BEING PLEASANT TO EVERYBODY ELSE WOULD MAKE FOR A BETTER WORLD.

What do you have to lose if you are pleasant? Most people appear pleasant when you know them in a shallow social setting. Complications arise when the daily issues and pressures of life begin to influence your interactions with everybody in your path.

People's pleasantness is challenged when your actions interfere with their value system and their actions interfere with your value system and routines. That's when the task of being pleasant to everyone becomes a little more difficult.

As long as you play by the normally accepted rules of interaction and treat others with whom you interact with respect, you probably will find that most people are pleasant and courteous.

On the other hand, if you are pushy, expect everyone to cater to you, and you do not extend to other's common courtesies that you would hope to be extended to you, of course, you will commonly find occurrences in which people are not particularly pleasant to you. Nor should you expect them to be pleasant to you. Don't be surprised when people are often unpleasant to you if you treat them like subjects and with scorn.

Oh yes, it would be a better world if everyone was pleasant to everyone else. If you find that not to be the case, do some soul searching because more than likely, you are the reason people are not pleasant to you.

What a pleasant world it would be . . .
If everyone was pleasant to you and to me?
And if they aren't, why . . . let me see . . .
It must be them, I'll suggest . . . erroneously!

51KK. SALADA TEA TAGLINES: THERE MAY BE TIMES WHEN YOU CAN'T FIND HELP—BUT YOU CAN ALWAYS GIVE IT.

There aren't many nobler actions than to help, or be helpful, to others. There are many opportunities each day when you can truly be helpful to others.

There are situations, though, when helping others is just not advisable. One that first comes to mind is the situation of assisting a motorist having car trouble along the highway. You never know what kind of situation you are stepping into, and it is just not advisable.

You can control most of the situations available to help others. In most cases, helping others can easily be accomplished. Just about any time carrying books, picking up paper, opening the door, letting someone go ahead of you in line, washing their car, taking someone out to lunch, taking someone flowers, running errands for someone, cleaning snow off a neighbor's driveway . . . will be helpful to others. There just is no limit to the variety of ways you can be helpful to others.

The great thing about all of these simple little acts of assistance you can give to others is the fact that you get much more from them than you give in return. That is a great opportunity. You initiate something by helping another person, and you get more from the situation than they do. It really will make you feel good to help others. They get helped, but you are made to feel better knowing that you actually can help other people.

And with well-thought opportunities to help others, you will likely not need much help from others. There will be many, many people who will think about you when you are likely to need assistance. Always be thinking about helping others, and the help is likely to be there when you need assistance.

Help is something you can always give.
Focus on what you can control.
Life holds time like a sieve.
You'll be the one they extol!

51LL. SALADA TEA TAGLINES: SOME PEOPLE ARE SO EAGER TO FIND FAULT THAT YOU'D THINK THERE WAS A REWARD.

Sure, there are many who are so eager to find fault with what you do, say, or what you stand for. They find fault for many reasons. They are jealous of what you are and what you have accomplished. They may believe that if you are made to look less good, they will look better. Others will try to make you look bad by pointing out your faults or mistakes so they might have the opportunities you forfeited by being exposed for some mistake, misstep, or action.

The people who are more likely to be on the receiving end of the tattler's initiative are the people with personalities that do not help, compliment, or act friendly to others with whom they come into contact. If a person is grouchy and not pleasant to the other people, they will find it less difficult to search for your faults. If you are always smiling at them, truly friendly to them, and are always helping them or others that they know about, they will, I assure you, find it much more difficult to search for your faults.

For no other purpose, this should be reason enough to do favors for other people. And there are many other reasons, including the advantage that for each of the small favors you give to someone else, you will get more positive out of the act of giving than the cost of your effort. Also when you give to others, there is the likelihood that they will treat you more favorably in the future and they will be less likely to search for your faults.

They work so hard . . .
To find mistakes you make . .
When you are off guard.
Oh they are such fakes.

52

"Regardless Of Your Excitement Over A Snowfall, Be Mindful That The Snow Will Soon Melt, And You Will Be Left With Just Your Overall Zest For Life To Provide Your Excitement For Living," Thomas R. Wallin

It occurred to me recently this the winter of 1996-1997 that people here in the Midwest as well as people generally all over the country get excited and somewhat happier when there is an expectation of an appreciable snowfall.

They buy extra food at the grocery stores and the children become excited with the expectation of getting out of school as a result of the snowfall. The youthful excitement of the potential of a deep snow and getting to go out and drive through the snow, play in the snow, or just walk in the snow is something different and something to look forward to during the winter.

The second and later snowfalls do not have quite the same affect but still ... a higher level of excitement for life and joy is there in anticipation of a significant snowfall. Often during the winter, all the local news people, talking heads, seem to cover is the snow and how people are getting around in the snow, snow-related accidents, other stories of snow removal, and amounts for the season, and the records, and so on.

Then when the snow fall stops and the snow plows begin to spread the salt and the roads are wet with a salty, watery, slushy mess, the luster comes off the snowfall. But if the kids were "lucky" enough to get out of school for the day because of snow, dealing with the mess of the salt and slush was all worthwhile, and they got to sled, build snow forts, make snow angels and snowmen, and throw snowballs!

Then in a day or so, the snow starts to disappear and melt off by the sun and warmer weather or it rains. People go back to the process of dealing with the cold weather. The snow melting and getting back to the routine is a little emotional comedown from the excitement of the snowfall. The trick is to continue focusing on the positive things we are have done and are doing and not let the snow melt and salty slush on the roads get to us.

A winter snow warning!
The weather map shows us in its path!
There will be a foot of snow in the morning.
The kids begin to laugh.

Then there is a warming ...
and winter's brown again.
Or is that a hint of greening?
Is springtime just around the "bend"?

53

"A Temptation Resisted Is A True Sense Of Character," Quote From The Movie *Papillon*, 1973.

A temptation to lie, to cheat, to take more than your share, to go against one of Ten Commandments must be faced and rejected daily by all of us. Daily, most of us are exposed to opportunities to lie, cheat, be greedy, or to violate one of the Ten Commandants. One's character can be a positive or a negative descriptive term.

Mold your image around the positive end of the character scale.

Resist the committing of a lie; cheating on a test or cheating a friend by telling something that they have asked you not to tell. These are all positive indication of your character.

The very first stories of the Bible involved the temptation of Eve and then Adam. They were tempted, and they failed to resist the temptation. What do you think of their character? Not much I presume! The entire adversity portion of the Bible was made necessary by Adam and Eve's failures to resist the temptation of eating the apple and other sins. It is especially relevant today because the eating the apple is very trivial compared to the temptations to which we are exposed. These can range from mere gossip to lying to thievery and on and on . . .

Take the road that is clearly expected of you. Even, exceed those expectations. Your character will move with you through life untarnished and will serve as a tool to gain you more positive influence. An "on again, off again" sense of achieving or exceeding expectations will weaken your message, since your reliability will certainly be questionable.

When exposed to the temptations of a negative act, my advice is to always take the high road.

Resisting temptation is your goal.
When you are tempted, step aside.
Taking the high road will be your role;
Character will be your pride!

54

"Doing What's Right When You Know No One Is Looking Is A True Measure Of Character," Congressman J. C. Watts In His Rebuttal To Pres. William Jefferson Clinton's State Of The Union Address, January 1997.

You must have the courage and be willing to do all that you do with full scrutiny, within view, and in the light of anyone willing or interested in what you are doing. Of course, there are some who meddle in the affairs of others and have no legitimate reason to do so. Perhaps they can be excluded, but you should do everything you do with correctness and pride such that you would be willing to do so, to live your life, in full view of anyone.

If what you do won't meet this test, sooner or later your deeds will put you in a bind, which you will regret.

A "sneak" is what I am writing about here. No courage or character is the sneak. They do not have the courage to speak up for what they want or need and will wait until no one is looking and then they make their move to undeservedly take what doesn't belong to them.

Doing what's right you say?
Does not depend on who can see . . .
You give quality and truth its day.
Being in the right is where to be!

55

"It Is Ok To Disagree Without Hating Someone," T. R. Wallin

Passion for an idea, a symbol or just pride promotes disagreements, which can result in hatred. The hatred can be short or long term depending on the issue. Hatred doesn't need to exist at all. Knowing and understanding their passions is the key to understanding and not hatred for them.

In the first place, people without passion are rated with the earthworms, snails, or perhaps even lower. Even an earthworm has passion when you pick it up. It is passionate about escaping. The worm "slims," wiggles, stretches, and wiggles, and slimes some more. All this is done in an attempt to escape. It is certainly easy to understand the worm's passion. The worm just does not want to be put on the hook. An understakable opinion and the reason for their passion is easy to see. They don't hate you for their predicament, but they use every strategy in their arsenal to escape and break your hold on them.

In our society, with few of our citizens experiencing a life-threatening attack, the passion they feel about an issue concerns less-exhilarating topics than "escaping a hook." This is the point of my subject. It is OK to disagree or have a different opinion without hating someone. If there is passion though, how far does it go? The level of the issue, which brings forth the passion, is significant. I see squirrels in the yard getting passionate about food. Our pet, Peaches . . . sorry, Gracie and Chrisie . . . certainly got extremely passionate about food.

One would think that religion would be high in the order of the topics on which to be passionate. Then, even concerning religion, is it OK to disagree without hating the other individual? Probably millions of people have been killed throughout history because of disagreements relative to religion. The crusades, the Middle Eastern conflicts, the continuing jihad, and the Northern Ireland terrorism campaign are all passionate, religion-based conflicts, which have evolved into hatred. Some religion based hatred is a struggle to the death of fear.

The Golden Rule, the Ten Commandments, and the Bill Of Rights, added for good measure, should guide how we relate to and think about others. Hatred is not acceptable, should not be allowed, but does exist. Disagreements, difference of opinions are acceptable and possible but should not go beyond just a minor difference of opinion if the Golden Rule, the Ten Commandments, and the Bill of Rights tossed in for good measure, are followed. But there is nothing comparable as a standard with Islam. Open discussion of what other people are thinking may help to understand each other. Without comparable religious guidelines a friendly solution is not likely. If one pauses to think about the other person and why they do what they do, you can understand their passion and give them the respect they deserve.

You can disagree without hate.
Who wins the series or who stays out late.
And as long as the structure you occupy . . .
Allows for agreement which both can satisfy.
Disagreement may exist . . .
Without a solution in sight, people are at risk.

56

"Assess Their Passion Before You Commit," T. R. Wallin

When you are deciding whether to support or oppose someone in a venture, assess their passion, their excitement . . . their commitment before you join in to the project.

A quote often attributed to former president Eisenhower is true: You lead men into battle by pulling them rather than pushing them. Yet after a while, if the men haven't exhibited some of the passion and drive of their own, the target is not going to be conquered."

Pull and then assess their response, pull and assess, pull and assess. Understand your ally's commitment before you commit.

Eventually, you have to be in the position to need to exert limited or no pull leadership. Their . . . your soldiers', your children's . . . response must reflect some passion or the mission will fail. The general, the leader eventually must turn the responsibility for passion and commitment over to the men without passion, the staff, the team, or the mission will fail, and the team will lose.

Eventually, a parent, and that is what this is all about, a father's advice . . . a parent must go on with other activities, or the frustration and resentment will build up within the parent.

Passion for life's fruits must be kindled in the children, the team, the army, or the mission will fail.

Take my word . . . to best be able to assess.
Know their passion before you commit.
To take them on . . . be it a full court press . . .
Or on a business deal or a World Peace Summit.
Assess their passion before you commit.

57

"Decisions, Not Conditions, Determine Who A Man Is," Vicktor Frankl, Unknown Media Quote, 9/2/, 1997.

Who are your parents? Where do you live? Are your parents wealthy? Are your parents intelligent? Are you overweight? Are you handsome? Are you tall?

All are conditions of the present and surely need not reflect the conditions of the future. They may have an impact on the future, but you can choose to not let the conditions of the past influence, if not dominate the future.

Your future is certainly dependent on the decisions you make from here on out.

Isn't that an exciting concept? Your future is dependent on the decisions you make. You can be and actually are in charge of your own destiny unless you turn your future over to someone else through your own action or inaction.

For those who are intelligent and athletic, please believe me when I say that if you begin early enough, there is absolutely no limit, *no limit*, to what you can achieve with your life. You can be a world-class athlete, and you can achieve world-class academic credentials and positions from PhDs, to medical doctors, to lawyers, to teachers, to engineers of all varieties. There just is no limit!

The longer you wait to begin your quest up the mountain, the more difficult it is to achieve the very-top positions . . . but many top possibilities are feasible, no matter when you start.

Without intelligence, some aspects may be limited, but many lower-intelligence levels certainly can be overcome with hard work.

The same is true for athletic ability: athletic ability can be created through hard work. Some natural ability can be replaced with hard work. You might not be able to achieve more than someone who has both the natural ability and work ethic. You certainly will be able to achieve more than someone who has natural ability but does not continue to work at it. Eventually, you will be able to defeat and overcome the natural athlete who does not work at fine-tuning his or her skills.

What you are; did you come from afar?
These are conditions of the present, do I sound bazaar?
Decisions you make to refine your repertoire . . .
Are most important . . . use them to become a star!

BIBLIOGRAPHY

(1) *Father's Instructions for Life* by H. Jackson Brown Jr., from *Life's Little Instruction Book*
(2) "How to Pursue Happiness," by Adair Lara, *Reader's Digest*, p. 155, June 1993.
(3) "Do unto Others . . ." by James R. Fisher Jr., *Reader's Digest*, p. 130, June 1993.
(4) "Trust in God but Lock Your Car," from *Life's Little Instruction Book*, vol. II., H. Jackson Brown Jr.
(5) "Win with Your Strengths," by Donald O. Clifton and Paula Nelson, *Reader's Digest*, p. 74, May 1993.
(6) "What Winners Know," *Reader's Digest*, March 1994, and condensed from *The Winner Within: A life Plan for Team Players*, by Pat Riley.
(7) *The 7 Habits of Highly Effective People: Powerful Lessons in Personal Change*, by Stephen R. Covey.
(8) "People Need Trouble . . ." by William Faulkner, *Reader's Digest*, March 1994.
(9) "Capacity of Government . . ." by Malcolm S. Forbes Jr., *Reader's Digest*, March 1994.
(10) "Hope Is Not the Same as Joy . . ." by Vaclav Havel, *Reader's Digest*, March 1994.
(11) "The Sight of a Gravestone . . ." by Donald Hall, *Reader's Digest*, March 1994.
(12) "Genius Is a Bend . . ." by Edgar Lee Masters, *Reader's Digest*, March 1994.
(13) "Snobs Talk . . ." by Herbert Agar, *Reader's Digest*, March 1994.
(14) "Self-Esteem Cannot . . ." by Aaron Wildavsky, *Reader's Digest*, March 1994.

(15) "This Grand Show Is Eternal . . ." by John Muir, *Reader's Digest*, March 1994.
(16) "It Doesn't Matter . . ." by Angie Papdikis, *Reader's Digest*, March 1994.
(17) "Are We Demanding Enough of Our Kids?" by Edwin Kiester Jr. and Sally Valente Kiester, *Reader's Digest*, April 1994.
(18) *The Book of Virtues* by William J. Bennett, 1993, Simon and Shuster.
(19) *Are You Trying Real Hard?* John H. Johnson and Lerone Bennett Jr., 1989, from *Succeeding Against the Odds*, 1989, Warner books.
(20) "I will permit no man to narrow and degrade my soul by making me hate him," by Booker T. Washington.
(21) "Of course, it's the same old story. Truth usually is the same old story," Margaret Thatcher.
(22) "We are all worms, but I do believe I am a glowworm," Winston Churchill.
(23) "What Really Is Worthwhile?" Nardi Reeder Campion, *Reader's Digest*, July 1994 (and "What Is Worthwhile?" by Anna Robertson Brown).
(24) "Raising a Can-Do Kid: Seven Traits That Encourage Self-Esteem in Your Children," John Rosemond, *Better Homes and Gardens*, March 1990.
(25) "A Millionaire's Notebook: How Ordinary People Can Achieve Extraordinary Success," copyright 1996, by Steven K. Scott.
(26) "How To Be the Best," my conversation with Jimmy Johnson, *Rush Limbaugh Newsletter*, June 1996.
(27) *My American Journey*, by Colin Powell, copyright 1995.
(28) President James A Garfield's Cherished Personal Principles:
(29) The only cure to an identity crisis is involvement in life outside of self; Sermon, December 15, 1996, Naperville, IL, St. Margaret Mary Parish, Pastor Rev. William O'Shea.
(30) "Idleness, selfishness, fecklessness, envy, and irresponsibility are the vices upon which socialism in any form flourishes and which it in turn encourages," Margaret Thatcher, *Washington Times Weekly*, December 1996.
(31) "Maturity is a high price to pay for growing up," Tom Stoppard, the Plays for Radio 1964-91 (Faber and Faber), *Reader's Digest*, August 1996.
(32) "When we seek to discover the best in others, we somehow bring out the best in ourselves," William Arthur Ward, *Reader's Digest*, August 1996.

(33) "Hot heads and cold hearts never solved anything," Billy Graham, *Reader's Digest*, August 1996.
(34) "A great many people mistake opinions for thoughts," Herbert V. Prochnow, *Reader's Digest*, August 1996.
(35) "Freedom, after all, is simply being able to live with the consequences of your decisions," James X. Mullen, The Simple Art of Greatness (Viking Penguin), *Reader's Digest*, August 1996.
(36) "Slow down, simplify and be kind," Naomi Judd, *Reader's Digest*, August 1996.
(37) "We may pass violets looking for roses. We may pass contentment looking for victory," Bern Williams; *Reader's Digest*, August 1996.
(38) "Words are plentiful, but deeds are precious," Lech Walesa, *Reader's Digest*, August 1996.
(39) "The harder I work, the luckier I get," Unknown Speaker, Talk Radio, December 26, 1996.
(40) "If you are going to get anywhere in life, you are going to have to go into business for yourself," Unknown Speaker, Talk Radio, December 26, 1996.
(41) Be Fair; Only Agreed to Need Comes before Fairness.
(42) "The most important trip you may take in life is meeting people halfway," Henry Boye in *National Enquirer*, *Reader's Digest*, January 1997.
(43) "In politics, there's a fine line between too much conviction and too little," Robert J. Samuelson in *Newsweek*, *Reader's Digest*, January 1997.
(44) "High station in life is earned by the gallantry with which appalling experiences are survived with grace," Tennessee Williams, Memoirs (Doubleday), *Reader's Digest*, January 1997.
(45) "The attempt to silence a man is the greatest honor you can bestow on him. It means that you recognize his superiority to yourself," Joseph Sobran, Universal Press Syndicate, *Reader's Digest*, January 1997.
(46) "Never let a problem to be solved become more important than a person to be loved," Barbara Johnson, The Joy Journal (Word); *Reader's Digest*, January 1997.
(47) "Love is what's left in a relationship after all the selfishness has been removed," Cullen Hightower, *Reader's Digest*, January 1997.
(48) "Treat a person as he is, and he will remain as he is. Treat him as he could be, and he will become what he should be," Jimmy Johnson, quoted by Jarret Bell in *USA Today*; *Reader's Digest*, January 1997.

(49) "Suggestions for making life more vivid, more enjoyable, more rewarding: try to be surprised by something every day; wake up in the morning with specific goals to look forward to; make time for reflection and relaxation," Mihaly Csikszentmihalyl, *Creativity: Flow and the Psychology of Discovery and Invention*.

(50) "Honesty, hope, faith, courage, integrity, willingness, humility, brotherly love, justice, perseverance, spiritual, service," Alcoholics Anonymous, Wilson and Robert Smith, 1935.

(51) Taglines, Salada Tea

(52) "Regardless of your excitement over a snowfall; be mindful that the snow will soon melt, and you will be left with just your overall zest for life to provide your excitement for life," Wallin.

(53) "A temptation resisted is a true sense of character," quote from the movie *Papillon*, 1973.

(54) "Doing what's right when you know no one is looking is a true measure of character," Congressman J. C. Watts in his rebuttal to Pres. William Jefferson Clinton's State of the Union Address, January 1997.

(55) Bonus: It is OK to disagree without hating someone.

(56) Bonus: Assess their passion before you commit.

(57) "Decisions, not conditions, determine who a man is," Viktor Frankl, unknown media quote, September 02, 1997.

CPSIA information can be obtained at www.ICGtesting.com
Printed in the USA
BVOW081929120613

323166BV00004B/314/P